NONCOMMERCIAL, INSTITUTIONAL, and CONTRACT FOODSERVICE MANAGEMENT

Mickey Warner

School of Hospitality Management
Florida International University

John Wiley & Sons, Inc.
New York • Chichester • Brisbane • Toronto • Singapore

Copyright © 1994 by John Wiley & Sons, Inc.

Recognizing the importance of preserving what has been written, it
is a policy of John Wiley & Sons, Inc. to have books of enduring
value published in the United States printed on acid-free paper, and
we exert our best efforts to that end.

Library of Congress Cataloging in Publication Data:

Warner, Mickey
    Noncommercial, institutional, and contract foodservice management
    Mickey Warner.
        p.   cm.
    Includes index.
    ISBN 0-471-59573-X
    1. Food service management.   2. Industrial feeding--Management.
    3. Food service--Contracting out.   I. Title.
    TX911.3.M27W377   1994
    647.95'068--dc20   93-3883
                                                              CIP

Printed in the United States of America

10 9 8 7 6 5 4 3 2

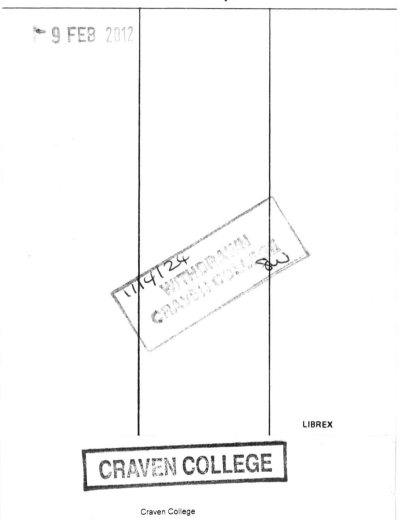

To Frank, Pam, Mandy, and Sparky

Contents

Foreword

This book by Dr. Mickey Warner, *Noncommercial, Institutional, and Contract Foodservice Management,* is further evidence of an individual who strives for perfection, an individual who knows that in the race for excellence there is no finish line, and that accomplishments such as writing this book are merely points along the way. The book is a solid accomplishment, a book both for industry professionals and for students.

This book is not only a broad, philosophical approach to an ever-expanding area of the foodservice industry, but it is also an action book, an operating manual filled with the nitty-gritty of how to get the job done.

With forms, charts, tables, and figures to illustrate the principles discussed, this is a book that tells one how to **establish** an objective and then takes one **step-by-step** through the actions needed to reach it. Throughout one is shown: here's **how** to plan, here's **how** to organize, here's **how** to staff, here's **how** to lead, and here's **how** to control.

Mickey Warner is one of the leading instructors on our staff and a distinguished colleague to whom I look up. He has faith, vision, and a strong will to succeed. Mickey never finished grade school because he had to go to work; he remedied his lack of formal education by returning for his Doctorate at age 70. He is recognized by both industry professionals and his academic colleagues as a leading authority in the fields of contract, noncommercial, institutional, and recreational foodservice management.

Noncommercial, Institutional, and Contract Foodservice Management is a true testimony to Dr. Warner's accomplishments. This is not a book that will find its way into a bookstore to be sold as used. Instead, it will go onto a shelf above one's desk where it will become well worn from the many times it is used as a reference. It is a concrete, down-to-earth, practical working manual that is not only for our time, but for all time.

LENDAL H. KOTSCHEVAR, PH.D.
DISTINGUISHED PROFESSOR
SCHOOL OF HOSPITALITY MANAGEMENT
FLORIDA INTERNATIONAL UNIVERSITY

Foreword

In 1978, after many formative years in airline, military, and commercial foodservice operations, I entered the noncommercial world of business & industry foodservice, or what many of us now affectionately call corporate dining. Despite the confidence that comes from a wealth of foodservice experience, an undergraduate degree in hotel and restaurant management, and a graduate MBA degree, I was unprepared for the uniqueness and dynamics of this new foodservice challenge. Unprepared, that is, until I purchased Mickey Warner's book *Industrial Foodservice and Cafeteria Management*. This book, published in 1973, was, for all intents and purposes, my guide and bible as I began to understand that which I was called upon to manage. Indeed, through Mickey's book, I had at my side as a mentor Mickey Warner himself, whose own reputation within the noncommercial sector was, and still is, legendary. The legions of operating forms, from labor scheduling to weekly sales summaries, are as germane and important to management today as they were when first developed by Mickey and introduced to a cadre of managers who worked for him in the 1960s.

Mickey Warner's book has never gathered dust on my shelf and neither has this most talented citizen of our industry and academia. *Noncommercial, Institutional, and Contract Foodservice Management* is more than just an update of his original 1973 publication. It is a paradigm for learning and action. It is a blending of **what's happened** and **what's happening** held together with instructions on **how to make more things happen**. Indeed, it is everything one should know about the noncommercial sector, but only Mickey Warner thought to find out. And find out he did.

His love for and dedication to this industry is evidenced by the currency and detail of this work. His *mise en place* layout of basic, foundation-building information and industry examples serves to welcome students in an unintimidating fashion to new career opportunities. The in-depth coverage of even the most routine operations for all noncommercial sectors will be a most welcome management tool for seasoned foodservice professionals everywhere. *Noncommercial, Institutional, and Contract Foodservice Management* is the only book anyone will ever need to be guided and mentored through the world of noncommercial and contract foodservice management. Indeed, it is the only book that can now replace my favorite, Mickey Warner's 1973 classic, *Industrial Foodservice and Cafeteria Management*.

NEIL S. REYER, VICE PRESIDENT
DINING AND TRAVEL SERVICES
CHEMICAL BANK, NEW YORK

Preface

The first edition of this book was written in 1972 as a teaching text to be used at the Culinary Institute of America. It was entitled *Industrial Foodservice and Cafeteria Management*. At that time, the term "industrial" was commonly used to describe what is now known as institutional foodservice; the term "noncommercial" was not generally used.

At the time of publication of the first edition, there was very little in print on the subject. In the preface of that book I wrote, "The purpose of this book is to open the door for the student to the vast area of industrial foodservice opportunities."

That was 1972; this is 1994. What a difference 22 years has made.

In 1972, the industry was primarily self-operated and the contract management companies were small- or medium-sized, and numerous. Today, some segments of the industry are heavily contracted by large and small management companies. The big ones got that way by consuming the small ones. And new small companies have sprung up as entrepreneurial executives from the large contractors left to form their own firms.

European companies have acquired some American contractors and entered the U.S. market. New contractor markets, such as correctional foodservice and recreational foodservice, have become identified. The entire marketplace, and the professional and academic approach to that marketplace, has changed dramatically.

When I wrote the first edition of this book, a friend made the comment to me, "Mickey, you are twenty years ahead of your time. No one's written a college textbook like this." Well, perhaps he was right. That edition sold few copies to academia and didn't really help add foodservice management courses to college curricula. But thousands of copies were sold to the industry before it went out of print in 1983.

In 1994, as in 1973, I am again addressing this book to students of foodservice management and industry professionals.

Many HRI and hospitality schools and colleges now offer several specialized courses in noncommercial and institutional foodservice. Books have been written on recreational foodservice management as well as health care, school, and other noncommerical foodservice areas.

Still, there is no single comprehensive text that may be used to support a general course on the subject of institutional and noncommercial foodservice. This book is intended for that purpose. It may also be used by industry professionals as a basic reference.

This edition maintains the same format as the first. It reviews the basics of each industry segment and the differences between self-operated and the contract-managed facilities.

I present four case reviews that carry through the book. While there are other examples that could have been reviewed—schools, correctional facilities, and others—these four are basic. The principles presented in them apply to other industry segments.

The book offers both an overview and a how-to approach. Each reader, student, or professional should use it to suit his or her individual needs.

Noncommercial foodservice, both contracted and self-operated, has become a recognized field for both academic study and promising careers.

Perhaps there will be no need to wait another 22 years before every school and college with a hospitality management program offers noncommercial foodservice management courses. I sincerely hope so.

MICKEY WARNER, ED.D
APRIL 1994

Acknowledgments

Every book is the product of authors and those who contribute to their efforts. This book is no exception; the contributions of many people made this book possible. Among them are students from my classes, foodservice contractors, self-operators, suppliers, associates, and friends.

Foremost have been my students, particularly graduate assistant Jonathan Probber, who patiently transformed the student module into a publishers draft, making valuable editorial suggestions along the way.

Maria Theresa Zancudo, *another* graduate assistant, maintained a current student copy of the workbook for classroom use while the text was in preparation. John D'Olivera reviewed all of the arithmetic to ensure its accuracy. Several classes of graduate and undergraduate students ensured that the material was relevant to classroom work and project preparation.

Much help was received from contract management organizations and personnel. Some were old friends willing to share new material. Others were new friends willing to share current concepts. Among the old friends are Gary Horvath of Service America Corporation, Dick Kresky of Marriott Management Services, Rich Grund of Total Food Service Direction, and Joel Katz of ARA Services. Among the new friends are Judd French of the Canteen Corporation, Bob Wood of the Wood Company, Tony Wilson and his staff at ARA, and others. Each provided current organizational charts, sales and cost information, marketing methods and materials, and other relevant information that ensures the timeliness of this book.

Among the self-operators, a number of individuals were helpful by offering current materials from their fields of interest. Particular among them are Neil Reyer of Chemical Bank in New York, Richard Ysmael of the Motorola Company, Peg Lacey of Cornell University, and Ruby Puckett of Shands Hospital.

Several suppliers provided valuable current data, particularly Dan Gallery of CARTS of Colorado, Craig Held of Taco Bell, and Mike Jalbert from PepsiCo.

Other old friends also proved invaluable; a call to any of them provided a quick response with current information and encouragement to "go for it." Particular among them are Sheldon Silver of the National Automatic Merchandising Association and Les Lenzner, the nation's leading vending management expert.

A particular effort by Assistant Dean Lee Dickson, FIU, deserves special acknowledgment. It was Professor Dickson who encouraged my return to teach a course on the subject and write this book. Without his encouragement, this book may not have been written.

There were others too numerous to mention, but all share in the credit for this book, as do all of the professionals I've worked with along the way.

1

Noncommercial Foodservice: An Overview

Noncommercial foodservice management is a major career opportunity for the hospitality management student. Nevertheless, few schools and colleges offer courses specifically designed to prepare students for such a career. As foodservice management students prepare to enter the industry, they should consider which segment meets their personal and professional goals. Questions to ask include:

- What are the various foodservice industry segments?
- What are the career opportunities in each segment?
- Which are of interest to me?
- What are the requirements for success in the various segments?

Other academic disciplines provide students with certain options to make career decisions. Engineering students elect a specific field of study such as electrical, chemical, civil, and so on. In a business school, students choose to major in accounting, finance, information systems, or other areas. Medicine, education, and arts and sciences each have their own areas of major study. In each case, a student makes a decision to enter a general field of study and then selects an academic major in a specific segment of that field.

Hospitality schools and college hospitality programs usually provide curricula in hotel, foodservice, and travel (HFT), or hotel, restaurant, and institutional management (HRI). Students usually work through a base curriculum and take more specialized courses in the different fields. Further narrowing is possible, allowing students to select a curriculum that tightly matches their career objectives. Noncommercial foodservice management is one possible track.

Foodservice management is a recognized profession. It has a number of identified segments, each with its own specific requirements for success. Institutional foodservice management encompasses several of the noncommercial industry segments.

The word *noncommercial* is controversial, defined differently by different researchers and authors. The terms *institutional* and *noncommercial* could well be used interchangeably and in fact often are.

Contract foodservice is the domain of the major contract foodservice management companies. A sizable portion of this activity is in the institutional foodservice field.

This chapter introduces various fields of institutional foodservice management and their contract management components. Upon completion of this chapter, readers should know and understand the following:

1

- the scope of the foodservice industry
- the nature of the institutional segments of the industry
- the history of the various segments
- the structure of the various segments
- career opportunities in institutional and contract foodservice

THE FOODSERVICE INDUSTRY

The foodservice industry is the nation's third-largest employer. The National Restaurant Association's (NRA) 1993 annual survey divides the industry into three different areas:

1. Commercial
2. Institutional or noncommercial
3. Military

Foodservice contractors are listed as commercial, although a major portion of their activity is institutional. The NRA projects total 1993 sales at $267.2 billion. Figure 1.1 details the NRA Report.

Restaurants and Institutions (*RI*), a trade magazine, also prepares an annual survey. It uses a somewhat different approach. Figure 1.2 details the 1992 report.

RI summarizes the institutional and commercial segments and reports further on the several different areas it categorizes as institutional. The "military" area is shown as an institutional segment by *RI* but as a separate category by the NRA. This is just one example of the lack of common reporting formats among different publications in the industry.

FIGURE 1.1

**National Restaurant Association Research:
Projected 1993 Sales by Industry Sector**

	Projected 1993 Sales (Billion $)
GROUP I COMMERCIAL FOODSERVICE	
Eating Places	173.6
Drinking Places	9.3
Foodservice Contractors	16.4
Hotel/Motel Restaurants	15.9
Retail, Vending, Recreation	21.3
TOTAL GROUP I	236.5
GROUP II INSTITUTIONAL FOODSERVICE (Self-Operated)	
Business, Schools, Colleges and Universities, All Health Care, Clubs, Community Centers	29.5
TOTAL GROUP II	29.5
GROUP III MILITARY FOODSERVICE	
Officers and NCO Clubs, (Open Mess) Military foodservice	1.2
TOTAL GROUP III	1.2
GRAND TOTAL	267.2

FIGURE 1.2

A Comparison of Institutional and Commercial Segments:
Estimated Sales and Number of Units

	Estimated 1993 Sales (Billion $)	Estimated 1993 Real Growth	Estimated 1993 Market Share	1992 Units
INSTITUTIONAL				
Employee Feeding	17.913	0.6	6.6	16,000
Schools	15.242	1.7	5.6	89,000
Hospitals	11.872	0.2	4.4	6,985
Colleges and Universities	8.025	0.3	0.2	3,350
Military	6.236	−0.9	2.3	3,320
Nursing Homes	4.406	1.7	1.6	18,000
Transportation	3.508	1.1	1.3	300
Child Care	2.807	1.5	1.0	29,000
Elder Care	1.112	2.5	0.4	10,000
TOTAL INSTITUTIONAL	71.121		23.4	175,955
TOTAL COMMERCIAL	199.080		73.8	
TOTAL INDUSTRY	270.201		100.0	

Other researchers and publications also differ in reporting segmentation of annual sales. For purposes of this text, the term *institutional* means all areas of the industry that are not classified as commercial (having profit as an aim).

In 1987, the International Foodservice Manufacturers Association (IFMA) published *FOODSERVICE: A Segmented Industry* as a service to its members—suppliers of food, equipment, and supplies to the foodservice industry. IFMA detailed 12 different foodservice industry segments and how they affect the sales efforts of suppliers. Figure 1.3 is a summary of the different segments reported by IFMA.

Of the 12 segments reported by IFMA, six are institutional:

1. Business and industry foodservice
2. College and university foodservice
3. Health care foodservice

FIGURE 1.3

IFMA Industry Segments Report

1. Full-service Restaurants
2. Quick-service Restaurants
3. Health Care Foodservice
4. Elementary and Secondary School Foodservice
5. College and University Foodservice
6. Hotel/Motel Foodservice
7. Military and Correctional Foodservice
8. Transportation Foodservice
9. Business and Industry Foodservice
10. Retail and Convenience Grocery Foodservice
11. Recreational Foodservice
12. Contract Foodservice/Vending

4. Elementary and secondary school foodservice
5. Military and correctional foodservice
6. Contract foodservice vending

These six segments comprise the institutional or noncommercial foodservice industry.

HISTORY OF THE INDIVIDUAL INDUSTRY SEGMENTS

Each part of the industry has a unique history that affects the present-day structure and operation of each segment. How a segment began, its objectives, and how it is managed are all relevant to modern-day institutional foodservice management. Take a look at the different segments in that light.

Business and Industry Foodservice

Also known as *B & I foodservice* or *business dining service*, business and industry foodservice is provided by employers in the nation's manufacturing plants, office buildings, and other business locations. In this segment, approximately 20 percent of the facilities are operated by the employers themselves (*self-operators*), and the remaining 80 percent are operated by contract management companies.

B & I foodservice has its roots in the historical effort of employers to provide food and housing to employees. The early cave dwellers had helpers whom they protected from harm and provided with food and shelter. Later, families gathered in groups, forming villages and towns, and developed trades as a means of livelihood. Tradespeople and craftspeople formed guilds and began to teach their trade or craft to apprentices. These apprentices, or employees, were housed and fed on the job—an early example of employee foodservice.

History's giant construction projects provide their own examples of employee foodservice. While the workers in most cases were slaves and no wages were provided, they were given food and shelter. The building of the Pyramids, the irrigation of the Nile valley, the construction of the Roman roads, and other major construction projects required a planned foodservice to provide for the workers. As the great civilizations formed armies and marched against each other, special groups within the armies were used to provide foodservice to the soldiers. These construction and military foodservices are early examples of mass feeding and quantity cooking.

In America, farmers had hired hands to whom they provided food as part of their pay. The Western cowboys were constantly on the move, and the chuck wagon was the employee foodservice. Railroad building required a mobile foodservice that traveled with the work force. Early lumber camps required both foodservice and housing for the timber workers. All of these are examples of organized employee foodservice—each had as its objective the provision of meals to a work force.

With the advent of industrial revolution, groups of workers were organized in a single location to produce various products. The mills of England are an example: the individual craftsmen gave way to groups of workers at a single mill. Working conditions in the 1700s and early 1800s were deplorable. The work hours were long, and workers provided for their own meals in any manner they could.

Around 1800, Robert Owen, a mill operator in Scotland, theorized that better working conditions would produce a better employee, greater productivity, and a better product. With his new ideas for treating employees fairly, he was the forerunner of what became known as "personnel management." Among these ideas was the provision of an eating room in a separate building that housed various employee services. Owen was so successful that his methods were copied by other employers, ultimately resulting in legislation in Great Britain that changed the way management treated its employees.

In the United States, employee foodservices were originally known as "industrial" foodservices. Many businesses provided a midday meal at a modest and/or subsidized price. The cafeteria, which was to become the generally accepted method of employee foodservice, was originated in 1891 by the Young Women's Christian Association (YWCA) in Kansas City, Missouri. The YWCA was interested in providing its members with a good, low-cost foodservice. It had visited the Ogontz Club for Women in Chicago, which was providing its members a quality, self-service arrangement. Using the Ogontz Club as a model, the YWCA developed the cafeteria style of service and implemented it at their location.

The earliest known business-based employee foodservice was at the Bowery Savings Bank in New York. In 1834, the bank opened a dining room for its employees and provided a wait staff–served lunch to them at no charge. Other banks followed the lead. In 1893, the First National Bank of Chicago served meals without charge to its clerical employees and at a small charge to its officers. The Philadelphia National Bank, the Chase Bank (now the Chase Manhattan Bank), and others followed suit.

Today, almost all major banking houses have a foodservice for their employees—usually an employee cafeteria—and a dining-room service for their executive staff. Meals are still served at a lower-than-commercial price, with part of the cost of the operation borne by the employer.

Insurance companies were also among the first employers to provide a midday meal to their employees. The Metropolitan Life Insurance Company of New York initiated a free service to its employees in 1893. In the late 1970s, they were still offering that free service daily to over 15,000 employees at their New York headquarters. Their professionally managed foodservice staff numbered more than 700. Today, they still have the service but levy a modest charge for the meals. The Prudential Insurance Company in Newark, New Jersey, started a similar service in 1895. Figures 1.4a and 1.4b are pictures of that early service offered at Prudential. That service is still operating, but is now run by a foodservice contract management company.

Most other major insurance companies now operate both employee cafeterias and executive dining rooms as part of their employee benefit programs. Meals are generally priced well below those available at commercial operations, with the company subsidizing the difference in cost.

The New York and Chicago telephone companies were pioneers in employee foodservice. Both initiated a lunchroom service for operators around 1890. As the telephone industry grew, the various companies operated a complete chain of foodservice facilities. The kitchens used standardized menus, recipes, documented operating procedures, and other professional methods. Individuals working in the foodservice department had complete career opportunities within the company. The Bell System of 1960 had over 400 cafeterias operating in the United States and Canada, all using the latest in management techniques. Although the federal government disbanded the Bell System as part of its antitrust case settlement in 1984, the surviving Baby Bells are still operating the same facilities.

On the manufacturing scene, (the "industry" of the business and industry segment) factories began operating a foodservice for their employees as early as 1890. The Warner Corset Company of Bridgeport, Connecticut, established the Seaside Institute, an employees' club that contained a lunchroom along with other amenities. The National Cash Register Company of Dayton, Ohio, opened a dining room for department heads in 1890. This was a forerunner of today's

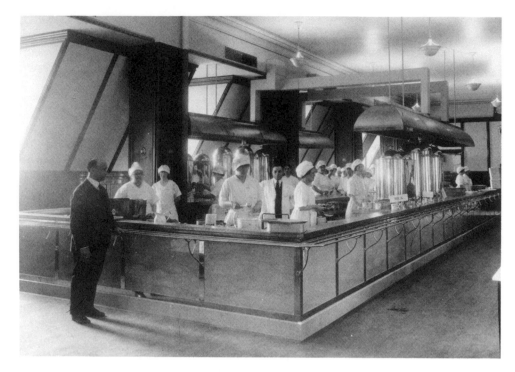

FIGURE 1.4*a* Prudential Insurance Co. Cafeteria Service, Newark, NJ, 1895

FIGURE 1.4*b* Prudential Insurance Co. Employee Dining Room Area, Newark, NJ, 1895

executive dining rooms. One year later, they added an employee foodservice facility seating 1,800 people, reported to be the largest dining room in the world at that time.

Other companies followed these early examples, further popularizing the idea of an employee foodservice and executive dining rooms. A survey prepared by a British researcher in 1905 lists over 50 American companies that provided an employee and/or executive foodservice.

The concept of a subsidized service was prevalent from the beginning. An 1899 study by an American student reports that in Europe, many employers provided a lunchroom where employees could eat meals they had brought from home, with a supplemental beverage service available at cost; in effect, a 100 percent food cost. The study also reports that American employers provided a full service with meals sold below cost or provided free.

At the time of World War I (1914), foodservice had become a part of personnel services in many industries. It was estimated that over 50 percent of the larger companies provided some sort of service. The advent of the war and the need for a shorter lunch hour further accelerated this trend. The cafeteria became the dominant method for providing a foodservice to the large numbers of people employed in the various plants and office buildings. Supervisory and executive personnel were still provided a sit-down service with a wait staff.

By the time of World War II (1941) and the expansion of mass production, industrial (institutional) foodservice expanded rapidly. It was estimated that by 1945, when the war ended, there were over 12,500 industrial plants, employing over 16 million people. Almost half the plants provided a foodservice at the job site. Industrial foodservice, as it was then called, was well established, and there were food management careers in that industry segment.

College and University Foodservice

Oxford University of England was founded in the late twelfth century, followed by Cambridge University in the thirteenth century. Students lived in their own quarters and had their meals prepared by servants. Universities were established in the rest of Europe during the twelfth century, but they were really only societies of teachers and students; there were no groups of buildings with classrooms and administrative facilities. Oxford and Cambridge are reputed to be the first universities with an organized administration and classrooms. Both Oxford and Cambridge ultimately provided a common dining room where the evening meal was served to all students in a ceremonious fashion. The custom still exists.

This country's oldest college is Harvard University, established around 1638. By the time of the American Revolution, ten universities existed in the various colonies. Figure 1.5 provides a list of these ten universities and their founding dates. These educational institutions all had some form of foodservice for both students and faculty.

In 1862, Congress passed the Morrill Act granting public lands for the establishment of educational institutions, which later became known as land grant colleges. Every college thus created contained an organized foodservice facility for both students and faculty.

Numerous institutions were also formed and endowed by religious and private organizations. These were sometimes specialized colleges for the study of medicine, law, business, or engineering. In later years, some of these colleges grew to encompass other schools and became major universities.

In 1987, author Lendal Kotschevar reported over 2,500 schools and colleges above the secondary school level with a professionally managed foodservice. Some were self-operated; others were managed by contract companies.

FIGURE 1.5

Ten Early American Universities and Their Founding Dates

1. Harvard University	1638
2. William & Mary College	1693
3. Yale University	1701
4. Princeton University	1746
5. Washington & Lee University	1749
6. Pennsylvania University	1751
7. Columbia University	1754
8. Brown University	1764
9. Dartmouth University	1770
10. Rutgers University	1776

College and university foodservices, sometimes called campus dining, now provide student cafeterias, student board plans, faculty dining rooms, student union foodservice, catering, and many other on-campus foodservices. Foodservice directors are professionals with their own trade association and recognized operational and certification standards.

Health Care Foodservice

Crude hospitals are reported to have existed in India and Egypt as far back as six centuries before Christ. Records exist of the first hospital, which was established in England in 1004. Mexico is reported to have established the first hospital on the American continent in 1524.

Despite this extensive history, it was not until the nineteenth century that standards of treatment and diet were created. Florence Nightingale, an English nurse, is considered the founder of the modern hospital organization, including the dietary department. During the Crimean War in 1854, she was sent by her government to serve the wounded. Her resulting organization of the army hospitals and kitchens reduced the high mortality rate. The chef Alexis Soyer, who worked with Miss Nightingale in the Crimea, is reported to have invented the first camp stove, developed specific recipes, and taught other soldiers how to use them—all with excellent results. Some consider this the first "dietary" work performed in the military.

After the war, Miss Nightingale continued her work in the hospitals of England. She improved the management of the hospitals by devising an organizational structure and developing a formally organized dietary department. In effect, she became both the first hospital administrator and the first hospital dietician.

The term *dietician* originated in 1899 at a home economics conference held in Lake Placid, New York. At that time, physicians in American hospitals had solicited the help of women to control their patients' dietary regimen. They felt that food held a therapeutic as well as a nutritional value and required special study. The conference selected the term to denote people devoting themselves to this study.

Early dieticians were all female. Today, the American Dietetic Association, founded in 1917, has more than 62,000 registered dieticians (RDs) of both sexes, all considered professionals by the medical community. Many of these RDs are also qualified foodservice directors at various schools, hospitals, and business and industry foodservice locations.

Today, a modern hospital provides patient foodservice with special-diet kitchens, employee cafeterias similar to those in the business and industry segment, special staff dining rooms, public facilities for hospital visitors, catering services for special occasions, and foodservice vending for off-shifts and remote areas. The foodservice director of such a facility is a professional skilled in all of these departments. Very often, the director may also be a registered dietician or employ one or more RDs as part of the staff.

Health care foodservice is no longer limited to hospitals. Extended care facilities, nursing homes, retirement homes, and similar locations are all considered part of the health care foodservice field. Many are managed by contract foodservice companies with separate divisions specifically organized to meet the needs of this growing market.

Primary and Secondary School Foodservice

Primary and secondary schools have a long history of providing foodservice to students. Serving food at school began with volunteer efforts of the Children's Aid Society of New York in 1853. In the early 1900s, lunch service in schools was primarily a volunteer effort. In 1921, the Chicago Board of Education claimed that it was serving lunch in all of its high schools and most of its elementary schools. Many other major cities also had impressive school lunch programs at that time.

The first federal funding for school lunch programs came as part of the Roosevelt Administration's Reconstruction Finance Corporation (RFC) in 1932. The funds paid the labor costs for lunch preparation in several Missouri towns. The project grew and, by 1934, was expanded to 39 of the existing 48 states.

In 1934, the Roosevelt administration initiated the Works Progress Administration (WPA), a Depression-era welfare/work program. WPA assigned workers in needy areas to the school lunch programs and paid the labor costs. By 1941, the program had standardized menus, recipes, and procedures and was operated in all 48 states, the District of Columbia, and Puerto Rico. It encompassed over 23,000 schools, served over 2 million lunches daily, and employed over 64,000 people.

In 1942, the federal government provided surplus food and funds to serve lunch to over 5 million students in over 78,000 schools daily. It was not unusual for the food to be delivered directly from local farms that received federal subsidies. These commodity deliveries were stopped during World War II (1942–1946) when they were used for the war effort instead. This change dropped the number of schools receiving federal food assistance to below 36,000.

In 1946, with World War II over, the federal government passed the National School Lunch Act. Known formally as the National School Lunch Program (NSLP), the act's purpose was ". . . to safeguard the health and well-being of the nation's children and to encourage the domestic consumption of nutritious agricultural commodities and other food. . . ." The new legislation came about as a result of three basic findings by the government:

■ During physical examinations, many of those drafted were found to be malnourished.
■ There was a need to use farm surplus that did not have a ready market after World War II.
■ There was a need for a nourishing lunch at school to facilitate learning.

The federal government enacted the NSLP to provide some relief from these problems.

In 1966, Congress passed the Child Welfare Act, providing additional funding for the NSLP. The program helps provide a nutritious lunch to malnourished children, either free or at a reduced price, at participating schools. Any primary or secondary school may participate if they are either public or nonprofit private with tuition less than $2,000 per year. The program provides three categories of assistance: paid, free, or reduced price. In addition, commodities are also provided under a federally regulated program.

The NSLP is administered by the United States Department of Agriculture and by the state departments of education. In addition, the National School Breakfast Program (1975) has been added to the earlier programs, as well as the Donated Commodities Program and the Special Milk and Kindergarten Milk Programs. Still another program called Head Start, for pre-school children, falls under the NSLP.

Originally, the federal programs prohibited participating school districts from utilizing the services of a contract management company. During the 1970 White House Conference on Nutrition and Health, it was reported that some school districts were not meeting the nutritional needs of their children. As a result, a law was passed allowing school districts to use an outside management company without losing their qualification for NSLP and commodity support.

Foodservice managers directing a school lunch program must now be professionals. They must be familiar with the special needs of their customers, the laws and regulations required to obtain financial assistance, and other specialized needs of this segment of the industry. Whether they are employed by a school district or a contract management company, they all require the same professional credentials.

Currently, management companies operate an estimated eight to ten percent of all school district programs. The school lunch program is a major market for the contract companies and is expected to continue. Running a cost-effective program is now part of the professional management requirements.

Correctional Foodservice

Correctional foodservices are operated by various city, county, state, and federal agencies. With the increase in crime due to drug use and trafficking, prisons are overflowing. New facilities are being built by every level of government, and foodservice facilities have assumed an important role.

Historically, the foodservice in a correctional institution was given little, if any, special attention. Originally jails were not places of incarceration; they were privately operated facilities where lawbreakers were kept until sentenced or punished. Punishment typically meant flogging, slavery, exile, or death. The concept of incarceration did not develop until the end of feudalism, around the eighteenth century. The feeding of inmates was not a consideration before this development.

Early prisons were private enterprises. A governmental agency contracted with a private jailkeeper to maintain the facility. The jailkeeper fed, clothed, housed, and hired out prisoners. In return he received a per diem fee. In some cases prisoners had to pay for their food, bedding, and water by working to earn credit for their keep.

A typical early prison menu consisted of bread and water, porridge and beans, and bitter coffee. Gruel, a grain mixture, was a mainstay. The jailer's attitude was to provide the minimum necessary to sustain life and the ability to work. A 1960 report by one prison commission noted that an average dinner menu consisted of soup as a course, potatoes, and a sweet dish and that the supper menu was commonly cold ham, tomato pieces, and a cup of tea. In one state, gruel was still served as late as 1976.

In 1970, a major riot took place at Attica Prison in New York, followed by similar riots in other locations. Poor quality food was an important cause of these riots, which attracted public awareness and legal attention. Inmate rights were defined, and an effort was made to impose standards for the prisons, including the foodservice.

In 1977, the American Correctional Association (ACA) developed the first set of standards that has since been followed by numerous other agencies. ACA requirements include:

- Menus that meet the Recommended Daily Allowances (RDAs) of the National Academy of Science.
- A documented foodservice policy that keeps records of food served, menus planned, and so on.
- Provision of special diets for inmates with dietary law restrictions such as Jews, Moslems, and so on.
- Provision of three meals per day, two of which must be hot.
- Provision of appropriate staff supervision.

In effect, these standards require the operation of a professional foodservice management facility, which is fast becoming the rule rather than the exception.

The advent of interest by the contract management companies in this area is accelerating the professionalism of correctional institution foodservice management.

Foodservice Vending

Foodservice vending is now an integral part of most institutional foodservice operations. Whether the setting is business and industry, college and university, health care, or other areas, vending is almost always a part of the service. Originally a means of providing simple products from machines, vending is now capable of providing many of the menu items appearing in manual facilities, via sophisticated equipment. The history and present status of this segment is of such magnitude that it requires special attention and is covered in Chapter 6.

CONTRACT FOODSERVICE MANAGEMENT

Contract management of the industrial foodservice facility had its beginning in 1897. At that time Nicholas Cease quit his job at the locomotive plant in Richmond, Virginia, to sell ice-cold lemonade for a penny a dipper to his fellow employees. The management of the plant noted a drop in the accident rate, which they attributed to the availability of cold drinks, and invited Cease to expand his operation to an indoor service.

When the plant moved to Dunkirk, New York, as the American Locomotive Works, Cease moved with it. He and his brother William opened the first American contracted foodservice. While it was a profit and loss operation, the company provided the equipment and space. This allowed the Cease brothers to sell food more cheaply than the adjacent facilities. Figure 1.6 is a copy of their first menu. The Cease company grew to become the foodservice management company of many locomotive and steel plants in the Northeast.

OUR MENU

DINNER

Chowders	3c	Tomatoes	3c
Vegetable Soup	3c	Boiled Onions	3c
Vermicelli Soup	3c	Beets	3c
Split Pea Soup	3c	Boiled Cabbage	3c
Tomato Soup	3c	Pies, (all kinds) per slice	3c
Queen Olives	3c	Custards	3c
Lamb and Beef Stews	3c	Plum Pudding with Hard Sauce	3c
Roast Pork and Apple Sauce	3c	Jellies	3c
Roast Prime Beef, Dish Gravy	3c	Cakes	3c
Spring Lamb and Mint Sauce	3c	Domestic Cheese	3c
Cold Ham	3c	Swiss Cheese	3c
Pickled Pigs' Feet	3c	Fruit	1 and 2c
Mutton	3c	Coffee	3c
Mashed Potatoes	3c	Milk	3c
Sweet Potatoes	3c	Horseradish	
Turnips	3c	Pepper Sauce	
Peas	3c	Worcestershire Sauce	} free
Corn	3c	Table Sauce	
Salads	3c	Catsup	

BREAKFAST and SUPPER

Fruit in Season	3c	Small Steak, Potatoes, Bread, Butter	10c
Coffee	3c	Sugar Cured Ham	3c
Milk	3c	Chops	3c
Tea	3c	Liver and Onions	3c
Chocolate	3c	Hamburg Steak	3c
Oatmeal	3c	Bacon	3c
Force	3c	Fried Oysters, two for	3c
Shredded Wheat Biscuit	3c	Hot Frankforts, two for	3c
Cod Fish Balls	3c	Porterhouse Steak	15c
		Sirloin Steak	15c

EGGS (One)

		POTATOES	
Boiled	3c		
Scrambled	3c	French Fried	3c
Fried 3c, Poached on Toast	3c	Hashed Brown	3c
Boston Baked Beans	3c	Baked	3c
Potato Salad	3c		

BREAD

SANDWICHES

Ham	3c	Pullman Loaf, Boston Brown Rye	—
Chicken	3c	Corn Cakes	3c
Domestic Cheese	3c	Buckwheat Cakes	3c
Swiss Cheese	3c	Syrup and Butter	3c
Egg	3c	Buttered Toast	3c
Oyster Sandwiches	3c	Waffles	3c
		Bread or Rolls with Butter	3c

SOAP, PEPSIN GUM, TOBACCO and CIGARS at Low Prices.

AMERICAN LOCOMOTIVE WORKS

Cease Lynch System

Any inattention or uncivil remarks of Waitresses reported to Manager will be appreciated.

MAY 5th, 1904—

FIGURE 1.6 The Cease Company's First Menu

Other companies followed, usually operating on a regional basis. United Food Management was founded in the Cleveland area in 1919 by two partners, Tom Blum and A. P. Doron. They invested two hundred dollars each to form Factory Stores, which later became United Food Management. They sold asbestos gloves, tobacco, food and beverage items, and related products. Figures 1.7a and 1.7b show the small building that served as a start to a full-fledged foodservice management company.

By 1945, United was operating over 300 separate accounts in 14 states from the Mississippi to the East Coast and from the Canadian border to Alabama. They were completely organized, with standard recipes, cost control systems, and management development methods that rival anything on the food management scene today.

Other companies that became national corporations also began regionally. The Fred B. Prophet Co. was formed in Detroit, Nationwide Food Services was formed in Chicago, Foodcrafts was started in New England, and Al Green Enterprises was formed in Detroit.

The market potential of industrial foodservice led to a number of restaurant companies starting industrial foodservice divisions. Many of them already had an efficient commissary and distribution system, and it was not difficult to expand them to the new market. Harding Williams, Inc., grew out of the Chicago company John P. Hardings. The Waldorf Systems and Bickford's, both with commissaries in New York City, formed new divisions to serve this expanding market. Morrison's cafeteria company in Alabama initiated a new division to serve the southern United States. Manning's Cafeterias in California followed the Morrison's style. Contract foodservice management was now a part of the foodservice industry in the business and industry segment.

Many institutional foodservice operations are now managed by contract management companies. One National Restaurant Association survey estimates that about one-third of the more than 8 million employees in the foodservice industry work for contract companies.

Universally accepted hard data is difficult to find. Most of the reliable market statistics used by the contractors are also prepared by them and are thus proprietary. This notwithstanding, it is estimated that contractors now operate a significant percentage of all segments of the industry. Some researchers feel the following to be an accurate summary of industry segments operated by contractors:

- 80 percent of all business and industry locations
- 40 percent of colleges and universities (campus dining) locations
- 15 percent of all health care locations
- 15 percent of primary and secondary school locations
- 5 percent of correctional facilities

One fairly reliable source of information is the "Annual 400" issue of *Restaurants and Institutions* magazine that lists the top-grossing 400 companies in foodservice with some subcategories.

A review of this report details that 25 of these companies classified as *contract* operate over 15,000 locations, have gross sales between $30 million and $3,950 million, and have a total of $11,393 million in annual sales. A further detailed breakdown of these companies is presented in Chapter 3, "Contract Foodservice Management."

Contractors are professional foodservice managers in all fields of institutional foodservice. They have separate organizational structures for each of the specialized segments of the industry. They also offer full career opportunities to managers at all levels of the corporation, across segment lines, and in both staff and line positions.

FIGURE 1.7a An Early United Food Services Management Canteen Building

FIGURE 1.7b United Food Services Management Canteen

CAREER OPPORTUNITIES

New managers entering the foodservice field have a wide variety of career opportunities. They can select any of the various segments, self-operated facilities, or contract management companies. Many of today's contract management companies have been founded by managers who initially worked for others. The entrepreneur is alive and well in the institutional foodservice field.

A manager may start as a supervisor in a self-operated location, become general manager of that facility, move to a contract management company, and continue to rise in the ranks, going on to a larger facility and so on up the corporate ladder.

Others may start with a contract management company, enter as management trainees from college or some other area of the foodservice industry, become general managers of progressively larger operations, and ultimately become multi-unit managers or executives.

Still another career path is to start as a trainee or manager with a contract company where it is possible to grow and learn the basics of contract management, and then start a new company. Many managers have done just that—built a sizable company and then sold it to one of the major contractors.

The career opportunities are numerous and varied. There are no specific obstacles; there are many successful individuals from all groups. The only requirement is professional knowledge of the selected segment and management effort. The rest is up to the individual.

SUMMARY

Institutional foodservice management is now a major career opportunity for the hospitality student. Students should consider preparing themselves for specific industry segments during their academic tenure.

Contract foodservice management is the operation of a foodservice facility by an unaffiliated professional management company. A sizable portion of this activity is in the institutional foodservice field. A career in institutional foodservice management can be a career in contract foodservice management as well.

Of the 12 major segments of the foodservice industry, six are considered to be institutional. They are business and industry foodservice, college and university foodservice, health care foodservice, primary and secondary school foodservice, correctional institutions foodservice, and foodservice vending. Each of the six are sometimes referred to as *noncommercial*. This term is often used interchangeably with *institutional* by various areas of the industry.

Business and industry foodservice, also called *business dining* by some contractors, is centered in the plants, factories, and office buildings of the nation's manufacturing, banking, insurance, and other service industries. The foodservice may comprise employee cafeterias, foodservice vending, executive and/or guest dining rooms, and other similar services.

College and university foodservice operations may include weekly board plans, student cafeterias, faculty dining rooms, on-campus fast food operations, catering, foodservice vending, pub-type operations, and other activities.

Health care foodservice operations may include dietary service for patients, employee cafeterias, executive and physician dining rooms, public coffee shops and/or fast food–type operations, foodservice vending, catering, and others. The service may be in a hospital, extended care facility, nursing home, retirement home, or other facilities.

Primary and secondary school foodservice is strongly based around the federally funded school lunch program. The school market is rapidly becoming a major target for contract management companies.

Correctional foodservice has recently emerged as a specialized management area. Foodservice vending is present in almost all areas of institutional foodservice. When present, vending is almost always operated by contractors, even if the facility is self-operated. Vending services are usually used to supplement the primary foodservice, for off shifts, remote areas, and smaller populations.

2

Management:
Establishing Operating Objectives

There are many definitions of the word *management*. A few of the more popular ones are:

- Management is accomplishment.
- Management is accomplishment through people.
- Management is making the best use of available resources to achieve organizational goals and objectives.

Other definitions are used by various experts; some say there are as many definitions as there are managers.

Regardless of how it's defined, the driving force behind all management effort is a clear definition of the goals and objectives of the manager and/or the organization. Unless these are crystal clear, the management effort is usually impaired.

The basic tasks of a manager are:

- Planning
- Organizing
- Staffing
- Leading
- Controlling

Different experts may have different lists, but the tasks are similar.

This chapter reviews the fundamentals of management, shows the importance of establishing operating objectives and goals as the driving force behind management, and provides the reader with an example of clear operating goals for the various segments of institutional and contract foodservice management.

Upon completion of this chapter, readers should know and understand:

- The fundamentals of the management process
- The place of objectives and goal-setting within that process
- The nature of financial and service objectives
- The specifics of operating goals for different areas of institutional and contract foodservice management

THE MANAGEMENT PROCESS

A workable model of the management process for institutional and contract foodservice managers is:

- **Establish** the foodservice objective
- **Plan** to achieve it
- **Organize** the plan
- **Staff** the organization
- **Lead** the staff
- **Control** the results

Using this model, the six basic tasks of a manager are establishing the objective, planning, organizing, staffing, leading, and controlling. They are performed for one reason only: to achieve the foodservice objective. Unless the objective is clear and understood by everyone involved, the process will be flawed.

This chapter does not attempt to offer a flawless, sure-fire management formula; it does offer a brief review of a process well-suited to managing a foodservice operation. Those who wish to delve further into the study of management are encouraged to do so with a more profound review of the literature on the subject.

Let's take a look at the five basic tasks of a manager and how they apply to institutional foodservice management. Establishing objectives will be covered in greater detail later in this chapter.

Planning

Planning can be defined as making the best use of the resources available to the manager. The plan must be rooted in the objective. If it is not part of the objective, it should not be part of the plan. The resources usually available to the manager are the five Ms:

- Manpower
- Money
- Materials
- Methods
- Machines

The key phrase is *rooted in the objective*. Unless the objective is clear and precise, understood and accepted, the plan will be faulty. My own philosophy is, *if the plan is sound, success is possible but not guaranteed; if the plan is faulty, failure is absolutely guaranteed*. Obviously, if the goals and objectives are not clear, the plan will be faulty.

Labor hours (manpower) is the quantitative expression of the human element in foodservice. It means the number of employees used multiplied by the number of hours they are scheduled to work. In the foodservice industry these are the administration, production, service, and sanitation personnel that comprise the work staff. The plan to best utilize their efforts requires job descriptions, work schedules, and training programs.

Money is the working capital necessary to operate the foodservice. Working capital is used to provide the initial capital investment, the cash needed for the daily requirements, and the inventory required to maintain the operation. Unless sufficient working capital is available, the foodservice can't properly function.

Materials in the institutional foodservice business are primarily the foodstuffs purchased for production. The plan must include purchasing procedures, ordering, receiving, storing, and using the food. Materials also include paper goods, cleaning supplies, laundry, and other consumables. All must be given consideration as part of the plan.

Methods are the techniques that make people productive and control the results of their efforts. The methods must be consistent with the originally stated objectives and details of the plan. In a foodservice facility a recipe is a method, a production system is a method, and a cost control system is a method.

Machines in an institutional foodservice are the various ranges, mixers, cash registers, and all other equipment used. The plan must take into consideration constraints imposed by existing equipment as regards production, service, and sanitation, or it must consider the capital required to provide the machines necessary to improve the present operating condition.

All five resources—manpower, money, materials, methods, and machines—must be coordinated into the plan. Each must have its place in accomplishing the objectives of the plan.

Organizing

Organizing can be defined as deciding who will be responsible for what. *Who* refers to the men and women of the plan, and *what* is the operating objective. Who will be held responsible for the achievement of what portion of the operating goal? The answer to that question is the basis of the organizational effort.

The task of the foodservice manager is to establish lines of authority and responsibility based on the objectives delineated in the plan. While this may be considered an oversimplification, it neatly sums up the idea of organization.

Staffing

Staffing is the selection of personnel to fulfill organizational objectives. Its purpose is to provide the men/women of the planning process, properly trained to perform their jobs, accept responsibility, and achieve organizational objectives. Staffing is part of management and is driven by the organization's objectives.

A model used to delineate this function, called the *personnel cycle*, is shown in Figure 2.1. The personnel cycle utilizes the organization chart as a base.

Leading

Leading means motivating workers to achieve the company's objectives. Here again the functions of leadership will depend on the industry segment, the objectives of the facility, the nature of the work force, and the abilities of the manager.

A manager of a health care facility will use a different management style to lead the workers in a dietary kitchen than the manager of a vending branch uses. The manager in a correctional facility may require still different uses of motivational skills.

Although operating goals may have little to do with leadership, the methods used by managers to achieve those goals will necessarily differ in the various segments of institutional and contract foodservice operations.

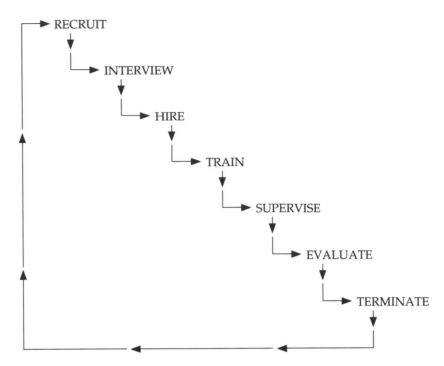

FIGURE 2.1 The Personnel Cycle

Controlling

Controlling is the opposite of planning. It is a method; it is part of the plan. If there is a checkpoint in the plan, it is part of the control system. For example, the objective calls for the achievement of specific sales and cost goals. The plan provides a method to achieve those goals. The control system must provide periodic reports on the status of goal achievement.

When clear objectives are established, a sound plan can result. When the plan is sound, control is concrete and helps achieve the plan. Again, the emphasis is on clearly established objectives as the driving force behind both the plan and the control process.

Putting it all together, the five tasks of a manager are driven by the original decision to establish the operating objectives. In institutional and contract foodservice operations, these decisions are varied and differ from segment to segment.

THE OPERATING OBJECTIVE

While a commercial foodservice facility has profit as its primary objective, the noncommercial facility does not generally have this goal. Operating policy of a restaurant is controlled solely by its owner. Operating policy of a foodservice is generally controlled by the company or organization offering the foodservice.

Establishing the Objective

All institutional foodservice operations, contracted or self-operated, have two primary objectives: to establish and fulfill service requirements (need) and to understand and work within their financial limitations (money).

While the specifics of service and finance differ with each foodservice, they are always considered when objectives are established. Each type of facility (B&I, campus dining, health care, school, correctional, and others) has different service needs and financial limitations that affect the operating objectives. Let's take a look at some of the major areas and examples of operating objectives for each.

Example One: Business and Industry (Office Building)

Most business and industry operations provide employee and executive foodservice facilities as an employee benefit. The purpose is to increase productivity through good working conditions. Many companies once provided large subsidies to give these services at well below market prices. Today, with widespread downsizing and heightened competition, many companies are now reluctant to provide the same degree of subsidy for the employee foodservice. Therefore, if an employee cafeteria is not considered a benefit by employees, they will not patronize it.

The sample corporation occupies a major portion of a midtown office building and provides a foodservice for its 2,000 employees and 100 executives. Its service and financial objectives might include:

Service

1. Provide a breakfast service to employees who commute and desire that meal.
2. Provide lunch service to the 2,000 employees within an 80-minute time frame—a quarter of the employees eat every 20 minutes.
3. Provide morning and afternoon coffee break service via vending machines at appropriate locations throughout the building.
4. Provide a quality dining room and guest dining room service to the 100 executives of the company plus 30–40 executive guests per day. Fulfill special catering requirements for board of directors' luncheons, sales meetings, and similar functions. The cost of corporate catering is borne by the company.
5. Provide corporate catering services as required by both employee and executive groups within the limits of company policy.

Financial

1. Offer all employee cafeteria and vending services at selling prices substantially below the outside commercial market. A sufficient price differential should exist so that employees regard the service as a company benefit.
2. Offer executive dining services at a menu price that covers the cost of food and service labor only.
3. Price the company-catered services (Board of Directors' meetings, sales meetings, etc.) at operational cost.
4. Price catering services offered to employees at least 25 percent below comparable commercial operations.
5. Recover, within the foodservice department, the costs of all food, labor, direct expenses, and management fees, if contracted. Capital investment, space charges, and related costs will be borne by the company.

Example Two: Business and Industry (Manufacturing Plant)

While a company with a midtown office building housing corporate staff personnel may have one set of policies and objectives at the corporate office, that same company may have a different set in one of its manufacturing plants.

Historically, manufacturing plants have unionized work forces. The particular union may have a say in the policies of the employee foodservice. In some cases the policies, both for service and selling price, may be written in the union contract.

More recently, many plants have nonunion work forces. While this precludes the workers determining service policies and selling prices in the employee cafeteria, there is still a desire on the company's part to provide an employee benefit similar to the first case.

In some manufacturing plants, separate services are provided for factory workers and administrative employees. There is a specific difference where the production workers are unionized and the office staff is not. While discrimination is hopefully not practiced, the placing of facilities at different points in the plant encourages the appropriate work groups to use the desired service.

A case history sample manufacturing plant employs 10,000 people (including administrative and executive personnel) on two shifts and operates five days per week. Its service and financial objectives might be:

Service

1. Provide cafeteria services at three locations for pre-shift, mid-shift, and post-shift manufacturing and administrative personnel; to offer breakfast, lunch, and dinner at the appropriate times.
2. Provide full dining-room service for 100 executives at lunch.
3. Provide continuous vending refreshment service to all plant personnel and all areas of operation via sufficient machines.
4. Provide catering services for all company events including sales meetings, training sessions, and company picnics.

Financial

1. Maintain all employee cafeteria and vending item prices within the constraints of the union contract.
2. Provide menu prices in the executive dining room below the cost of comparable services adjacent to the plant.
3. Provide company-required catering services at operating cost for each service.
4. Pay a commission on vending services to the union welfare fund or host company.
5. Operate the entire foodservice without subsidy from the host company. The company will provide the capital investment for fixed facilities, maintenance and repair of company-owned equipment, and utilities for the foodservice. Where a contractor is employed, the contractor will provide the necessary capital investment for all vending equipment and related services.

Example Three: Health Care Facility (Nonprofit Hospital)

Health care facilities may include a voluntary (nonprofit) hospital, a proprietary (for-profit) hospital, a nursing home, an extended care facility, a life-care facility, or a combination of these. They may be operated by a federal, state, county, or city government, or a nonprofit organization such as a church or religious group. Some may be operated by professional profit-making organizations. The type of ownership will have a direct effect on the hospital's objectives.

Some hospitals are teaching facilities and include a medical and nursing school, while others are devoted strictly to patient care. Regardless of the mission of the facility, all hospitals must provide patient and employee foodservices.

Additional services for visitors, such as catering and vending, may or may not be provided.

A case history sample for a 500-bed voluntary (nonprofit) hospital with an outpatient surgical center, an MRI (Magnetic Resonance Imaging) center, and an emergency room might have the following as its service and financial objectives:

Service

1. Provide a centralized tray service to all resident patients.
2. Provide an employee cafeteria to offer three meals per day to all staff members of the hospital, plus an overnight meal to night-shift workers.
3. Provide a doctor's dining room to offer lunch service to all doctors on the premises at lunch time.
4. Provide a visitor's coffee shop to operate from 7:00 AM to 7:00 PM, offering a menu appropriate to the meal period.
5. Provide a catering service to fill the hospital's needs for medical meetings, employee meetings, retirement affairs, and other such needs.
6. Provide vending (beverage and snack) service at the emergency room area and selected sites in the support service areas of the hospital.

Financial

1. Keep patient services within the allowable cost of $10.00 per patient day and to meet all governmental and most insurance reimbursement schedules.
2. Offer menu prices in the employee cafeteria that reflect only the cost of food and direct labor.
3. Price the doctor's dining-room luncheon buffet low enough to attract the attendance of all doctors on staff and in the hospital at the time of lunch service.
4. Provide commissary support (cooked food and storeroom services) to the Ladies' Auxiliary to operate the coffee shop. All merchandise must be supplied at cost.
5. Develop a catering pricing package to cover all catering costs and produce a 10 percent net profit on catering sales.
6. Utilize vending commissions for employee service programs such as award luncheons.

Example Four: College or University

Colleges and university foodservices include small resident operations with all students provided a three-meal-per-day board facility; large operations with board students, pay cafeterias, and other services; and community colleges or commuter schools where pay services are provided but boarding services are not.

Some state universities have 20,000 to 50,000 students registered. Community college systems may equal that enrollment with a combination of day and night students. Small liberal arts colleges may only have 600 to 1,000 resident students. Other schools fall somewhere in between.

Board students at a college or university may opt for a 15-meal (three meals per day, five days per week) program, a 19- or 21-meal (add the weekend days) program, or a combination of the three. Students are usually charged their board rate per semester by the college or university.

A case history sample for a large university with both board and cash operations, an enrollment of 8,000 students, administration and faculty dining services, and other operations may have the following service and financial objectives:

Service

1. Provide board rate services at breakfast, lunch, and dinner for all resident students at two cafeterias.
2. Provide cash foodservice at regular hours for nonresident students, administrative personnel, and faculty at a third cafeteria.
3. Provide catering services as required by students, administration, and other campus groups.
4. Provide student union snack bar, hofbrau, and specialty food services at afternoon and evening hours at various locations throughout the campus.
5. Provide snack and beverage service via vending machines at selected locations throughout the campus.
6. Offer student employment to those looking for on-campus positions at fair market pay rates.

Financial

1. Maintain a board rate for 15/19/21 meals per week at prices equal to or below comparable college/university operations.
2. Maintain a pricing structure in the pay cafeteria at 10–20 percent below outside market prices.
3. Maintain an attractive catering service at prices 10 percent below outside catering prices.
4. Operate the student union snack bar, hofbrau, and other services at a 10 percent or better net profit on sales.
5. Utilize contractor-provided campus vending services on a commission basis; utilize vending commissions to offset food service operating costs and price subsidies.
6. Operate the entire foodservice complex on a break-even or better basis to cover all operating costs from revenues (sales and commission incomes).
7. Provide maintenance to university-owned equipment, pest control services, and trash removal.
8. The contractor will provide board-rate students a choice of 15/19/21 meals per week and will provide a commission rate to the university on all cash sales in all areas.

Some major universities establish complete management policies with a mission statement for the foodservice operation as part of that policy. Cornell University is known for the quality of its total foodservice program. Figure 2.2 is a copy of the missions and goals statement from its policy manual. While this format differs somewhat from the previous examples, it serves the operating objectives for the foodservice at Cornell. These objectives drive management at the university.

Institutional foodservice facilities for schools, correctional facilities, and vending operations can all establish financial and service needs in this same fashion. Regardless of the situation, identifying why the foodservice is in operation is the key to the development of an operations plan.

SUMMARY

Establishing organizational objectives is the driving force behind management. Management has five basic tasks: planning, organizing, staffing, leading, and controlling. Each of these tasks is performed for the sole purpose of achieving the organizational objective(s).

FIGURE 2.2

Cornell University Mission and Goals Statement

Mission: In support of the University mission, Cornell Dining strives to meet nutritional, social, aesthetic and economic needs of its diverse consumer market with varied and innovative Dining programs in an enterprise framework.

Goals: *Customer Satisfaction*—to enhance customer satisfaction by offering a variety of quality dining programs that are flexible and affordable, giving the customer all possible options in time, location and type of service.

Staff Excellence—to ensure staff excellence by recruiting, training and maintaining a professional management, employee and student staff that meets the challenges and opportunities of a dynamic foodservice program.

Environment—to maintain diverse dining facilities for efficient production and customer-oriented service that address safety, sanitation, energy conservation, comfort and aesthetic quality.

Resource Management—to maintain financial stability with effective planning, decision making and accountability. Continually assessing the short-term possibilities and the long-range perspective.

University Support—to support the University mission with an ongoing commitment to student education, employment and programs as well as encouraging staff participation in University and community projects.

Industry Leadership—to foster industry networking through education, and participation in professional organizations.

Courtesy of Margaret Lacey, Cornell University.

Objectives for an institutional and/or contract foodservice operation take two forms:

■ Service requirements (needs)
■ Financial limitations (money)

Each of these categories will differ with the various segments of the institutional and contract foodservice fields.

Specific operating goals and objectives should be established to provide the manager with a clear-cut guideline to operational planning and other management tasks. Without clearly established objectives, management's efforts will almost always go astray.

Where compatible with other policies of the organization, a mission statement should be prepared detailing the foodservice operation's mission. This leads to service and financial objectives for management guidance.

3

Contract Foodservice Management

Contract foodservice management is the business of professional management companies. It is present in every segment of the foodservice industry. A recent issue of *Food Service Director (FSD)*, a trade publication, presented an overview of the various contractors active in the field, separating them into three tiers. According to *FSD*, tier one (national contractors) has four corporations with gross sales between $873 million and $4 billion. In tier two (midsize contractors) there are 18 companies with gross sales between $50 million and $455 million. Tier three (regional specialty contractors) contains 36 companies with gross sales between $486,000 and $46 million. Figure 3.1 details the *FSD* report.

This chapter reviews contractor origins and their role in noncommercial foodservice operations and provides the reader with an overall understanding of contractor activities. Upon completion of this chapter, readers should know and understand:

- The scope of contractor companies active in all segments of institutional and noncommercial foodservice management
- The origin of the four major national contract management companies; where they began and how they reached their present status; their organizational structure and how they plan to grow in and service the market place
- Types of contracts offered by management companies; differences in management fees; profit and loss and subsidized contracts
- The role of a client liaison as it relates to contractor operations; a definition of the title and explanation of the responsibilities and duties of the position
- Career opportunities within contract management (This section can be helpful both to students reviewing this area for the first time and industry professionals preparing a career plan to meet personal goals and objectives.)

CONTRACTOR ACTIVITIES

Foodservice is a $267 billion industry, according to the National Restaurant Association; $13 billion of that market is operated by professional management companies in the institutional and noncommercial foodservice segments. Their share continues to increase as more and more host organizations, in all segments, seek professional management of their foodservice activities.

Contractors can be classified as national, midsize, or regional. National contractors operate in all 50 states with some international operations in Canada, Europe, and Asia. They operate in all noncommercial segments and consider all segments and geographic regions their markets.

Performance Report for 3-tier contract companies

	1992 Volume	1992 Total Contracts	1991-1992 Vol. + or -
TIER 1 (4 companies)	$9,150,000,000	9,094	+2%
TIER 2 (18 companies)	$2,990,281,000	5,074	+11%
TIER 3 (36 companies)	$640,861,000	1,841	+8%
1992 TOTALS	**$12,781,142,000**	**16,009**	**+4%**

TIER 1: NATIONAL CONTRACTOR CHAINS

Contractor (home office location)	1992 Volume	1992 Total Contracts	1991-1992 Vol. + or -
MARRIOTT (Bethesda, MD)	$4,000,000,000	3,393*	+6%
ARASERVE (Philadelphia, PA)	$2,977,000,000	2,767	+6%
CANTEEN (Spartanburg, SC)	$1,272,290	1,884	+1%
SERVICE AMERICA (Stamford, CT)	$873,000,000	1,050	-5%

TIER 2: MIDSIZE CONTRACTOR CHAINS

Contractor (home office location)	1992 Volume	1992 Total Contracts	1991-1992 Vol. + or -
MORRISON'S C/M (Mobile, AL)	$455,000,000	904	+8%
SEILER/FDI (Waltham, MA)	$400,000,000	430	n/a
RESTAURA (Phoenix, AZ)	$350,000,000	400	n/c
SERVICEMASTER (Downers Grover, IL)	$250,000,000e	300e	n/a
WOOD CO. (Allentown, PA)	$250,000,000	292	+12%
GARDNER MERCHANT (Trumbull, CT)	$225,000,000	680	+10%
DAKA (Wakefield, MA)	$200,000,000	232	n/c
GUEST SERVICES (Fairfax, VA)	$107,656,000	128	+19%
HDS SERVICES (Farmington Hills, MI)	$102,000,000	142	+10%
VALLEY INNOVATIVE (Jackson, MS)	$97,125,000	162	+5%
PROFESSIONAL F/S MGMT. (Jupiter, FL)	$96,500,000	124	+11%
WOMETCO F/S (Coral Gables, FL)	$85,000,000	770	-2%
GUCKENHEIMER (Redwood City, CA)	$75,000,000	163	+23%
ALL SEASONS (Braintree, MA)	$75,000,000	116	+7%
RESTAURANT ASSOC. (New York, NY)	$63,000,000	26	+15%
SOUTHERN F/S (Birmingham, AL)	$55,000,000	105	+8%
LACKMANN F/S (Woodbury, NY)	$54,000,000	43	+5%
NUTRITION MGMT. (Kimberton, PA)	$50,000,000	56	+23%

LEGEND: e = estimated, not reported, n/a = not available, n/c = no change, * includes Host contracts, volume

FIGURE 3.1   Performance Report for Three-Tier Contract Companies

Midsize contractors operate in one or more industry segments in several geographic areas but do not usually consider all segments and areas as their markets. Their spheres of activity usually depend on their origin, ownership, and management skills.

Regional specialty contractors operate in smaller geographic regions, usually in only one or two industry segments. Their markets are limited both by their management skills and financial capacity.

The large national and international organizations have been formed by over 30 years of merger and acquisition activity. They entered many specialty markets (i.e., health care, corrections, colleges and universities) by acquiring a successful regional or midsize company. They continue to do so and consider this option a major vehicle for growth.

The midsize operators follow the example of the national organizations. They, too, continue to view acquisition and merger as a viable means of growth. Many

TIER 3: REGIONAL SPECIALTY CONTRACTORS			
Contractor (home office location)	1992 Volume	1992 Total Contracts	1991-1992 Vol. + or -
THE LEVY ORGN. (Chicago, IL)	$46,000,000	8	+12%
BON APPETIT (San Francisco, CA)	$43,200,000	42	+37%
FLIK, INTL. (Mamaroneck, NY)	$42,000,000	74	+22%
SERVOMATION (Clinton Park, NY)	$37,000,000	60	+5%
BLUE RIBBON (Philadelphia, PA)	$35,000,000	65	-3%
SERV-RITE CORP. (Pittsford, NY)	$32,500,000	221	n/c
ALLEN & O'HARA (Memphis, TN)	$28,000,000	24	n/c
MGR FOOD SVCES. (Atlanta, GA)	$26,215,000	7	+1%
PREMIER F/S (San Diego, CA)	$25,650,000	9	+18%
ARCH. CHICAGO (Chicago, IL)	$24,630,500	268	+7%
AMBASSADOR F/S (Kansas City, MO)	$24,000,000	80	+2%
BUSINESS F/S (Mineola, NY)	$22,000,000	97	+10%
S.H.R.M. CATERING (Lafayette, LA)	$21,509,000	19	-13%
CVI SERVICE GROUP (Plainfield, NJ)	$20,000,000	129	n/c
REST. MKTG. ASSOC. (Media, PA)	$19,000,000	24	+8%
TOTAL F/S DIR. (Miami, FL)	$18,000,000e	32	-10e%
BROCK & CO. (Malvern, PA)	$17,400,000	46	+7%
PCS MGMT. (Raleigh, NC)	$16,800,000	44	+8%
SANESE SVCES. (N. Andover, MA)	$14,700,000	71	+4%
ARBOR MGMT (Addison, IL)	$13,500,000	41	+8%
GOURMET SERVICE (Atlanta, GA)	$13,200,000	16	+41%
SERVICE DYNAMICS (Nutley, NJ)	$12,500,000	68	+9%
SUN WEST SERV. (Tempe, AZ)	$12,345,000	54	+4%
WHITSONS F/S (Huntington Sta., NY)	$12,000,000	43	+31%
HALLMARK MGMT. (Columbus, OH)	$11,143,000	15	+9%
CORPORATE CHEFS (Haverhill, MA)	$10,000,000	64	+20%
CENTURY MGMT. (Forty Fort, PA)	$9,000,000	35	+30%
NORTHWEST F/S (Boise, ID)	$8,500,000	17	+7%
IDEAL MGMT. (Ronkonkama, NY)	$6,500,000	15	+10%
CONSOLIDATED MGMT. (Des Moines, IA)	$5,900,000	34	-8%
SIERRA F/S (Carlstadt, NJ)	$5,800,000	46	+11%
QUALITY F/S MGMT. (Troy, NY)	$4,953,000	22	+6%
FOOD SERVICES, INC. (Milwaukee, WI)	$2,210,000	15	+12%
DIETARY ASSOC. (Beavercreek, OH)	$555,000	8	+12%
SPECTRA SVCES. (Naperville, IL)	$486,000	4	+77%
INTERPACIFIC MGMT. (Bothell, WA)	n/a	30	+19%

LEGEND: e = estimated, not reported, n/a = not available, n/c = no change

FIGURE 3.1 (*continued*)

of them intend to become national organizations in much the same manner as the four companies discussed below.

Regional specialty companies are targets for acquisition by larger midsize or national companies. Some do not wish to grow beyond their present area or industry segment but wish to remain specialty operators in a limited region. Others have been in business for many years. The founder and entrepreneur may not have a bona fide succession plan and may want to "cash out" by selling to a larger corporation.

THE FOUR MAJOR NATIONAL CORPORATIONS

Four corporations now dominate the contract foodservice management field. The four tier one corporations, with a combined $9.15 billion market share, control

71 percent of the $12.78 billion contract foodservice market. The rest of the market is shared by 54 smaller midsize and regional companies.

The market continues to grow as contractors make further inroads into foodservices still operated by host organizations. In particular, health care, corrections, campus dining, and schools are prime targets for contractors because a large percentage of these markets are still self-operated.

Each of the major organizations evolved to its present size in a different way. Their historic origins have had an effect on their market activities, organizational structures, management philosophies, and sources of financing. Following is a closer look at the big four.

ARA Services

ARA began in Chicago before World War II as Automatic Retailers of America, a vending company. During the war it expanded to the Detroit market and was generally a subcontractor to the primary institutional foodservice contractor. When the fresh brew coffee machine became available in the early 1960s, it entered that market and utilized it to penetrate the institutional foodservice industry. After numerous acquisitions of both food and vending companies, it became a national organization. One of those acquisitions, the Slater Company of Philadelphia, became the forerunner of what is now ARASERVE.

Slater was a well-organized contract foodservice management company. When ARA acquired Slater, ARA moved its Chicago corporate headquarters to Philadelphia to capitalize on the Slater reputation and organizational strengths. ARA then used Slater's foodservice management methods to expand its business nationally, primarily through acquisition of numerous smaller regional contractors.

Today ARA is a multifaceted international contract management company active in every field of noncommercial and institutional foodservice. This part of the corporation operates under the name ARASERVE. ARA has a number of other business activities with both domestic and foreign operations.

ARA is active in other markets besides foodservice. It has interests in book and periodical distribution, linen and laundry services, equipment maintenance, and other activities. Figure 3.2 is their organizational chart. ARA operates in the United States, Europe, and Asia. Its corporate headquarters are still in Philadelphia.

In 1984, ARA became a privately held corporation through a leveraged buy out, common at that time. It is currently owned solely by the executives and managers of the corporation.

ARASERVE Organizational Structure

ARA Services is organized into four sectors: ARASERVE, Leisure-International, Distributive Services, and Health and Educational Services.

Each sector has its own president, staff specialists, and line operating organization. ARASERVE is the contract management group for noncommercial and institutional segments. The other three sectors are distinctly different major business activities of the corporation. Figure 3.3 diagrams ARASERVE's structure.

Each sector is further apportioned into market groups to better address target markets within each group. ARASERVE is divided into four groups as shown in Figure 3.3: business services, educational dining, health care nutrition services, and ARA/Cory refreshment services. Each has its own president, group staff, area vice-presidents, regional managers, district managers, and location food service directors.

FIGURE 3.2

ARA Services' Organizational Chart

ARASERVE	Leisure-International	Distributive Services	Health & Education Services
Business Services Group	Leisure Services Group	Magazine & Book	Children's World Learning Centers
Educational Dining Group	• Concessions	Aratex	
Health Care Nutrition Services	• Convention Centers	• Wear-Guard	Spectrum Emergency Care
ARA/Cory Refreshment Services	• Parks and Resorts		Correctional Medical Services
	• Fine Dining		
	• Special Events		
	Encore		
	Environmental Services		
	International		
	• Canada (Versa, Ltd.)		
	• Japan (AIM Ltd.)		
	• U.K.		
	• Belgium		
	• Germany		

Courtesy of ARA Services, Philadelphia, PA.

The business services group is divided yet further into three specialized segments: business dining, conference center management, and correctional foodservice. The correctional division is called Szabo Correctional Food Services because ARA acquired the Szabo corporation, a specialist in contract correctional food service.

The educational dining group includes campus dining and elementary and secondary school operations. Each of these segments uses the staff services of the group president but has its own organizational structure.

The health care and nutrition group is divided into acute care (hospitals) and continuing care (nursing homes and other nonhospital areas). This group has its own staff specialists such as dieticians and nutritionists to service specialized client needs.

ARA/Cory Refreshment Services provides office coffee services and runs numerous retail convenience stores. This is a specialized business that is totally unrelated to contract foodservice management but has similar support needs and is therefore assigned to the ARASERVE sector.

FIGURE 3.3

ARASERVE Contract Foodservice Management—Corporate Sector

Business Services Group	Educational Dining Group	Health Care Nutrition Services	ARA/Cory Refreshment Services
Business Dining Services	Campus Dining Services	Acute Care Services	Office Refreshment Services
Conference Center Management	School Nutrition Services	Continuing Care Services	Retail Services
SZABO Correctional Food Services			

Courtesy of ARA Services, Philadelphia, PA.

Marriott Corporation

Marriott began as a small family restaurant in the Washington, D.C., area in 1927. It expanded to airline catering and hotels and by 1970 was a leader in both fields.

In 1959, Marriott entered the contract foodservice management field with business and industry accounts. Internal growth and development was slow so it decided to grow in the business, health care, and education segments via acquisition.

Marriott acquired several major contract management companies. The acquisition of Service Systems of Buffalo, New York, provided geographic balance and a large sales force in the in-plant foodservice segment. Saga Corporation of Menlo Park, California, expanded Marriott's scope of activities in campus dining and health care, and Corporate Food Services of New York provided further penetration into law firms, major banks, and corporate foodservice. Through these and other acquisitions, Marriott became a major player in most areas of contract foodservice management.

Marriott Management Services' Organizational Structure

Marriott Management Services (MMS) was formed by various acquisitions made over the years. Two major acquisitions—Service Systems and Saga Corporation—are the basis of MMS.

Service Systems was founded and later expanded by executives from Cease Commissaries (see Chapter 1). The firm had expertise in manual and vending foodservice in manufacturing plants. Its organization used management systems that were developed earlier by Bill Cease and became the basis for Marriott management. These methods are still used in these B&I industry segments.

SAGA operated some of the finest campus foodservice facilities in the country. It was also well known for health care foodservice. As did Cease, SAGA had strong management expertise in these two specialized segments of the industry.

Marriott consolidated the strengths of both Service Systems' B&I base (with its Cease Commissaries heritage) and SAGA's campus dining and health care base to form Marriott Management Services as a separate operating group similar to the ARASERVE sector of ARA.

The 1992 organizational structure of MMS was divided into staff and operating divisions, as follows:

Staff Services
■ Senior vice-president, finance/planning
■ Senior vice-president, total quality management

Operating Divisions
■ Corporate services (B&I)
■ School services, elementary and secondary
■ Education services (campus dining)
■ Health care, food and nutrition services
■ Canadian division
■ Laundry division

In addition, each operating division of MMS had facilities management services that operate housekeeping and maintenance in many contracted locations as well as some noncontracted locations. Each division directs its own facilities management services. Each division has a separate organizational structure. A division president divides his or her geographic operating areas between several senior vice-presidents.

Canteen Corporation

Canteen is the oldest of the big four. It manufactured candy vending machines and later cigarette vending machines and operated a national vending organization beginning in the early 1940s. It was the only company to use franchises to operate vending branches in various parts of the country. This is still their practice.

A Canteen employee has been credited with inventing the fresh brew coffee machine around 1960. It was this machine that changed the nature of the contract foodservice industry and helped give it its current structure.

The fresh brew coffee machine brought foodservice and vending management together. Canteen grew from a vending company to a contract management company by acquiring many contractors for whom it previously provided a vending subcontract.

In 1988 Canteen acquired Interstate-United Corporation, a major competitor, and became one of the largest contractors in the country. Interstate-United had been formed from a previous acquisition by Interstate Vending Company of United Foods, which had itself previously acquired Cease Commissary. As a result, Canteen has a historical basis in all three companies.

Today, Canteen can boast of being the oldest contract company (due to its Cease roots) as well as the originator of the fresh brew coffee machine.

Canteen Corporation's Organizational Structure

Canteen is a subsidiary of Flagstar Corporation, a publicly held corporation. Flagstar was formed as TW Holdings by a group of Wall Street investment bankers as a buy-out vehicle to acquire what was then TW Corporation, the parent company of Canteen. TW Holdings' name was later changed to Flagstar.

Flagstar owns several other foodservice companies in addition to Canteen. These are public restaurants such as Denny's, Quincy Steakhouses, and Spartan Foods—a major franchisee of Hardee's restaurants. The corporate headquarters for all Flagstar companies is in Spartanburg, South Carolina.

A single individual is president and CEO of all of the corporation's foodservice subsidiaries, including Canteen. Canteen in turn has its own structure, with staff and line personnel organized on a regional basis. Like ARASERVE and Marriott Management Services, Canteen delegates its operating responsibility to a single individual with a dual title: senior vice-president, chief operating officer. Here, though, the similarity ends.

Whereas ARASERVE and Marriott Management Services organize their operations by market segment groups, Canteen uses eastern and western division vice-presidents of operations to direct all Canteen functions in their respective geographical areas. Each division vice-president is responsible for all Canteen business in all industry segments, with the exception of recreational foodservice, which falls under an operating subsidiary, Volume Services, headed by a division vice-president.

Figures 3.4a and 3.4b depict the organizational structure of the eastern and western divisions of Canteen. Note that each division president has an identical support staff of four people: food director, vending director, vice-president/sales and marketing, and controller. The controller is an assignee from the Flagstar corporate office and does not report directly to the division president. Operating responsibility is geographic, halved by the Mississippi river. Each division president is responsible for all Canteen business in his or her region.

The western division president, with a larger area, has 16 regional vice-presidents (RVPs), and the eastern division president has 13 RVPs. Each has a single city within his or her region (i.e., St. Louis, Seattle, Boston) where there is a major

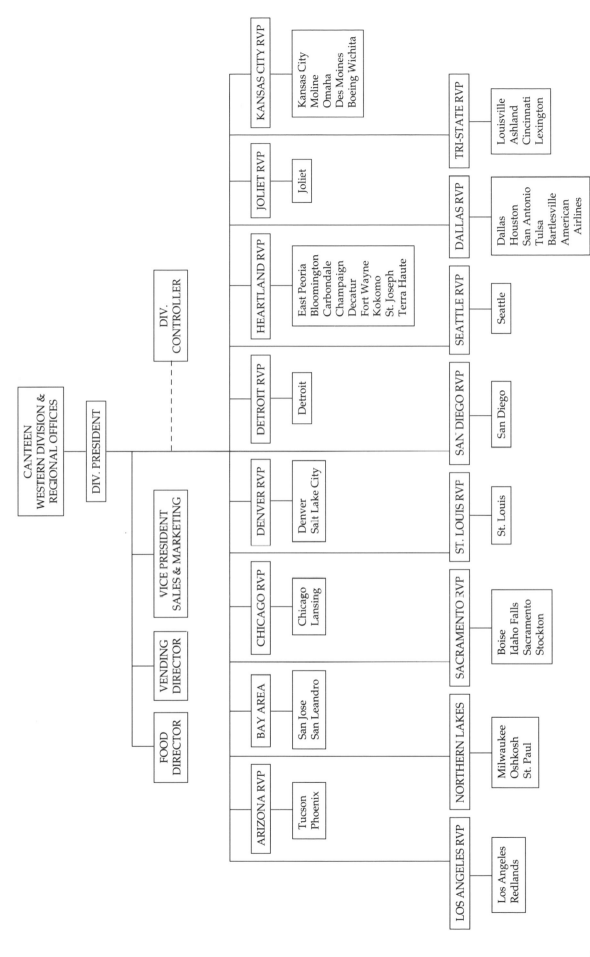

FIGURE 3.4a Canteen Organizational Chart—*Western Division* (Courtesy of Canteen, a division of Flagstar Corp., Spartanburg, SC)

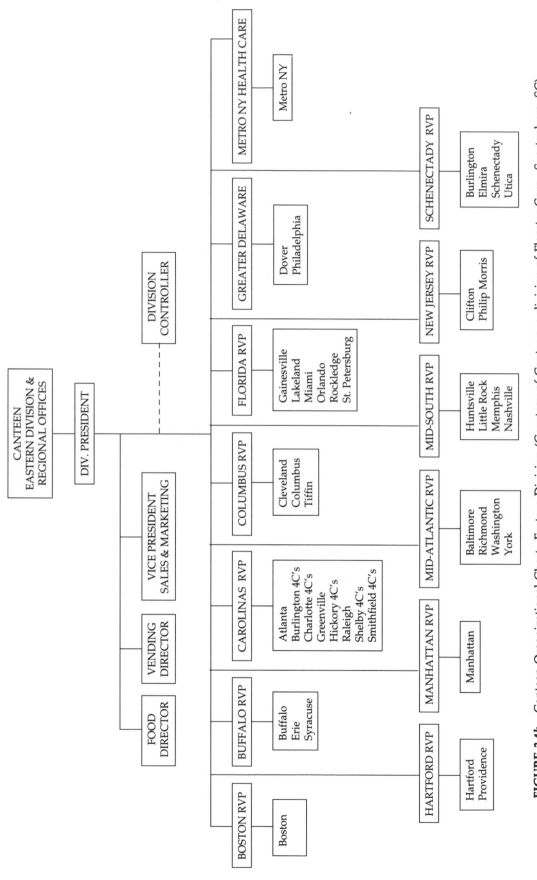

FIGURE 3.4b Canteen Organizational Chart—Eastern Division (Courtesy of Canteen, a division of Flagstar Corp., Spartanburg, SC)

concentration of both the number of accounts and sales-dollar volume. Each RVP operates as an independent entrepreneur and is responsible for all industry segments in his or her region, financial and service objectives, and staffing.

Note that Canteen differs from ARASERVE and Marriott primarily in the regional division of staff service management.

Service America

Service America corporation began as the Macke Company around 1926. Macke was a small vending company in the Washington, D.C./Maryland area. It grew as other vending companies grew—through the advent of the fresh brew coffee machine—to become a major regional food and vending service contractor.

In 1985, Allegheny Beverage Company, a Pepsi-Cola bottler, acquired both Macke and Servomation, a company founded in Kansas City, Missouri, around 1960 that also began by capitalizing on the fresh brew coffee machine and later expanded into both vending and foodservice management. They were combined to form Service America, which operates in all areas of the country and in all market segments. The corporate headquarters are in Stamford, Connecticut.

Service America's Organizational Structure

Service America uses yet another organizational form somewhat different from either ARA's or Marriott's. It has organized its operating divisions into three segments: dining services, vending services, and recreational services. Each division is headed by a senior vice-president.

Service America's dining services division identifies three regional vice-presidents for what it calls *specialty markets*, which are positioned geographically. These VPs are responsible for schools, colleges and universities, and health care.

The B&I markets are organized regionally, with three vice-presidents in charge of geographic areas. They have separate divisions for correctional and recreational foodservices. Unique to Service America are positions for vice-president/customer retention and manager/customer services.

Vending services is a separate division headed by a senior vice-president and divided into six geographic areas. There is also a vice-president for customer retention in the vending area.

The Service America organization chart is, in some ways, a mix of those of ARA, Marriott, and Canteen. Service America separates major markets (B&I and vending), combines minor specialty markets, and isolates a growth market (correctional). Like all of its competitors, Service America identifies recreational foodservice as a separate semicommercial market.

Like Marriott, some of Service America's efforts are directed towards selling cleaning and maintenance contracts in facilities where it presently operates a foodservice. This is accomplished by establishing separate cleaning and maintenance divisions to support the foodservice contract. Figure 3.5 is the Service America 1992 organization chart.

The big four have grown to their present status by acquiring midsize and smaller regional specialty companies, and they show no signs of having lost interest.

The future of the four tier one companies appears to be still more expansion, more diversity, and greater overall growth in both revenue and profits.

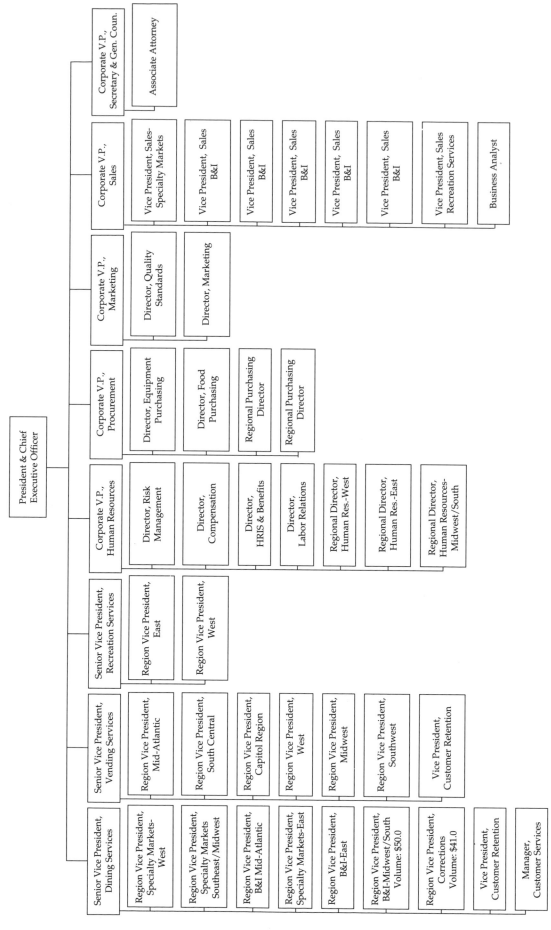

President & Chief Executive Officer

Corporate V.P., Secretary & Gen. Coun.
- Associate Attorney

Corporate V.P., Sales
- Vice President, Sales-Specialty Markets
- Vice President, Sales B&I
- Vice President, Sales B&I
- Vice President, Sales B&I
- Vice President, Sales B&I
- Vice President, Sales B&I
- Vice President, Sales Recreation Services
- Business Analyst

Corporate V.P., Marketing
- Director, Quality Standards
- Director, Marketing

Corporate V.P., Procurement
- Director, Equipment Purchasing
- Director, Food Purchasing
- Regional Purchasing Director
- Regional Purchasing Director

Corporate V.P., Human Resources
- Director, Risk Management
- Director, Compensation
- Director, HRIS & Benefits
- Director, Labor Relations
- Regional Director, Human Res.-West
- Regional Director, Human Res.-East
- Regional Director, Human Resources-Midwest/South

Senior Vice President, Recreation Services
- Region Vice President, East
- Region Vice President, West

Senior Vice President, Vending Services
- Region Vice President, Mid-Atlantic
- Region Vice President, South Central
- Region Vice President, Capitol Region
- Region Vice President, West
- Region Vice President, Midwest
- Region Vice President, Southwest
- Vice President, Customer Retention

Senior Vice President, Dining Services
- Region Vice President, Specialty Markets-West
- Region Vice President, Specialty Markets Southeast/Midwest
- Region Vice President, B&I Mid-Atlantic
- Region Vice President, Specialty Markets-East
- Region Vice President, B&I-East
- Region Vice President, B&I-Midwest/South Volume: $50.0
- Region Vice President, Corrections Volume: $41.0
- Vice President, Customer Retention
- Manager, Customer Services

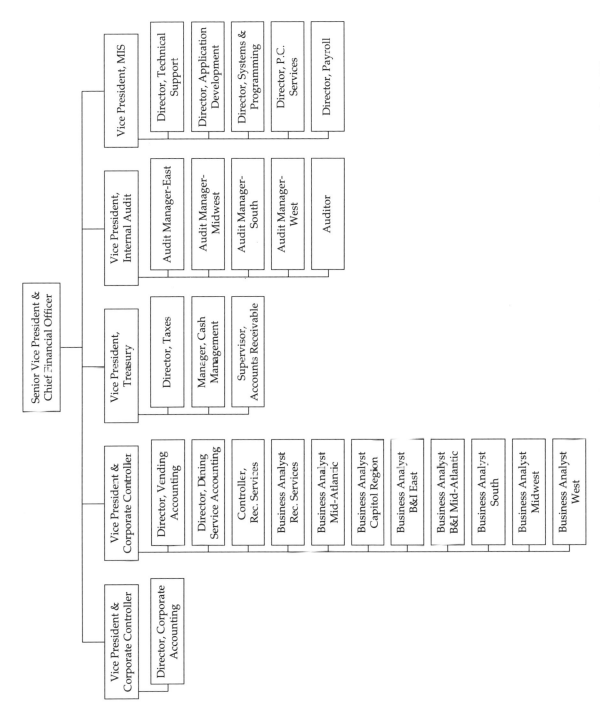

FIGURE 3.5 Service America's Organizational Chart (Courtesy of Service America Corporation, Stanford, CT)

TYPES OF MANAGEMENT CONTRACTS

Contract management companies use the management contract as the vehicle for their agreement with the host organization. There are four basic types of contracts:

■ Management fee
■ Profit and loss
■ Commission-paid
■ Subsidy

Management Fee Contracts

A management fee contract is just that—the client pays a fee for the contractor's management of the foodservice. This takes the form of a fixed dollar amount, a percentage of gross sales or costs, or a combination of both. In the business and industry segment, it was the most common method used by the early operators. This is generally how a management fee contract works:

■ For each client, the contractor establishes a separate account within its own organization, to which it credits revenues and charges costs.
■ The contractor adds an administrative charge for home office expense (in addition to the management fee mentioned above).
■ The contractor prepares monthly and annual statements for the client, detailing the results of operations.
■ The contractor bills the client for operating losses incurred or pays the client if operating profits are realized.

Under a management fee contract, the client controls all policy decisions regarding menu pricing, hours and types of service, and other conditions affecting the employees of the facility. The contractor provides advice on technical matters, operates the facility within the policy established by the client, and maintains financial controls as dictated by that policy. Capital investment costs are usually paid by the client. The contractor provides working capital as part of its administrative function. The contractor therefore spends heavily on labor (professional staff) but has low, if any, capital costs (renovation, equipment, and the like).

In all industry segments, fee structures may be established to reflect the degree of management and corporate staff support required by the operation. The key elements in all management contracts are little, if any, capital risk for the contractor and control over all policy decisions for the client. Appendix B is a typical management fee contract of a regional contractor.

Profit and Loss Contracts

With a profit and loss (P & L) contract, the contractor operates the facility at its own financial risk. If a profit results, the contractor keeps it; if a loss results, it sustains that loss. However, it's rarely that simple. In most B&I facilities operating under a profit and loss contract, there are other considerations.

Different B&I accounts have different needs that affect the sort of P & L contract employed. Manufacturing plants have operating needs geared to manufacturing; office buildings must serve their white-collar, (usually) single-shift staff. Companies are reluctant to offer a contractor carte blanche to operate company facilities at the contractor's discretion regarding hours of operation, menu pricing, and other company policy matters.

In many manufacturing situations the plant has a trade union. The foodservice's hours of operation, menu pricing, and other policies are often contained in the union contract. They are considered part of the bargaining agreement, and a contractor is obliged to honor all of these conditions. Such an arrangement would certainly have an effect on a contractor's levels of profit and loss.

Profits, obviously, are crucial under a P & L contract. If vending is a part of the foodservice contract, it is usually highly profitable, especially where populations are large. Contractors can offer a commission on vending sales to the client or use vending income to offset potential manual foodservice operating losses. If vending profits exceed losses from the manual foodservice, the contractor can offset those losses and still provide a commission to the client. In some unionized manufacturing plants, the union has contractual rights to vending commissions, so the contractor can't use the money to offset manual foodservice operation losses.

In the campus dining segment, the contractor usually must bid on board rates for a 15-, 19-, or 20-meal-per-week plan. This provides board students with established rates for their meal requirements. Contractors also operate cash sales locations for those not desiring a board plan, as well as staff cafeterias, faculty dining, and other services.

It is not unusual for a contractor to provide a guaranteed controlled board rate for students, limited menu pricing on cash facilities for other locations, and a commission on cash sales to the college or university. So there are many different kinds of outlets (and therefore revenue sources) at a college that contribute to the profit of a P & L contract.

In health care facilities that operate on a profit and loss basis, the contractor usually bids a specific charge per patient meal or day. That charge must cover all of its operating expenses for food, labor, and supplies.

In addition, the contractor may operate the employee cafeteria, the visitors' coffee shop, a catering service, and foodservice vending all under agreement with the hospital. These operational areas are negotiated much the same as those in the B & I segment. If sales volume is high enough, as it often is for the coffee shop or foodservice vending, commissions are paid to the hospital.

In the corrections segment, contractors bid to provide inmate meals at specific rates per meal or per inmate day, similar to a health care operation. Again, employee meals are provided at fixed rates or menu prices.

In all segments where a profit and loss contract is utilized, any capital investment costs, space charges (rent), equipment maintenance and repair, trash removal, exterminator services, area cleaning costs, and such are negotiated, though generally borne by the client. So in contract foodservice, a P & L contract is often not truly a profit and loss situation; many of the costs normally associated with operating a foodservice are absorbed by the client.

Commission-Paid Contracts

A commission-paid contract is a variant of a P & L contract; besides retaining any operating profits or sustaining losses, the contractor pays the client a commission. This can be based on profit limitation or a percentage of gross sales. This sort of arrangement is often found in highly populated, high–sales volume manual operations where menu prices and service requirements allow for a satisfactory operating profit. Commissions are almost always paid on vending operations.

Campus dining facilities, with high–cash sales outlets, are often commission-paid accounts; if the contractor also operates vending machines on campus, the college collects commission on those, too.

Subsidy Contracts

Subsidy contracts are the opposite of commission-paid contracts. They are used where the client wishes the operator to maintain a profit and loss perspective but the operator can't make a profit from the limited foodservice sales because the cost burden of service requirements makes profit impossible.

Where this is the case, contractors often bid a profit and loss contract but require the client to provide a fixed dollar subsidy. In some B & I profit and loss operations, downsizing reduces employee populations and causes an existing profit to become a loss.

Some contractors have successfully renegotiated contracts (converting them to subsidy) when an employer reduces population below a certain amount, eliminates some shift services, or makes other changes harmful to the contractor's business levels. Other contractors have convinced the employer to change the service requirements to less labor-intensive manual operations or more cost-effective vending operations.

Most employers still regard the foodservice as an employee benefit. The operation of the foodservice must meet the needs of the employer whether or not it provides a profit to the contractor. In these situations a subsidy is not unusual.

Subsidy contracts aren't the norm in health care or correctional foodservice. These segments are more suited to management fee or profit and loss agreements.

CONTRACTORS VERSUS COMMERCIAL FOODSERVICE OPERATIONS

No matter what sort of contract or type of account, there are dramatic differences between institutional and commercial foodservice operations. In commercial segments, the owner/operator has total control over operating policy and objectives. In institutions, the client makes demands on the operator not found in the commercial segments.

In a B&I unit, the employer is required to deal with office hours, employee benefits, executive dining needs, and other constraints. Accurate production and other types of records must be maintained. In health care foodservice, the hospital must attend to patient dietary needs, offer foodservice to all shifts, accommodate visitors, and more. On a college or university campus, the foodservice must provide board-rate dining halls, cash sale outlets, and other staff and student services. A correctional facility must provide three meals a day to inmates, shift meals to staff personnel, and more, all while using inmate labor and maintaining security.

Different foodservice operations mean different types of management contracts. Depending on circumstance, each type has its proper place.

In the past, most employers viewed the foodservice as an employee benefit. They would provide subsidized operations offering low cafeteria prices, service styles and hours to accommodate all, and other amenities to satisfy employees. This is changing as the economy forces cost consciousness on client companies; now, almost all companies want controlled costs, limited subsidies, and profit and loss–type foodservice operations. Some are also insisting on commissions. While these are their desires, it's not always feasible in view of the obligations to employees. As a result, all four types of contracts continue to flourish.

THE CLIENT LIAISON

A question commonly asked of institutional contract foodservice directors is . . . "Who do you work for?" The answer is twofold: Directors work both for their employer—the contract company and their client. They must keep both happy in the interest of the account, the contractor, and their own career prospects.

Certainly, if the client is happy, just about everyone else will be. But who or what is the client? The client is both the organization for whom the contractor provides the service and the individuals within the organization for whom services are provided. They may be managers in a position to affect the contractor's fortunes, employees at a B & I foodservice, students in a campus dining facility, patients using foodservice in a health care facility, pupils and parents using a school foodservice, or inmates who eat at a correctional institution foodservice. They all have a voice in the operation and ultimate disposition of the foodservice.

To coordinate the various constituents' sometimes diverse interests, organizations employing a contract management company usually identify a single individual to act as liaison between the contractor and the client company. That individual is responsible for monitoring the foodservice's performance and presenting client concerns to the director.

The qualifications of a client liaison can have a direct bearing on the success of the contractor. Many a contractor has difficulty because the liaison has no special qualifications toward, or interest in, fulfilling his or her responsibility. The location manager must then be sufficiently astute to fill the vacuum created.

In B & I locations, client liaisons may be assigned from several areas. The foodservice contract and its supervision may be delegated to any of a number of departments and/or individuals. Some common choices are:

- Industrial Relations, which handles all union services and negotiations
- Human Resources or Personnel, which handles all employee benefits
- The Office Services Department, which handles all administrative chores for the office
- The Real Estate Division, which handles all operations of the office building
- Plant Services, which handles all physical facilities

The liaisons are as varied as the organizational structures and management philosophies of the clients.

In a health care contract, liaison responsibility may be assigned to the hospital administrator, his/her assistant, the purchasing department, the personnel department, or a specific coordinator for special contracts.

In a campus dining account, liaison responsibility may be assigned to the purchasing department (which negotiated the contract), the college business manager, a dean of student affairs, an administrative assistant to one of the above, or someone specially assigned by the administration.

In a school district foodservice, the responsible assignee(s) may be the school principal, a school business manager, a member of the school board, a specially assigned individual, or a committee chairperson.

In all cases the liaison is unlikely to have extensive foodservice management experience or skill in managing the services of a major contractor.

One exception is the current trend by larger corporations in the B & I segment to hire a professional corporate liaison for foodservice. This is particularly true of businesses in major metropolitan areas and, to some extent, large manufacturers with multiplant operations and a corporate foodservice director. Some larger organizations that use contractors have appointed professional foodservice executives as liaisons, including those from former contractors. This is common with major insurance companies, banks, and urban office complexes.

Large organizations maintain a major capital investment in their employee foodservice operation. In addition, they have specific policies they enforce to maximize their investment in productive employees.

A liaison, coordinating the efforts of a contract management company with the objectives of the host company, requires certain skills and knowledge. That individual must understand the real world of foodservice management, the nature of contracting for such a service, and the needs of the company providing the benefit.

Some organizations, particularly large banking institutions, give other duties to their foodservice liaison depending on that person's background and management skills. It is not unusual to find organizational structures, such as Chemical Bank in New York, with a restaurant and travel services department headed by a foodservice executive. That person has a staff overseeing all foodservice management contracts for the bank's locations, all bank travel services, and related departments.

The restaurant and travel services department works with contractors at various bank locations to ensure that services meet the bank's needs. Activities of the liaison, who heads the department, include:

Financial: Preparation of annual budgets based on contractor revenue and expense forecasts for the coming year

Menu Planning: Work with the contractor to design and plan appealing menus for the executives and employees utilizing the foodservice

Sanitation: Maintain an inspection system that monitors the degree of sanitation provided by the contractor

Salary Decisions: Ensure that wages and salaries correspond to client specifications, particularly where a management fee contract is in force

Marketing: Maintain food committees to ensure direct lines of communication between the foodservice and the personnel it serves; maintain a promotional program for menus, branded items, and sales materials to increase patron awareness of the foodservice

Policy Decisions: Ensure that all policy decisions of the contract management company affecting the foodservice serve the operating objectives of the client

Capital Investment: Maintain a credible capital investment policy so that the facility is properly maintained

The corporate liaison is the key to the successful performance of the contractor. If he or she maintains credibility in communication, transmits accurate information to the contractor, and evaluates the foodservice on a professional basis, the resulting operation will meet both the client's and contractor's objectives.

In a corporation where there is either no liaison or an ineffective one, the contractor must act alone. This means that decisions regarding menus, merchandising, marketing, capital investment, and other areas may or may not meet client needs. The liaison is the client's agent; an effective liaison, in practice, becomes the client. Where there is no liaison or an incompetent one, the client is left without a voice in the foodservice operation.

Contract management companies and their assigned food service directors must encourage clients to assign competent individuals to the role of liaison. Liaisons must be adept at maintaining a clear understanding of client conditions, goals, policies, and all other items that have an effect on the foodservice operation. Even if there is no liaison or a bad one, the contractor is still ultimately responsible for client satisfaction.

CAREER OPPORTUNITIES

Career opportunities within contract management are plentiful. There is as much or more potential for a successful career with a contract management company as there is in any other area of foodservice.

Entry level positions are filled directly from school or college or from the ranks. Both paths have produced success stories. Many current contract executives began their careers with the company as management trainees, directly from college, or by working their way up.

A review of the organizational structure of any company can indicate a career path within that company. A successful career may require moving from one company to another if opportunity is not abundant in the present situation. A classic career path within a single corporation would look like this:

Entry Level Position

- Management trainee
- Up-from-the-ranks supervisor
- Lateral transfer

First Promotional Level

- Department manager of a large account
- Assistant manager of a smaller account
- Chef-manager of a smaller account

Second Promotional Level

- General manager of a large account
- Foodservice director of a small account
- Vending branch manager of a vending branch

Third Promotional Level

- Multi-unit manager; either assistant district manager, district manager, or other position responsible for multiple operations
- A staff position at district, regional, or corporate level

Future Promotions

- Positions in either staff or line departments; movement within divisions of the corporation to a different industry segment

If a career within a company is not progressing as desired, a change in employment might be in order. The industry is professional and growing fast, and opportunity is vast. A successful and rewarding career in contract foodservice management is there for the taking. An individual must match the job opportunity with qualifications and temperament to achieve personal goals.

SUMMARY

Contract foodservice management is now a $13 billion business. Contractors are active in all segments of the institutional and noncommercial foodservice industry. Contractors can be classified as national, midsize, and regional/specialty.

The organizational structures of contract management companies may be designed along industry segment lines (ARASERVE and Marriott Management Services) or regional lines (Canteen Corporation). Others may be a hybrid (Service America).

Management contracts are divided into four types: management fee, profit and loss, commission-paid, and subsidy. Capital investment costs are normally borne by the client.

The client liaison is key to a successful contract management foodservice.

Career opportunities within the field of contract foodservice management are vast. Typical entry level positions are management trainee and up-from-the-ranks supervisor.

4

The Self-Operated Market

"Self-op" is industry shorthand for a company that runs its own foodservice. Self-ops flourish in most industry segments, require professional management, and offer career opportunities.

The percentages of contractor-operated facilities presented in Chapter 1 can be used to calculate the percentage of self-ops within each industry segment:

- 10–20 percent of all business and industry locations
- 40–50 percent of all colleges and universities (campus dining)
- 55–65 percent of all hospital locations
- 90–95 percent of all primary and secondary school locations
- 95–98 percent of all correctional facility locations

Self operators dominate in all segments except B&I, but the 10–20 percent of B&I self-ops are also major operations. This constitutes a substantial market for the professional food service director or manager.

This chapter reviews self-operated foodservices in all industry segments and provides the reader with a better understanding of self-ops.

Upon completion of this chapter, readers should know and understand:

- The scope of self-operated facilities by market segment
- Example organizational structures of major operations in B&I, health care, college and university, and elementary and secondary school foodservices
- Career opportunities within each segment
- Professional qualifications required for success as a self-op manager

SCOPE OF THE SELF-OPERATED MARKETS

Figures 4.1*a* and 4.1*b* are derived from the 1992 survey "Foodservice Growth by Market Segment," published by *Restaurants and Institutions* magazine, and statistics from Technomics, Inc., a consulting firm.

This indicates that a $25–29 billion market with 87,000–94,000 locations would still be self-operated in various noncommercial and institutional segments in 1992. This is notwithstanding that correctional and health care, other than hospital facilities, are not included in these totals.

Following are some examples from the various segments of the industry.

FIGURE 4.1a

1993 Projected Gross Annual Sales and 1992 Number of Units for Institutional and Noncommercial Foodservice

Segment	Projected 1993 Sales (Billion $)	Number of Units in 1992
Employee Feeding (B&I)	17.913	16,225
Schools		
Elementary and Secondary	15.242	89,000
Hospitals	11.872	6,730
Colleges and Universities	8.025	3,460
TOTALS	$53.052	115,415

Figures for hospitals do not reflect the total health care industry. There are no figures for the correctional market.

FIGURE 4.1b

Anticipated Gross Annual Sales for 1993—Self-Operated Units

Segment	Sales (Billion $)	Number of Units
Business and Industry 10–20%	1.79–3.58	1,622–3,244
Schools Elementary and Secondary 90–95%	13.71–14.48	80,100–84,550
Hospitals 55–65%	6.53–7.71	3,701–4,374
Colleges and Universities 40–50%	3.21–4.01	1,384–1,730
TOTALS	$25.24–29.78	86,807–93,898

BUSINESS AND INDUSTRY: THE MOTOROLA CORPORATION

Motorola has world and corporate headquarters in Schaumburg, Illinois and offices and manufacturing plants all over the world. The majority of its facilities—22 plants—are in the continental United States.

To provide employee foodservices at all of its plants, Motorola established a separate department called Food Works as a division of the company. This department operates much like any independent foodservice organization except that its market is strictly the employees of Motorola company operations.

Figure 4.2 is a 1992 organizational chart detailing the structure of Food Works. Note that there are a director and two staff services positions—corporate secretary and MIS manager. Food Works is supported by the staff services of Motorola Corporation, the same as any other corporate department.

The Food Works' line departments are organized geographically to provide direction and supervision to four regions: Illinois, Florida, Texas, and Arizona. Each state/region has its own area manager; area managers for Florida and Arizona have some offshore responsibility. Florida provides management support to operations in Puerto Rico, while Arizona provides similar services to some outlets in the Pacific and Asia.

Food Works is an approximately $20 million-a-year enterprise. Its mission is to provide all the necessary services to all employees at all locations of the cor-

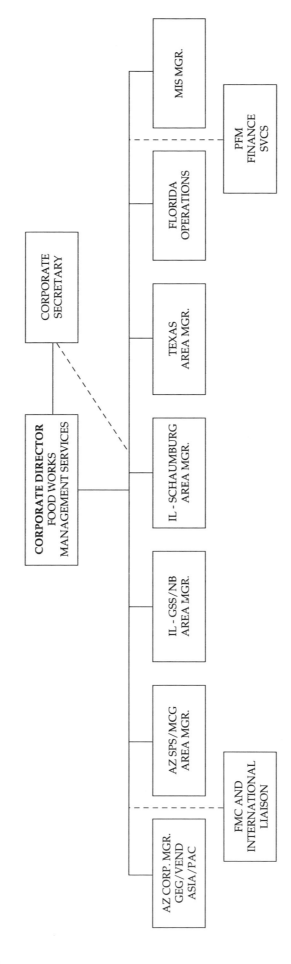

FIGURE 4.2 Organizational Structure of Motorola Corporation's Food Works (employee foodservice) Department (Courtesy of Motorola Corporation, Schaumburg, IL)

47

poration and to recover all direct operating costs within the operation. The director of Food Works is an executive of Motorola Corporation.

Career opportunities within Food Works are comparable to any other food-service company except that growth within Food Works is limited by the growth of Motorola itself. There is no opportunity for the food division to grow in new markets apart from the corporation.

Note that Motorola has an organizational structure similar to that of a contract foodservice organization in the B&I segment. Each region has a director, a small staff, and line operations managers. Each receives additional staff support from the parent corporation.

Remember that a contract foodservice manager must understand the concept of working for two bosses—the client and the contractor. That's not the case with self-op managers; the host organization is both client and company.

Many other companies are self-ops. Careers can be made by changing employers among self-ops in much the same way as one would with contractors. But realize that career potential within the self-op sector is limited because there are many more contract-managed B&I institutions and more self-ops are going to contractors every year.

The Kodak Corporation of Rochester, New York, is a recent example. This $30 million per year, 55-outlet foodservice, self-operated since its first employee cafeteria in 1905, recently contracted with Marriott Management Services. Long regarded as one of the premier B&I self-ops, Kodak's move to a contractor is particularly significant, highlighting the strength of this trend.

HEALTH CARE SERVICES: SHANDS HOSPITAL

The health care market, as defined by contractors, includes hospitals, nursing homes, extended care residences, retirement homes, and other facilities. Self-ops generally operate only one hospital, nursing home, or other facility at a time.

For purposes of this example, we will explore the self-operation of a single hospital.

Hospital foodservice management has become a distinct specialty. In Chapter 1, the early work of Florence Nightingale was reviewed; recall that she developed an organizational structure for hospital administration and, within that structure, a dietary department. Little has changed since then. A modern hospital has a well-defined organization, within which functions the dietary department.

Figure 4.3 is the organizational chart for the Food & Nutritional Services Department of Shands Hospital of the University of Florida in Gainesville. This is a large teaching hospital that has extensive patient and public facilities and maintains a staff of 168 in the foodservice department. It is a typical large teaching hospital and provides a good example of a self-op and the career potential therein. Its service objective is threefold: to provide a satisfactory service to patients, employees and staff, and the public.

Shands Hospital is governed by a board of directors and administered by a chief executive officer who directs five operating divisions. One of those divisions is operations, overseen by a vice-president. Within the division is a director of clinical services. Under that position is the food and nutrition services department. It is important to note the chain of command and the location of the food and nutrition services department. This structure is totally different from what is typical in the B&I segment and contractor-managed operations.

The food and nutrition services department of the hospital has its own organizational structure designed to meet the needs of the facility. Note that the organization has three operating departments: nutrition services, commercial services, and foodservice systems.

The three operating departments serve the three populations targeted by the

SHANDS HOSPITAL, the University of Florida

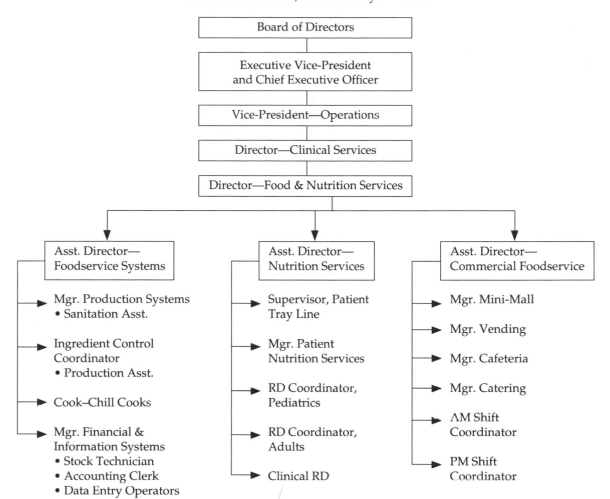

FIGURE 4.3 Organizational Chart of Shands Hospital Detailing the Food and Nutrition Services Department (Courtesy of Ruby B. Puckett, MA, RD, LD, Shands Hospital, Gainesville, FL)

hospital's service objectives—the patients, the employees, and the public. The departments are supported by a centralized foodservice division.

Note that the assistant director of nutrition services has specialized areas of responsibility, typical of a dietary department, supported by registered dieticians (RDs) and dietetic technicians.

The assistant director of foodservice systems is responsible for a commerical-type cook-chill system. The assistant director of commercial foodservice has a B&I-type structure with an employee cafeteria, foodservice vending, company catering, and minimall. Both of these areas have commercial and noncommercial counterparts and do not require medical foodservice management experience.

Annual food purchases for the dietary department of Shands are estimated at $2.14 million. A standard method used to convert the value of food purchases to a comparable value of retail sales is to consider food purchases as 40 percent of sales or to multiply the food purchase value by 2.5. Multiplying 2.5 by $2.14 million equates the Shands dietary department to $5.35 million in annual sales for a commercial facility. This is in addition to the potential commercial (non-dietary) food sales previously described. Shands is a sizable operation with opportunities and problems to match.

Food Service Director magazine provides an annual survey (Figure 4.4) of the top 100 self-op hospitals detailing gross annual food purchases and meals served.

HOSPITAL (location)	1992 $ PURCHASES (food, labor, operating exp.)	TOTAL BEDS (Avg. Daily Cesnus)	1992 $ FOOD PURCHASES	+or- 1992 Pct.	1992 $ LABOR	1992 MEAL COUNTS	+or- 1992 Pct.
NYU Medical Ctr. (New York, NY)	$12,130,000	840 (672)	$4,000,000	-5	$7,400,000	2,500,000	+2
Univ. of Iowa Med. Ctr. (Iowa City, IA)	10,818,209	890 (785)	3,500,000	+3	6,605,426	2,073,179	+1
VA Medical Ctr. (Palo Alto, CA)	9,600,382	1,380 (1,075)	1,843,906	+3	7,612,322	1,310,400	n/c
Henry Ford Hosp. (Detroit, MI)	8,743,940	732 (638)	2,887,526	-2	5,246,208	1,400,000	-6
Univ. of Calif. Med. Ctr. (San Francisco, CA)	8,720,000	560 (400)	2,400,000	-10	5,500,000	438,000	-5
Carolinas Med. Ctr. (Charlotte, NC)	8,196,000	777 (700)	3,023,520	+3	4,068,199	1,682,601	+6
Methodist Hosp. (Indianapolis, IN)	8,100,000	1,120 (952)	2,800,000	+3	5,000,000	2,300,000	n/c
Franciscan Health Syst. (Cincinnati, OH)	7,550,000	737 (650)	2,400,000	-3	3,308,000	1,610,000	-1
Little Co. & Mary Hosp. (Evergreen Park, IL)	7,300,000	401 (289)	2,300,000	+7	1,500,000	324,000*	—
Ohio State Univ. Hosp. (Columbus, OH)	7,262,000	824 (640)	2,469,370	+6	4,230,000	1,576,346	+5
Anderson Cancer Ctr. (Houston, TX)	7,150,000	514 (452)	2,682,000	+3	3,750,000	1,250,000	+2
Hermann Hosp. (Houston, TX)	7,100,000	560 (500)	2,700,000	--	3,700,000	570,000	n/c
St. Vincent Med. Ctr. (Little Rock, AR)	7,000,000	699 (475)	3,000,000	-7	3,200,000	2,336,034	+4
Miami Valley Hosp. (Dayton, OH)	6,609,163	652 (510)	2,602,852	-7	3,443,453	1,572,961	n/c
VA Med. Ctr. (Los Angeles, CA)	6,500,000	1,400 (1,100)	2,000,000	-4	3,000,000	1,204,500	+2
Camarillo State Hosp. (Camarillo, CA)	6,472,846	1,175 (1,175)	1,758,000	-5	4,399,961	429,474	+2
Baptist Med. Ctr. (Little Rock, AR)	6,317,715	889 (630)	2,915,680	+1	2,986,343	3,281,017	-15
NY Hosp./Cornell Univ. (New York, NY)	6,300,000	940 (846)	2,000,000	+2	3,500,000	2,000,000	n/c
Beth Israel Hosp. (Boston, MA)	6,300,000	504 (485)	2,400,000	n/c	3,200,000	1,250,092	+5
Laguana Honda Hosp. (San Francisco, CA)	6,225,000	1,100 (1,080)	2,340,000	+4	3,600,000	1,410,000	+1
The Med. Ctr./U of CA (San Francisco, CA)	6,019,649	476 (380)	2,322,559	-4	3,045,053	1,249,200	-3
St Joseph Hosp. (Milwaukee, WI)	6,007,172	500 (420)	1,626,883	+2	1,559,539	787,817	+5
Buffalo Gen. Hosp. (Buffalo, NY)	6,000,000	710 (580)	n/a	—	n/a	1,184,693	-5
South Oaks Hosp. (Amityville, NY)	5,900,000	656 (550)	1,900,000	n/c	2,000,000	793,000	n/c
Shands Hosp. (Gainsville, FL)	5,709,049	564 (479)	2,100,000	+5	3,209,049	2,130,000	+14
Metro Health Med. Ctr. (Cleveland, OH)	5,700,000	750 (650)	2,500,000	-3	3,500,000	1,350,500	n/c
Hackensack Med. Ctr. (Hackensack, NJ)	5,656,770	531 (531)	2,000,407	+5	3,270,557	1,208,374	+2
Kettering Med. Ctr. (Kettering, OH)	5,654,157	630 (397)	1,917,209	n/c	3,463,948	891,953	-3
St. Francis Regl. Ctr. (Wichita, KS)	5,506,000	866 (500)	1,800,000	+10	2,897,000	288,000	+2
Sarasota Memorial Hosp. (Sarasota, FL)	5,500,000	963 (512)	2,200,000	+5	2,700,000	1,200,000	+2
Huntington Memorial Hosp. (Pasadena, CA)	5,450,000	616 (400)	2,200,000	+2	2,400,000	341,763	-5
Florida State Hosp. (Chattahoochee, FL)	5,317,409	1,200 (1,200)	1,916,135	+6	2,931,412	1,314,000	-5
Univ. of Kansas Med. Ctr. (Kansas City, KS)	5,200,000	483 (325)	1,300,000	+1	3,300,000	889,000	-10
Univ. Hosp. & Clinics (Columbia, MO)	5,170,473	400 (285)	1,751,238	-14	2,604,354	4,282,000	-6
St. Francis Hosp. (Tulsa, OK)	5,028,812	660 (500)	1,820,537	+4	2,840,354	1,296,738	+3
Loma Linda Univ. Med. Ctr. (Loma Linda, CA)	5,000,000	570 (476)	1,750,000	+2	2,500,000	1,460,000	+2
Presbyterian Hosp. (Albuquerque, NM)	4,936,289	1,000 (675)	2,182,909	+2	2,168,305	1,095,000	n/c
Schrumpert Med. Ctr. (Shreveport, LA)	4,983,000	625 (410)	2,500,000	+7	2,000,000	1,683,210	+6
Oakwood Hosp. (Dearborn, MI)	4,949,848	574 (400)	1,833,700	+5	2,755,348	957,685	+1
Christ Hosp. (Cincinnati, OH)	4,872,728	496 (314)	1,683,962	-3	3,094,888	924,878	-7
Einstein-Weiler Hosp. (Bronx, NY)	4,800,000	431 (385)	1,000,000	n/c	3,000,000	750,000	n/c
Univ. of Wash. Med. Ctr. (Seattle, WA)	4,660,000	460 (370)	1,500,000	+2	2,000,000	1,250,000	+3
Albert Einstein Med. Ctr. (Philadelphia, PA)	4,400,000	600 (450)	2,200,000	+2	2,000,000	600,350	+2
Memorial Med. Ctr. (Savannah, GA)	4,645,528	515 (474)	1,802,226	n/c	2,020,858	1,500,630	+5
Greenville Mem. Hosp. (Greenville, SC)	4,505,000	700 (510)	2,500,000	-10	2,000,000	1,453,584	-2
Fairview Development Ctr. (Costa Mesa, CA)	4,500,000	1,080 (1,080)	1,800,000	+3	2,700,000	1,095,000	n/c
Mohawk Valley Psych. Ctr. (Utica , NY)	4,360,000	900 (750)	1,250,000	-9	3,000,000	821,250	-10
St. Anthony's Hosp. (St. Louis, MO)	4,339,028	863 (642)	2,395,120	+2	1,633,081	n/a	—
Franklin Square Hosp. (Baltimore, MD)	4,330,000	789 (405)	1,500,000	+2	1,250,000	600,000	+2
Univ. of Utah Med. Ctr. (Salt Lake City, UT)	4,300,000	388 (334)	1,600,000	-15	2,200,000	760,000	+10

FIGURE 4.4 *Food Service Director* Magazine's 1992 Annual Survey of Top 100 Self-Op Hospitals

HOSPITAL (location)	1992 $ PURCHASES (food, labor, operating exp.)	TOTAL BEDS (Avg. Daily Census)	1992 $ FOOD PURCHASES	+-or- 1992 Pct.	1992 $ LABOR	1992 MEAL COUNTS	+-or- 1992 Pct.
Crozer Chester Med. Ctr. (Upland, PA)	$4,266,502	480 (400)	1,491,998	n/c	2,730,504	1,062,213	+2
New Britain Gen. Hosp. (New Britian, CT)	4,200,000	325 (290)	1,700,000	+6	1,900,000	803,000	+3
St. Joseph Mercy Hosp. (Pontiac, MI)	4,149,921	531 (320)	1,610,000	n/c	2,294,000	1,850,904	-3
Irvine Med. Ctr. (Orange, CA)	4,108,081	493 (302)	1,171,220	-3	2,595,618	661,000	n/c
Moses H. Cone Mem. Hosp. (Greensboro, NC)	4,100,000	568 (334)	1,100,000	-2	1,500,000	760,445	+3
San Mateo County Hosp. (San Mateo, CA)	4,020,000	250 (205)	1,500,000	+3	2,000,000	850,000	-1
Sparrow Hosp. (Lansing, MI)	4,000,000	504 (400)	1,000,000	-3	1,000,000	1,400,000	+12
St. Peters Hosp. (Albany, NY)	3,994,976	452 (400)	998,000	-2	1,402,072	570,884	n/c
Jackson Madison Hosp. (Jackson, MS)	3,928,000	682 (400)	1,428,000	+1	1,700,000	1,563,000	+1
Norwalk Hosp. (Norwalk, CT)	3,872,000	300 (300)	1,350,000	-1	2,000,000	1,277,500	+1
Grady Memorial Hosp. (Atlanta, GA)	3,843,668	992 (750)	1,869,730	-15	329,352	1,642,500	-15
Park View Memorial Hosp. (Ft. Wayne, IN)	3,830,000	725 (575)	2,040,000	+5	1,500,000	1,318,330	-4
Medical Center Hosp./VT (Burlington, VT)	3,700,000	548 (395)	1,000,000	+9	2,000,000	1,100,000	+8
El Camino Hosp. (Mountainview, CA)	3,680,000	300 (200)	1,010,000	-5	2,400,000	493,851	-10
Mt. Sinai Med. Ctr. (Cleveland, OH)	3,675,000	375 (285)	1,212,943	-10	2,212,091	957,207	-10
Fairview General Hosp. (Cleveland, OH)	3,590,000	467 (230)	1,200,000	-2	1,200,000	252,000	-15
E. Jefferson General (Matarie, LA)	3,565,000	600 (400)	1,645,418	-15	1,810,452	938,992	+10
Riverview Med. Ctr. (Redbank, NJ)	3,550,000	496 (440)	1,700,000	-2	1,500,000	730,000	-2
Hosp. of St. Raphael (New Haven, CT)	3,525,000	500 (475)	1,800,000	n/c	2,000,000	1,500,000	n/c
JFK Med. Ctr. (Edison, NJ)	3,500,000	550 (550)	1,677,000	+2	1,320,000	1,535,000	+30
Hinsdale Adventist Hosp. (Hinsdale, IL)	3,500,000	438 (250)	1,300,000	+4	1,600,000	700,000	n/c
Kennestone Hosp. (Marietta, GA)	3,433,672	539 (377)	1,590,990	-7	1,601,146	783,813	-1
Selinsgrove Med. Ctr. (Elysberg, PA)	3,400,000	694 (689)	1,900,000	+4	1,300,000	876,000	-2
Lakeland Reg. Med. Ctr. (Lakeland, FL)	3,266,450	891 (475)	1,769,450	n/c	1,477,000	550,000	-5
Blodgett Memorial Hosp. (Grand Rapids, MI)	3,161,000	410 (256)	1,478,000	-10	1,472,000	520,000	-6
St. Elizabeth Hosp. (Beaumont, TX)	3,000,000	500 (400)	1,000,000	+5	1,500,000	1,084,000	+3
St. Francis Hosp. (Evanston, IL)	2,970,885	426 (280)	1,070,595	-13	1,483,409	635,000	-13
Emanuel Hosp. (Portland, OR)	2,800,000	554 (225)	1,100,000	+5	1,400,000	880,000	-5
St. Joseph Hosp. (Orange, CA)	2,778,000	380 (240)	1,133,000	-10	1,137,000	583,000	-10
Glen Falls Hosp. (Glen Falls, NY)	2,668,000	440 (300)	946,000	-4	1,461,000	905,547	n/c
Southern Regl. Med. Ctr. (Riverdale, GA)	2,600,819	367 (260)	1,051,615	n/c	1,307,102	821,437	n/c
Bridgewater State Hosp. (Bridgewater, MA)	2,580,000	n/a	950,000	-2	1,500,000	2,738,000	n/c
McLean Hosp. (Belmont, MA)	2,505,000	328 (100)	1,500,000	-2	1,000,000	672,000	-1
Christ Hosp. (Jersey City, NJ)	2,470,000	367 (340)	1,400,000	n/c	900,000	505,000	+7
Jersey City Med. Ctr. (Jersey City, NJ)	2,465,000	550 (425)	1,000,000	+3	1,300,000	347,280	+6
E. Tennessee Baptist Hosp. (Knoxville, TN)	2,410,000	330 (260)	945,447	n/c	1,470,743	565,000	+2
Froedert Mem. Lutheran (Wauwatosa, WI)	2,400,000	280 (190)	900,000	+1	980,000	695,000	+1
Memorial City Med. Ctr. (Houston, TX)	2,226,000	250 (150)	1,125,000	+6	1,034,940	886,000	+5
Spohn Hosp. (Corpus Christi, TX)	2,225,000	450 (400)	975,000	+4	850,000	1,095,000	+3
Bethesda Memorial Hosp. (Boynton Bea., FL)	2,200,000	306 (198)	822,321	+6	1,038,000	449,794	-5
Cape Cod Hosp. (Hyannis, MA)	2,196,420	247 (225)	637,569	+1	1,460,592	479,300	n/c
Mercy Med. Ctr. (Cedar Rapids, IA)	2,131,000	453 (312)	1,009,000	n/c	892,000	754,000	-2
SW General Hosp. (Middleberg Hgts., OH)	2,049,600	350 (260)	870,000	-3	1,000,000	712,410	n/c
Comm. General Hosp. (Harris, NY)	1,908,187	300 (210)	908,187	+4	1,000,000	188,945	-7
Laurel Crest Manor (Bensburg, PA)	2,100,000	615 (611)	800,000	+4	1,200,000	650,000	n/c
Rosewood Center (Owings Mills, MD)	1,200,000	600 (300)	440,000	-5	600,000	400,000	-5
John L. Deaton Med. Ctr. (Baltimore, MD)	1,168,000	360 (212)	437,000	-4	600,000	182,800	+25
Mercy Med. Ctr. (Roseburg, OR)	850,000	111 (55)	230,000	+5	490,000	170,000	-5
Milwaukee Psych. Hosp. (Wauwatosa, WI)	670,000	147 (80)	325,000	-17	313,000	150,000	-3
Roswell Park Memorial (Buffalo, NY)	608,058	120 (100)	122,000	+2	464,221	109,800	+8
TOTALS/AVERAGES	$451,294,656	57,595 (44,904)	$161,516,616	+2%	$226,185,439	111,048,890	+1%

FIGURE 4.4 *(continued)*

51

Using the 40 percent conversion factor mentioned above, annual comparable sales would be $4-18 million.

Self-operated hospital food services are a major part of the industry. They offer excellent career opportunities for the foodservice manager. While credentials as a registered dietician are a plus, they are not required. In smaller locations dietetic service can be (and often is) contracted out to a visiting RD. In the larger facilities there is ample organizational space for staff dietitians.

In the early days of hospital foodservice management, the dietician was often the food service director also. She or he was seldom trained as a manager and was generally a poor one. That has changed; RDs desiring management positions now usually have the appropriate background. It is not unusual for a hospital's director of foodservice to have credentials both as an RD and as a manager.

For purposes of comparison, Figure 4.5 shows the organizational structure of a skilled nursing care facility, and Figure 4.6 shows the organizational chart of an intermediate nursing care facility. Note that the foodservice (dietary) department is always separate and headed by either a supervisor or manager. The title is dependent upon the size and operating scope of the facility.

COLLEGES AND UNIVERSITIES: CORNELL UNIVERSITY

College and university foodservices of today provide board-rate meals to students, cash sale operations, catering services, foodservice vending, and a myriad of other foodservices for the college community. Campus dining is now a major foodservice industry segment with a sophisticated customer.

Page 45 shows that about half of all college and university facilities are self-operated. This includes some of the largest and most complex schools in this segment. *Food Service Director's* annual survey of the top 100 self-op campus dining facilities is shown in Figure 4.7.

As with the health care example, we can estimate sales using the 40 percent food purchase ratio. Sales so calculated range from $5.3 to $34.9 million.

One of the operations covered in this survey is Cornell University in Ithaca, New York. With annual gross sales estimated at $20 million, it provides an excellent case study for our review.

Cornell is an Ivy League college. As such, it has comparatively high tuition and a student body that expects the quality of the foodservice to match that of the education.

Figure 2.2 in Chapter 2 is a mission statement of the goals of the food service department at Cornell. They are:

■ Customer satisfaction
■ Staff excellence
■ Environmental diversity
■ Resource management
■ University support
■ Industry leadership

Cornell's organizational chart defines three areas of operational responsibility:

■ Administrative services
■ Dining services (area 1 and area 2)
■ Food production

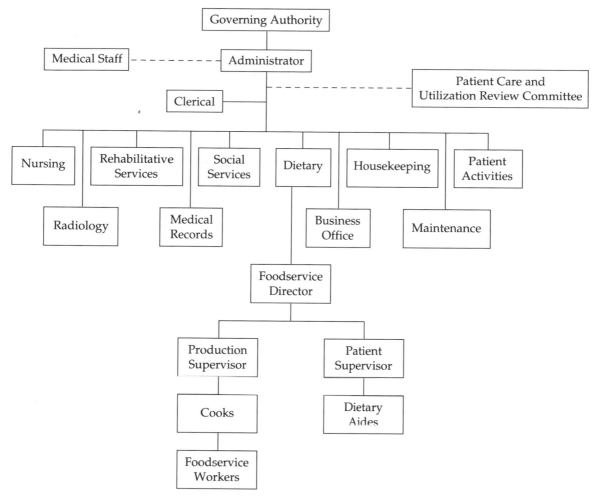

FIGURE 4.5 Typical Organizational Chart of a Skilled Care Facility (*Source: Management of Medical Foodservice*, 2nd ed. Catherine Sullivan, Van Nostrand Reinhold, 1990.)

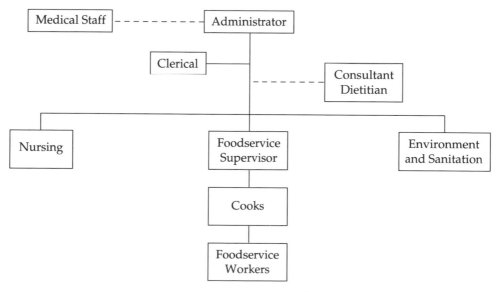

FIGURE 4.6 Typical Organizational Chart of an Intermediate Care Facility (*Source: Management of Medical Foodservice*, 2nd ed. Catherine Sullivan, Van Nostrand Reinhold, 1990.)

Performance Report for 100 top self-op colleges

COLLEGE (location)	1992 FOOD $ PURCHASES	+or- Pct.	1992 LABOR $ COSTS	1992 OTHER DIR. EXPENSES	'91/'92 ENROLLMENT	1992 MEALS (Board)	+or- Pct.
Univ. California/LA (Los Angeles, CA)	11,700,000	+5	12,600,000	7,700,000	32,000/32,000	7,000,000	-1
Penn State Univ. (University Park, PA)	10,300,000	+3	11,279,500	3,018,925	28,000/28,000	2,250,000	n/c
Michigan State Univ. (Lansing, MI)	10,158,000	-5	8,130,000	8,282,000	40,000/39,500	6,750,000	-2
Brigham Young Univ. (Provo, UT)	9,000,000	n/c	8,000,000	6,000,000	27,000/28,000	4,032,000	n/c
Purdue Univ. (W. Lafayette, IN)	8,500,000	+2	9,700,000	1,350,000	36,000/36,000	4,600,000	n/c
Univ. of Texas (Austin, TX)	7,638,000	n/c	7,636,000	5,554,000	49,700/48,600	6,056,000	n/c
Harvard Univ. (Cambridge, MA)	7,540,000	+6	12,650,000	8,945,000	35,500/35,778	5,000,000	+9
Syracuse Univ. (Syracuse, NY)	7,500,000	-6	6,298,000	6,687,000	16,000/16,000	1,541,561	-6
Rutgers Univ. (New Brunswick, NJ)	7,440,000	+4	9,730,000	7,200,000	50,000/60,000	4,000,000	+4
Ohio State Univ. Hosp. (Columbus, OH)	7,327,102	+3	4,238,708	1,070,000	33,000/33,000	4,647,120	-4
Univ. of Wisconsin (Madison, WI)	7,110,900	+3	3,663,188	678,682	42,000/40,000	7,000,000	-9
Notre Dame Univ. (South Bend, IN)	7,000,000	+1	7,500,000	4,000,000	10,000/10,0000	5,000,000	+2
Univ. Of Connecticut (Storrs, CT)	6,860,000	n/c	11,392,700	499,300	17,250/16,850	3,232,000	-6
Kent State Univ. (Kent, OH)	6,500,000	+7	7,200,000	1,500,000	31,500/31,700	4,400,000	+5
Univ. of Colorado (Boulder, CO)	6,340,000	+10	4,566,000	1,318,000	24,000/24,000	3,315,000	+4
Virginia Tech Univ. (Blacksburg, VA)	6,100,000	+4	7,000,000	1,000,000	23,000/23,000	3,650,000	-4
USAF Academy (Golden, CO)	6,000,000	—	n/a	n/a	n/a	2,342,530	-2
Yale Univ. (New Haven, CT)	5,600,000	-2	8,000,000	2,500,000	10,000/10,000	2,500,000	n/c
Univ. of Maryland (College Park, MD)	5,500,000	+2	6,000,000	n/a	30,000/30,000	4,000,000	+5
Ohio State Univ. (Columbus, OH)	5,272,064	+4	6,886,544	2,477,000	52,000/52,000	2,600,000	-7
Univ. of Kentucky (Lexington, KY)	5,154,000	n/c	4,600,000	689,000	22,150/22,400	2,900,000	+3
U.S. Naval Academy (Annapolis, MD)	5,000,000	-8	3,500,000	800,000	44,000/44,000	4,700,000	n/c
Univ. of Washington (Seattle, WA)	5,000,000	-2	6,000,000	3,000,000	34,000/34,000	n/a	n/a
U.S. Military Academy (West Point, NY)	5,000,000	+4	n/a	n/a	4,322/4,300	n/a	n/a
Bowling Green State (Bowling Green, OH)	4,953,557	+5	5,297,000	2,262,000	18,000/18,000	1,964,000	+6
Boston College (Boston, MA)	4,831,411	+3	6,434,820	2,610,532	14,400/14,400	4,625,210	+8
Illinois State Univ. (Normal, IL)	4,500,000	+5	3,100,000	2,100,000	22,000/21,000	2,500,000	n/c
Univ. of Pennsylvania (Philadelphia, PA)	4,400,000	+4	4,600,000	4,000,000	17,860/17,890	3,000,000	+10
Univ. of California (Santa Barbara, CA)	4,400,000	+3	4,400,000	880,000	18,500/18,500	4,000,000	n/c
N. Carolina State Univ. (Raleigh, NC)	4,200,000	+3	2,000,000	1,500,000	20,000/22,000	2,539,445	+20
Iowa State Univ. (Ames, IA)	4,115,000	+3	1,450,000	2,000,000	25,000/25,000	3,000,000	n/c
Univ. of Georgia (Athens, GA)	4,000,000	+1	3,700,000	n/a	28,000/28,000	2,464,000	+2
Univ. of California (Berkley, CA)	4,000,000	n/c	6,500,000	1,500,000	30,000/30,000	2,500,000	-n/c
Univ. of Iowa (Iowa City, IA)	3,900,000	+6	4,600,000	1,066,000	26,800/28,000	2,162,250	n/c
Columbia Univ. (New York, NY)	3,750,000	-3	4,000,000	600,000	10,000/11,000	1,700,000	-3
Villanova Univ. (Villanova, PA)	3,736,000	+1	4,661,198	8,165,556	11,485/11,485	3,136,000	+3
Dartmouth College (Hanover, NH)	3,600,000	n/c	4,000,000	2,000,000	5,700/5,700	n/a	n/a
Univ. of N. Dakota (Grand Forks, ND)	3,500,000	+4	3,600,000	1,100,000	11,800/12,000	1,000,000	+3
Univ. of Dayton (Dayton, OH)	3,500,000	+10	6,490,000	1,600,000	10,400/10,600	n/a	n/a
Duke Univ. (Durham, NC)	3,500,000	n/c	4,500,000	1,000,000	10,000/10,000	7,280,000	-3
W. Michigan Univ. (Kalamazoo, MI)	3,500,000	n/c	4,980,000	3,965,000	22,000/22,000	2,700,000	n/c
Cal Poly State Univ. (San Luis Obispo, CA)	3,230,928	n/c	3,845,939	1,962,676	17,575/16,300	1,052,000	n/c
Ohio Univ. (Athens, OH)	3,200,000	+5	4,900,000	500,000	18,500/18,700	2,078,239	+3
Rochester Institute (Rochester, NY)	3,200,000	n/c	3,320,000	3,480,000	13,000/13,000	957,000	+7
E. Michigan Univ. (Ypsilanti, MI)	3,132,000	+4	3,186,406	2,361,000	25,000/25,000	1,500,000	+3
Univ. of Kansas (Lawrence, KS)	3,107,875	+9	3,521,900	542,432	25,000/25,000	1,820,460	-9
Colorado State Univ. (Fort Collins, CO)	3,100,000	n/c	3,100,000	n/a	21,500/21,500	833,000	-n/c
Univ. of Arizona (Tucson, AZ)	3,048,854	-8	3,442,316	1,400,000	35,500/34,500	8,481,310	-11
Univ. of Nebraska (Lincoln, NE)	3,007,540	+2	2,721,854	959,897	22,000/22,000	2,214,400	+5
Vanderbilt Univ. (Nashville, TN)	3,000,000	-4	2,200,000	1,500,000	10,200/10,200	n/a	-9

FIGURE 4.7 *Food Service Director* Magazine's 1992 Report for Top 100 Self-Op Colleges

COLLEGE (location)	1992 FOOD $ PURCHASES	+or- Pct.	1992 LABOR $ COSTS	1992 OTHER DIR. EXPENSES	'91/'92 ENROLLMENT	1992 MEALS (Board)	+or- Pct.
Univ. of New Hampshire (Durham, NH)	3,000,000	+5	3,800,000	2,500,000	11,800/12,000	1,800,000	+2
Eastern Illinois Univ. (Charleston, IL)	2,956,520	n/c	3,015,100	1,576,080	10,400/10,400	3,000,000	-5
Univ. of Minnesota (Minneapolis, MN)	2,907,718	+2	2,908,722	n/a	40,000/37,000	1,613,000	n/c
Univ. of Maine (Orono, ME)	2,900,000	n/c	3,700,000	181,000	13,000/12,000	1,051,980	-10
Washington State Univ. (Pullman, WA)	2,900,000	n/c	3,750,000	3,000,000	16,800/16,800	1,600,000	n/c
Univ. of Oklahoma (Norman, OK)	2,808,000	-2	2,577,000	1,310,000	23,000/23,000	1,400,000	n/c
S. Illinois Univ. (Carbondale, IL)	2,768,000	+2	3,028,000	3,361,000	23,800/24,000	1,926,400	n/c
Univ. of Oregon (Eugene, OR)	2,703,000	+4	2,650,000	655,000	16,700/16,500	1,427,000	+3
Utah State Univ. (Logan, UT)	2,700,000	-9	1,890,000	588,340	14,500/16,000	425,000	+7
Louisiana State Univ. (Baton Rouge, LA)	2,606,800	+3	2,799,000	1,834,000	26,000/26,700	701,149	-4
Oklahoma State Univ. (Stillwater OK)	2,600,000	+5	2,425,000	600,000	18,000/18,000	1,600,000	-5
Radford Univ. (Radford, VA)	2,600,000	n/c	2,100,000	400,000	9,500/9,400	2,465,884	+11
N. Iowa Univ. (Cedar Falls, IA)	2,600,000	+7	3,300,000	1,000,000	13,100/13,100	1,700,000	-4
Bucknell Univ. (Lewisville, PA)	2,600,000	n/c	2,000,000	n/a	3,200/3,200	448,400	+4
Georgia Southern Univ. (Statesboro, GA)	2,500,000	+4	3,000,000	500,000	13,300/14,100	1,800,000	+6
Univ. of N. Texas (Denton, TX)	2,460,000	+1	3,460,000	1,160,000	27,000/26,500	1,500,000	+2
Oregon StateUniv. (Corvallis, OR)	2,420,000	-12	2,855,000	1,523,000	14,950/14,000	710,000	-26
Kansas State Univ. (Manhattan, KS)	2,405,000	+3	3,220,332	1,594,414	21,000/21,500	2,400,000	n/c
San Jose State Univ. (San Jose, CA)	2,400,000	+4	2,600,000	2,500,000	30,000/29,500	520,000	n/c
Appalachian State Univ. (Boone, NC)	2,302,551	-10	2,821,536	1,730,000	11,502/11,570	1,796,549	-5
Univ. of Rhode Island (Kingston, RI)	2,235,188	+5	3,628,046	2,639,939	12,000/12,000	n/a	n/a
Univ. of Rochester (Rochester, NY)	2,300,000	n/c	2,000,000	1,500,000	7,000/7,000	1,500,000	n/c
Bates College (Lewiston, ME)	2,225,000	+6	2,000,000	475,000	1,500/1,550	810,000	+2
Smith College (N. Hampton, MA)	2,200,000	+3	n/a	n/a	2,600/2,600	1,300,000	n/c
California State Univ. (Fresno, CA)	2,185,000	-6	1,864,028	n/a	19,500/19,000	474,240	+1
Univ. of S. Mississippi (Hattiesburg, MS)	2,140,000	+5	1,300,000	200,000	12,200/11,500	1,250,000	+2
Williams College (Williamstown, MA)	2,130,000	+2	3,276,000	687,000	2,132/2,200	740,000	+2
Ferris State Univ. (Big Rapids, MI)	2,109,515	-3	3,098,382	3,986,987	12,000/11,800	1,467,978	-6
Michigan Tech. Univ. (Houghton, MI)	2,102,450	+6	2,342,730	300,350	6,900/6,900	1,240,000	n/c
Montanta State Univ. (Bozeman, MT)	2,100,000	+2	2,200,000	1,200,000	10,300/11,000	775,000	+8
Univ. of Wisconsin (Milwaukee, WI)	2,000,000	n/c	2,000,000	1,500,000	25,000/25,000	n/a	n/a
Drake Univ. (Des Moines, IA)	1,921,513	+13	1,261,063	1,167,618	8,096/6,882	960,331	+5
Auburn Univ. (Auburn, AL)	1,882,000	+3	1,207,000	794,000	21,600/22,000	n/a	n/a
Univ. of Akron (Akron, OH)	1,802,850	n/c	2,227,050	530,250	30,000/28,500	1,600,000	-5
N. Dakota State Univ. (Fargo, ND)	1,717,000	n/c	1,938,000	197,000	8,600/8,600	1,300,000	-2
Univ. of California (Sacramento, CA)	1,700,000	n/c	2,900,000	1,600,000	26,900/25,000	270,000	-2
Cal State Poly Tech. (Pomona, CA)	1,686,850	-4	2,518,884	1,095,494	20,500/17,500	1,058,000	-25
SUNY/Fredonia (Fredonia, NY)	1,650,000	-3	2,100,000	500,000	5,000/4,800	1,429,400	-3
C. Washington Univ. (St. Ellensburg, WA)	1,600,000	+4	1,800,000	1,300,000	6,100/6,300	1,017,000	-2
Tennessee Tech. Univ. (Cookesville, TN)	1,500,000	+2	972,000	1,116,000	8,200/8,200	n/a	n/a
Amherst College (Amherst, MA)	1,460,000	-10	1,651,937	620,000	15,080/15,080	544,078	+3
Furman Univ. (Greenville, SC)	1,455,000	n/c	1,329,000	754,000	3,300/3,300	842,000	n/c
Univ. of California (Fullerton, CA)	1,200,000	+5	1,500,000	900,000	25,000/25,000	n/a	n/a
Rensselaer Polytech. (Troy, NY)	1,000,000	+4	1,170,000	1,500,000	5,000/5,000	806,000	+5
Univ. of Mississippi (Oxford, MS)	1,000,000	+3	1,200,000	800,000	11,200/11,000	541,800	-2
Old Dominion Univ. (Norfolk, VA)	948,000	n/c	1,036,436	697,540	16,100/16,500	352,000	+20
Mt. Holyoke College (S. Hadley, MA)	910,000	-7	2,017,075	771,695	1,866/1,900	904,538	+1
Delta State Univ. (Cleveland, MS)	680,000	-1	504,000	167,128	3,950/4,008	740,000	n/c
Pacific Lutheran Univ. (Tacoma, WA)	617,880	-2	838,000	n/a	3,500/3,400	756,000	-2
N. Illinois Univ. (DeKalb, IL)	605,000	+3	912,000	230,000	24,000/23,000	n/a	n/a
TOTALS/AVERAGES	$368,382,510	+4%	$388,671,394	$176,503,003	1,903,434/1,904,036	207,914,658	+1%

FIGURE 4.7 *(continued)*

55

Figure 4.8 shows the organizational chart of Cornell's foodservice department.

Students are offered a variety of meal plans at six campus dining rooms. Cornell also runs four restaurants and cafeterias, four other retail units—snack and yogurt shops—and more than 200 vending machines at 65 locations.

Cornell serves more than 25,000 meals per day and employs 800 students each year. Gross annual sales from all outlets, as previously stated, exceed $20 million. Figure 4.9 is a bulletin from Cornell detailing its various services.

There are many foodservice management opportunities in self-op campus dining. Cornell dining services has 35 full-time management positions and 175 full-time professional staff positions. A career can be fashioned at a single college or university or can include moves to different colleges and/or universities. Those interested in a career in college and university foodservice must possess strong management ability and a well-rounded food management background.

ELEMENTARY AND SECONDARY SCHOOLS: THE USDA SCHOOL LUNCH PROGRAM

More than 90 percent—80,000 to 84,000 individual locations—of elementary and secondary school systems are self-ops. Some operate individually, while others are part of larger school districts.

School foodservices range from single decentralized kitchens to large, multi-unit centralized operations (commissaries). A small single unit school may serve only 100 meals per day. A large, multi-unit centralized system may serve up to 800,000 meals per day.

A decentralized school generally runs without commissary support and has a single foodservice director. For a large school this might be a professional manager; for a small school, a supervisor.

A centralized school system is usually operated by a city or county school district with a director overseeing the schools. It is managed centrally with a centralized preparation facility and distribution system. There may be from 250 to 900 schools in the system. Each school also does some of its own on-site food preparation.

The U.S. Department of Agriculture administers the National School Lunch Program (NSLP) through seven regional offices. Each state runs its own program under guidelines from the USDA. Local school boards, in turn, contract state departments of education for federal and state regulations regarding school lunch programs in their schools. Compliance allows the local board and its schools to receive USDA-donated foods as well as state and federal cash reimbursements in accordance with the program. This is a primary financial objective of the school lunch operation. Figure 4.10 details the NSLP and its organization from the United States Congress down to the local school foodservice authorities.

Figure 4.11 details the organization of a typical large school system. Note that local citizens elect a school board that in turn hires a school superintendent. That superintendent becomes responsible for all school activities, including the foodservice department. The foodservice director, who heads the department, is responsible to the superintendent and ultimately the school board for the operation of the program in the system and the district.

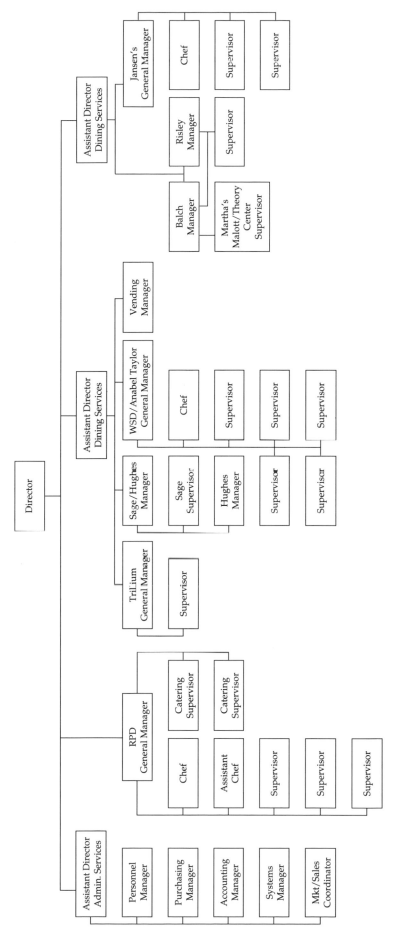

FIGURE 4.8 Organizational Chart (1992) of Cornell University's Department of Dining Services (Courtesy of Margaret Lacey)

Cornell Dining

Programs & Services

Program or Service	Definition of Clientele	Approximate # of Meals Served or Income per Day
Board Plan (Co-op)	Primary: Undergraduate campus residents Secondary: Upperclassmen off campus residents	15,300 meals
Cash ala Carte	Primary: Upperclassmen - off campus residents Secondary: Staff	$11,000
Catering	Primary: Non-Academic staff Secondary: Academic Staff	25-500 meals
Vending	Primary: Staff Secondary: Graduate Students	$3,200
Summer Programs	Cornell Community Members and Guests	300-3,000 meals
Convenience Store	Primary: Undergraduates Secondary: Staff/married graduate students	$3,500
Faculty Fellows/ Faculty-in-Residence	Primary: Faculty Secondary: Family members of faculty and Guests	85 meals

FIGURE 4.9 Cornell Dining Service—List of Programs (Courtesy of Margaret Lacey, Cornell University)

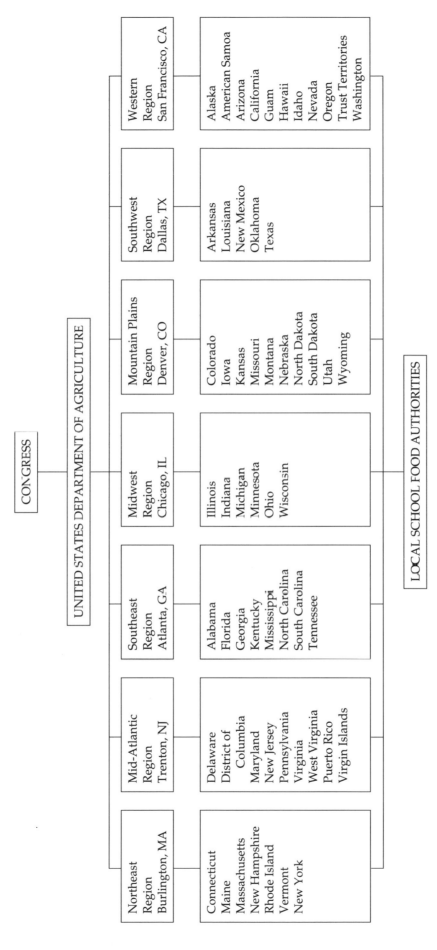

FIGURE 4.10 Organizational Chart of the National School Lunch Program (NSLP) (*Source: School Foodservice Management*, 4th ed. Dorothy VanEgmund Pannell, Van Nostrand Reinhold, 1990)

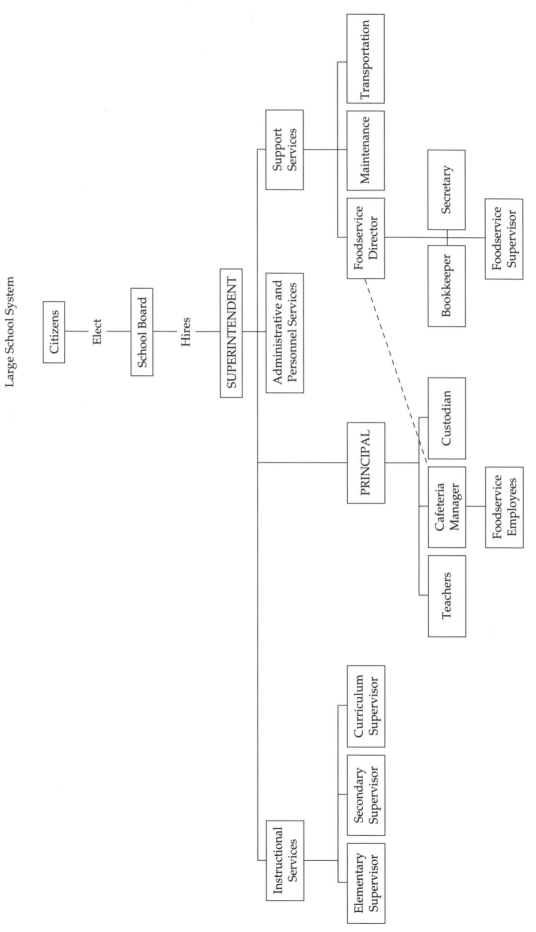

Large School System

FIGURE 4.11 Large School District Organizational Chart (*Source: School Foodservice Management*, 4th ed. Dorothy VanEgmund Pannell, Van Nostrand Reinhold, 1990)

FIGURE 4.12

Operating Objectives of Fairfax County, Virginia, Public School Foodservice System

1. Operate on a sound financial basis.
2. Serve good quality, nutritious food.
3. Teach good food habits.
4. Meet the needs of the students in a satisfying way.
5. Give employees an opportunity for personal development.

SOURCE: *School Foodservice Management*, 4th ed., Dorothy VanEgmund Pannell, Van Nostrand Reinhold, 1990.

Figure 4.12 lists the service objectives of the Fairfax County, Virginia, public school system. The list can serve as a model for any large school system.

Managers at individual schools must please the clients—students, teachers, and support staff. In this way a school district foodservice is analogous to a contract management firm, and the school-level managers are the unit directors. But in a school district there is a third boss (besides client and contractor): the USDA and its strict school lunch standards.

Food Service Director magazine published a 1993 report indicating that the top 100 school districts had estimated annual sales ranging from a low of $3 million to a high of $301 million. Some of this is reimbursement from the National School Lunch Program.

In *School Foodservice Management* (Van Nostrand Reinhold, 1990), Dorothy VanEgmund Pannell provides a guideline to plan local staffing for meal service with on-site production. The basis for evaluation is meals per labor hour (MPLH). The MPLHs are used to compare one location (or system) with another. Figure 4.13, an illustration of that planning system, demonstrates the degree of professionalism that exists within the school lunch management systems.

FIGURE 4.13

Typical Staffing Guidelines for an On-Site Production School Lunch Facility

| | Meals Per Labor Hour (MPLH)/Total Hours | | | |
| | Conventional System[b] | | Convenience System[b] | |
Number of Meal Equivalents[a]	MPLH	Total Hours	MPLH	Total Hours
Up to 100	8	9–12	9	9–11
101–150	9	12–16	10	11–14
151–200	10–11	16–17	12	14–16
201–250	12	17–20	14	16–18
251–300	13	20–22	15	18–20
301–400	14	22–29	16	20–25
401–500	14	29–35	18	20–28
501–600	15	35–40	18	28–34
601–700	16	40–43	19	34–37
701–800	17	43–47	20	37–40
800+	18	47+	21+	40+

[a]Meal equivalents include breakfast and à-la-carte sales. Three breakfasts equate to one lunch. A-la-carte sales of $3 equate to one lunch.
[b]Conventional system is preparation of food from raw ingredients on premises (using some bakery breads and prepared pizza and washing dishes). Convenience system is using maximum amount of processed foods (for example, using all bakery breads, prefried chicken, and preportioned condiments and using disposable dinnerware).

SOURCE: *School Foodservice Management*, 4th ed., Dorothy VanEgmund Pannell, Van Nostrand Reinhold, 1990.

The future of self-operated school systems is uncertain as costs increase and tax revenues decline. Despite this, there is every evidence that, by maintaining professionalism, school lunch managers will be able to maintain a strong self-op presence and resist contractors.

By the year 2000 it is expected that many school systems will provide service beyond the school lunch, including child day-care food service, meals for the elderly and the homeless, contracted service for other federal and state agencies, and more. This is discussed further in Chapter 10, "Sales and Marketing." Needless to say, school lunch programs, professionally operated, have potential markets as yet unrealized.

Those interested in school foodservice would do well to investigate larger school systems that have many management positions. With public school enrollments ballooning and school lunch budgets doing just the opposite, the need for professional school lunch managers and directors is greater than ever. The need for expert management is also making school districts give contractors a hard look.

School lunch programs will increasingly be required to defend their positions as taxpayer-supported services. Good management coupled with the obvious benefits of well-fed children should enable them to do so.

SUMMARY

A self-op is an organization that runs its own foodservice. Regardless of the industry segment, self-ops still flourish, providing career opportunities in professional foodservice management. Those interested in working for a self-op will need strong management ability and a deeper knowledge of the pertinent industry segment than those interested in employment with a contractor.

5

Financial Planning

Chapter 2 reviewed the concepts of management and the importance of establishing operating objectives, both service and financial. Establishing service objectives is the basis for management planning, and establishing financial objectives is part of that plan.

This chapter reviews the fundamentals of financial planning leading to the preparation of an operating budget. The same case histories used in Chapter 2 will be used here.

Upon completion of this chapter, readers should know and understand:

- The fundamentals of financial planning for a noncommercial foodservice operation
- How to prepare an annual budget for the foodservices of an office complex, a manufacturing plant, a college, and a hospital
- How to use these case examples to prepare an annual budget for any other type of institutional or noncommercial foodservice operation

THE FINANCIAL PROCESS

The foodservice director's financial projections and expectations, as well as the inevitable fiscal constraints he or she has to work with, are contained in the annual financial plan, also called the operating budget.

All institutions, whether self-operated or contracted, prepare annual operating budgets. The initial budget is usually submitted for review six to nine months before the new fiscal (budget) year. A final budget is prepared and usually approved three months in advance of the fiscal year.

The fiscal year may be the calendar year or any other 12-month period established by the organization. The manner in which an organization reports its financial results to stockholders, governmental agencies, or owners will determine the dates of the fiscal year. Most businesses use the calendar year (January to December) as their fiscal year; some use July to June. Many governmental agencies and departments use October to September as their fiscal year. The fiscal years of colleges and universities often parallel the academic calendar; those of hospitals, correctional institutions, and others vary.

Regardless of the dates chosen, the period in question covers one year of operations. That year may be divided into calendar months or accounting periods. Accounting periods are established by the organization to suit the schedule of the finance department. An accounting period is measured in weeks.

Organizations that use the calendar year as their accounting format prepare detailed statements for each month—their accounting period. The concept of multiple weeks is not used. They also prepare a quarterly report every three months. Those quarters are usually divided as follows:

- 1st Quarter . . . January 1–March 31st
- 2nd Quarter . . . April 1–June 30th
- 3rd Quarter . . . July 1–September 30th
- 4th Quarter . . . October 1–December 31st

Organizations that use weekly accounting periods as their format usually employ a "4-4-5" method of arranging the weeks into quarters. That is, they report two four-week periods and one five-week period to establish 12 annual accounting periods of equal length. Those 12 annual accounting periods usually look like this:

ACCOUNTING CALENDAR

FIRST QUARTER

PERIOD ONE	PERIOD TWO	PERIOD THREE
Weeks 1–4	Weeks 5–8	Weeks 9–13

SECOND QUARTER

PERIOD FOUR	PERIOD FIVE	PERIOD SIX
Weeks 14–17	Weeks 18–21	Weeks 22–26

THIRD QUARTER

PERIOD SEVEN	PERIOD EIGHT	PERIOD NINE
Weeks 27–30	Weeks 31–34	Weeks 35–39

FOURTH QUARTER

PERIOD TEN	PERIOD ELEVEN	PERIOD TWELVE
Weeks 40–43	Weeks 44–47	Weeks 48–52

The calendar year system has 365 operating days; the accounting period system has 364 (52 weeks × 7 days per week = 364 days). The accounting department makes periodic adjustments to pick up the missing day and, every four years, February 29th. Some organizations add a 53rd week when seven days accrue; others use various formulas to compensate for the missing day.

Regardless of the method, an operating location must prepare its annual financial forecast using the client's accounting calendar. (The accounting calendar has an effect on cost control, too. This is discussed in greater detail in Chapter 9, "Cost Control.")

THE BUDGET FORMAT

There is no one format for budget preparation suitable for all locations. Each location, type of facility, and company has different needs, and the budget format should match the organization's accounting calendar service needs.

Budget formats will vary with each type of facility. B&I, health care, corrections, school systems, and colleges and universities will use somewhat different models to prepare annual budgets. Despite the differences, the following steps are useful for all situations:

Step 1: Prepare a set of working forms for financial planning that include all areas of income and expense.
Step 2: Forecast revenues from all sources. (SALES)
Step 3: Forecast cost of sales. (COS)

Step 4: Forecast labor- and payroll-related costs.
Step 5: Forecast all operating expenses.
Step 6: Summarize all areas of revenue and expense to produce the annual budget forecast.

Follow these six steps to prepare a budget for any noncommercial foodservice.

The following examples examine budget preparation for an office building, a manufacturing plant, a college, and a hospital. The principles and procedures covered are applicable to other operations, such as correctional facilities and school systems.

CASE 1: URBAN OFFICE BUILDING

This is the same case examined in Chapter 2, with some modification. The location is the national headquarters of a large corporation in a major metropolitan city.

The facility services 2,000 employees and 100 executives. The employees are provided a 600-seat cafeteria for breakfast and lunch. There is also a 100-seat service dining room for employees desiring table service or lunch. There are also four executive/guest dining rooms for executives' business and entertainment needs. Special functions and some services are also provided in these rooms to employees and executives, with company approval.

Coffee break service is provided by vending machines located throughout the building. Full-line vending service is sufficient to meet the needs of the employees. In addition coffee delivery service is provided from the main kitchen for special meeting room needs.

Company policy dictates that the prices in the employee cafeteria reflect a major savings over comparable street prices. The prices in the full-service dining rooms can include only the additional cost of table service over prices for the same menu items in the cafeteria. Executive guest dining charges are departmental transfers and reflect only the direct operating costs of food, labor, and expenses for the service. Special function prices are evaluated on an individual basis.

The facility is operated by a contract management company. Its annual fee is a 5 percent administrative charge and a 5 percent management fee, both based on sales.

While the company operates the foodservice as an employee benefit, its policy is to recover all operating costs from operational revenue. The host company is willing to subsidize the management fee. Where necessary, vending commissions may be used by the contractor to offset manual foodservice losses.

Twelve accounting periods are used to present the necessary fiscal information desired by both the contractor and the client. A 13-week quarter with a 4-4-5 week format is used. The format in Figure 5.1 is used for the period operating statement as well as the annual statement.

Forecasting Revenue (Sales)

Forecasting sales for any foodservice operation are simply projected customer count multiplied by expected check average. For a B&I account, total sales are divided into periods and/or categories of sales; in this case that means cafeteria, service dining room, executive/guest dining, special functions, and catering, if any.

Potential customers of this facility are limited to employees of the client corporation and guests. One of the measures of the success of this employee benefit is the percentage of employees using the foodservice on a regular basis—

Period/Annual Statement
Urban Office Building

I.	SALES			
	Cafeteria		$_____	
	Service Dining Room		_____	
	Executive/Guest Dining		_____	
	Other		_____	
		TOTAL SALES	$_____	100.0%
II.	FOOD COST		$_____	__.__%
		GROSS PROFIT	$_____	__.__%
III.	LABOR COST			
	Payroll		$_____	__.__
	Payroll Related		_____	__.__
		TOTAL LABOR COST	$_____	__.__%
IV.	OPERATING EXPENSES			
	Paper Goods		$_____	
	Cleaning Supplies		_____	
	Linen and Laundry		_____	
	Replacements		_____	
	Insurance		_____	
	Repairs and Maintenance		_____	
	Exterminator		_____	
	Other Miscellaneous Costs		_____	
	Administrative Charge		_____	
		TOTAL OPERATING EXPENSES	$_____	__.__%
V.	TOTAL ALL COSTS		$_____	__.__%
VI.	NET OPERATING PROFIT OR (LOSS)		$_____	__.__%
VII.	MANAGEMENT FEE		$_____	__.__%
VIII.	NET PROFIT OR (LOSS)		$_____	__.__%

FIGURE 5.1   Typical Period Statement Used by a Contractor for a B&I Facility

the participation rate. Normally, a company expects an average daily participation of at least 50 percent. Some very successful operations achieve employee participation averages as high as 80 percent. The menu price structure, food quality, service, and attractiveness of the facility all contribute to the value perception of the customers (the employees) and, therefore, to the participation rate.

Workers in an urban office building are certainly not a captive audience. There is competition everywhere. Regardless of the lower prices charged in the employee cafeteria, the participation rate will be low unless the foodservice fulfills employee wants and needs.

Figure 5.2 is a form for potential annual sales evaluation. This form determines annual sales using meal period, participation percentage by meal period, check average per category of sales, and average daily sales.

The number of operating days per year is multiplied by average daily sales to forecast estimated annual sales. A forecast for each individual accounting period can be prepared by substituting the number of operating days in the accounting period for days in a year. In most cases a forecast by period (the 4-4-5 method) is also prepared to verify the annual forecast. For this example we will only review the annual forecast.

Sales Forecast Planning Form
Urban Office Building

A. Employee Population: _____

B. Executive Population: _____

C. Annual Operating Days: _____

(1)	(2)	(3)	(4)	(5)	(6)
Meal Period	Participation (%)	Average Daily Customers	Estimated Check Average ($)	Estimated Daily Sales ($)	Estimated Annual Sales ($)
Breakfast					
Lunch					
Service DR					
Exec. DR					
Special Functions					
Other					
D. Total Estimated Daily/Annual Sales				$	$

FIGURE 5.2 Typical Forecast Planning Form for a B&I Location

The following assumptions will be used to prepare an annual sales forecast:

	Participation	Check Average ($)
Breakfast Cafeteria	15%	1.00
Lunch Cafeteria	60%	2.50
Service Dining Room	10%	6.00
Exec/Guest Dining	60%	10.00
Special Functions	Estimated	15.00
Other	Estimated	15.00

There are numerous holiday closures—the foodservice operates an average of 250 days per year.

Using these assumptions, the following steps will produce the sales forecast shown in Figure 5.3:

Step 1: Verify that all meal period categories under column 1 correspond to the account's actual sales categories.

Step 2: Enter the population figures for employees and executives on lines A and B at the top of the form.

Step 3: Enter the annual operating days expected on line C at the top of the form.

Step 4: Enter the participation percentages for each category of sales under column 2.

Step 5: Multiply the percentages under column 2 by their respective population figure: employees, line A; executives, line B. Use estimates for executive dining and special functions. Enter the results under column 3.

Step 6: Enter the estimated check average for each category of sales under column 4.

Step 7: Multiply the figures under column 3 by the figures under column 4 and enter each result in the appropriate location under column 5.

Sales Forecast Planning Form
Urban Office Building

A. Employee Population: _____2,000_____

B. Executive Population: _____100_____

C. Annual Operating Days _____250_____

(1)	(2)	(3)	(4)	(5)	(6)
Meal Period	Participation (%)	Average Daily Customers	Estimated Check Average ($)	Estimated Daily Sales ($)	Estimated Annual Sales ($)
Breakfast	15	300	1.00	300	75,000
Lunch	60	1,200	2.50	3,000	750,000
Service DR	10	200	6.00	1,200	300,000
Exec. DR	60	60	10.00	600	150,000
Special Functions	Est.	10	15.00	150	37,500
Other	Est.	20	15.00	300	75,000
D. Total Estimated Daily/Annual Sales				$5,550	$1,387,500

FIGURE 5.3 Completed Sales Forecast Planning Form for Urban Office Building Example

Step 8: Multiply each figure in column 5 by the number of annual operating days shown in line C and enter the result in the appropriate line under column 6.

Step 9: Add columns 5 and 6 and enter results on line D.

You now have a forecast for:

■ Daily customer count by meal period
■ Daily estimated sales by meal period and total
■ Annual estimated sales by meal period and total

These figures can be used later for production planning, developing cost control data, and other relevant needs, some of which are discussed in subsequent chapters.

Forecasting Cost of Sales (Food Cost)

Accountants use two phrases, *cost of goods sold* or *cost of sales*, for what B&I operators call *food cost*. Regardless of the terminology, the concept is the same.

Food cost is the result of determining the categories of sales and the expected food cost percentage per category and then summarizing the results. Figure 5.4 has been designed for this exercise.

The procedure for using this form is as follows:

Step 1: Enter the appropriate meal periods under column 1. These are taken from column 1 of the Sales Forecast Planning Form shown in Figures 5.2 and 5.3.

Sales Mix/Cost Mix Analysis
Urban Office Building

(1)	(2)	(3)	(4)	(5)
Meal Period	Projected Annual Sales	Projected Food Cost (%)	Projected Food Cost ($)	Manager's Comments
Breakfast	75,000	35	26,250	
Lunch	750,000	40	300,000	
Service DR	300,000	35	105,000	
Executive DR	150,000	50	75,000	
Special Functions	37,500	50	18,750	
Other	75,000	30	22,500	
TOTALS	(A) 1,387,500	(C) B ÷ A = 39.5%	(B) $547,500	

FIGURE 5.4 Completed Sales Mix/Cost Mix Analysis for Urban Office Building Example

Step 2: Enter the projected annual sales under column 2. These are taken from column 6 of the Sales Forecast Planning Form.

Step 3: Enter the projected food cost percentage for each category of sales under column 3. These are evaluated by an analysis of the menu, pricing structure, company policy, and like variables. For this case history they have been estimated for illustration purposes only.

Step 4: Multiply each meal category sales amount in column 2 by each matching projected food cost percentage in column 3 and enter resulting dollar amount in column 4 as projected food cost.

Step 5: Sum column 2 to box A. This total should match the previous estimated annual sales figure shown on the Sales Forecast Planning Form. In this case, that number is $1,387,500. Sum column 4, the dollar amount of each category of food cost, and enter in box B. In this case, that amount is $547,500.

Step 6: Determine the annual projected food cost percentage based on the sales mix/cost mix analyzed by dividing the cost amount in box B ($547,500) by the sales amount in box A ($1,387,500). Enter the resulting percentage figure, 39.5 percent, in box C. This is the overall average food cost percentage resulting from the estimated sales and cost of sales for each meal period or area of sales.

Estimating Gross Profit Objectives

Recall that the food cost percentages used were determined by an analysis of the menu, pricing structure, company policy, and other variables. It was also stated that the facility was operated on a management fee basis by a contract management company and that the client considered the service an employee benefit. These details all have a bearing on the client's desire to recover all operating costs and the management fee from revenue.

When the annual budget is prepared, the gross profit must meet the bottom line objectives of management, or adjustments are required. Those adjustments may affect service hours, services provided, or pricing policy. Most often, adjustments are made to the pricing policy and the achievable gross profits. This will be covered in more detail in Chapter 9.

Forecasting Labor Costs

Forecasting labor costs requires the preparation of a complete survey of positions on the organization chart, the number of labor hours per position, the wage and salary scales for all employees, and an analysis of payroll-related costs and employee benefits. Consideration must be given to staffing patterns at the current service level and to any possible increases or cuts in service and, therefore, staff. Remember, service requirements are established by client policy, and the contractor must fill those requirements via adequate staffing.

There are four categories of personnel employed in any foodservice operation:

1. Management and administration
2. Production personnel
3. Service personnel
4. Sanitation and maintenance personnel (general utility)

An analysis using these four categories as a basis for cost projections can be prepared for this case history. The resulting information will provide a forecast of projected wage and salary costs for the coming (budget) year. A Labor Cost Planning Form work sheet is shown in Figure 5.5. The use of this or other such planning forms will allow for a potentially accurate forecast of annual labor costs for budget planning.

To use the Labor Cost Planning Form:

Step 1: Prepare a list of positions required for staffing to meet the service needs. List them in the four categories shown under column 1.
Step 2: Enter the number of workers required for each position under column 2. See Chapter 8, "Labor Hours Planning."
Step 3: Enter the number of weekly hours scheduled for work by each category of worker under column 3. Evaluate the sum of hours for both part- and full-time workers.
Step 4: Enter wage and/or salary rates for each category or individual worker. Use weekly pay scales for salaried personnel and hourly wage rates for hourly personnel.
Step 5: Evaluate total weekly wage and salary costs for each position using data from columns 3 and 4. Enter results on the appropriate line under column 5.
Step 6: Sum columns 2, 3, and 5. Enter the results at Totals.
Step 7: Multiply the subtotal of column 5 by the number of weeks in the fiscal year (usually 52). Enter the result at Projected Annual Wage and Salary Costs.
Step 8: Establish an expected reserve requirement for annual wage and salary increases. Enter that percentage figure at the ____% location. Multiply that percentage by the projected annual wage and salary costs. Enter the result in the space provided.
Step 9: Add the projected annual wage and salary costs to the estimated reserve for wage and salary increases. Enter at the bottom line.

Labor Cost Planning Form
Urban Office Building

(1)	(2)	(3)	(4)	(5)
Position	No. of Workers	Total Weekly Labor Hours	Wage Rate ($)	Present Weekly Wage Cost ($)
I. MGE./ADMIN.				
Subtotal				
II. PRODUCTION				
Subtotal				
III. SERVICE				
Subtotal				
IV. SAN. & MTE.				
Subtotal				
TOTALS				$ ___

Projected annual wage and salary costs (weekly cost X 52)	$___
___% reserve for wage and salary increases	$___
Forecast wage and salary costs for coming year	$___

FIGURE 5.5 Typical Labor Cost Planning Form for a B&I Location

Considerations

A manager preparing this form must consider the following questions:

- Is any change in service projected that will alter the staffing plan?
- Is there a union contract in effect that will establish a required wage increase for union personnel?
- Are there any client policies yet to be enacted that will affect the service requirements?

Budget time is when you evaluate present service and try to forecast any changes. Anything that will affect staffing patterns—and the resulting financial implications—must be considered.

Figure 5.6 is a completed analysis of this case history, using estimated salary rates that represent the current level of pay for a location of this sort.

Payroll-Related Costs

All employers have the same obligations for payroll-related costs. There are two categories: mandated taxes and employee benefits. Mandated taxes are those required by law. Employee benefits are provided the employee as a condition of

Labor Cost Planning Form
Urban Office Building

(1) Position	(2) No. of Workers	(3) Total Weekly Labor Hours	(4) Wage Rate ($)	(5) Present Weekly Wage Cost ($)
I. MGE./ADMIN.				
General Manager	1	40	650/wk.	650.00
Asst. Gen. Mgr.	1	40	500/wk.	500.00
Bookkeeper	1	40	350/wk.	350.00
Office Clerk	1	40	7.00/hr.	280.00
Subtotal	4	160		1,780.00
II. PRODUCTION				
Executive Chef	1	40	600/wk.	600.00
Cooks	2	80	10.00/hr.	800.00
Kitchen Worker	2	70	8.00/hr.	560.00
Baker	1	40	400/wk.	400.00
Kitch. Utility	2	70	5.00/hr.	350.00
Subtotal	8	300		2,710.00
III. SERVICE				
Cafeteria Sup.	1	40	400/wk.	400.00
Caf. Workers	10	350	5.00/hr.	1,750.00
Cashiers	3	75	6.00/hr.	450.00
Waitstaff	6	120	7.00/hr.	840.00
Subtotal	20	585		3,440.00
IV. SAN.& MTE.				
Head Utility	1	40	10.00/hr.	400.00
General Utility	6	210	5.00/hr.	1,050.00
Porters	2	70	5.00/hr.	350.00
Subtotal	9	320	—	$1,800.00
TOTALS	41	1,365	—	$9,730.00

Projected annual wage and salary costs (weekly cost X 52)	$505,960.00
Reserve for wage and salary increases (4%)	$ 20,238.00
Forecast wage and salary costs for coming year	$526,198.00

FIGURE 5.6 Completed Labor Cost Planning Form for Urban Office Building Example

employment. In a union shop, those benefits are spelled out in the union contract, in what is often termed the *welfare clause*.

Mandated Payroll Taxes

While the term *taxes* is used, these mandated benefits are actually various types of insurance. Some are paid to a government agency (i.e., Social Security) while others are paid to private insurers (i.e., Workers Compensation). These payments are all required and must be provided, by law, to every employee.

The four mandated benefits are Social Security and Medicare (FICA), state and federal unemployment insurance, worker's compensation, and in some states, state disability.

Employee Benefits

Various other employee benefits often provided for salaried and hourly workers include accident and health insurance, group life insurance, and pension plans. As mentioned above, a union work force may have some or all of these as a welfare package. The employer pays a fixed amount per employee for the total package.

Figure 5.7 is a summary of the payroll taxes and employee benefit costs an employer can expect. Note that some are variable costs, a percentage of wages paid (the payroll), while others are fixed costs, a set dollar amount per employee.

These rates change annually, and in recent years, rapidly. The United States Congress sets the FICA and Medicare rates. The various states and the employer's insurance rating establish the unemployment insurance rates. Past accident patterns and policies of the insurer determine the worker's compensation rates. Union welfare rates are negotiated at contract time for the life of the contract. Group life and pension plan costs fluctuate with insurance and annuity rates as well as inflation and interest rates.

Figure 5.7 is a payroll-related costs planner that can be used for the urban office building case, based on present tax levels. Figure 5.8 shows that form modified and used to evaluate projected payroll-related costs anticipated for the urban office building case example.

To use the Payroll-Related Costs Planning Form:

Step 1: Get the estimated annual payroll costs for salaried and hourly payroll from Figure 5.6, columns 4 and 5. Enter results at lines A and B.

FIGURE 5.7

Typical List of Fixed and Variable, Mandated and Voluntary Payroll-Related Costs

	Variable % of Payroll	Fixed Dollar Amount per Employee
Social Security and Medicare (FICA)	X	
State Unemployment Insurance	X	
Federal Unemployment Insurance	X	
Workers Compensation	X	
Health Insurance		X
Group Life Insurance		X
Pension Plan Insurance		X
Union Welfare Package		X

Payroll-Related Costs Planning Form
Urban Office Building

PROJECTED ANNUAL PAYROLL COST (from Figure 5.6)

A. Management and Administration (salaried)	$156,832
B. Hourly Wages	369,366
TOTAL SALARIES AND WAGES (payroll)	$526,198

PROJECTED NUMBER OF EMPLOYEES (from Figure 5.6)

C. Salaried	6
D. Hourly	35
TOTAL EMPLOYEES	41

(1) Cost Category	(2) % of Payroll Cost	(3) Fixed Cost per Employee ($)	(4) Total Dollar Cost
FICA	7.5		39,465
State Unemployment	3.0		15,786
Federal Unemployment	0.6		3,157
Workers Compensation	4.0		21,048
State Disability	0.6		3,157
Health Insurance (Mge. Only)		1,000	6,000
Life Insurance (Mge. Only)		200	1,200
Pension Plan (Mge. Only)		500	3,000
Union Welfare Plan (Hourly Only)		600	21,000
TOTAL DOLLAR COSTS			$113,813
Ratio to Payroll			21.6%

FIGURE 5.8 Completed Payroll-Related Costs Planning Form for Urban Office Building Example

Step 2: Get the number of salaried and hourly employees from the form in Figure 5.6. Enter the results at lines C and D.

Step 3: List all categories of payroll-related costs under column 1.

Step 4: List all percentages of total payroll under column 2.

Step 5: List all dollar amounts of cost per employee under column 3.

Step 6: Calculate the figure to be placed in column 4 by using the information at the top of the form.

Step 7: Sum column 4 for total dollar costs. For this example that figure is $113,813. Divide the total cost by the total payroll ($113,813/$526,198) to get a 21.6% payroll ratio.

Operating Expenses

To complete the budget, forecast operating expenses. This category covers all direct costs of operation. This may or may not include corporate charges, administrative fees, and similar internal charges. For this example we will include the 5 percent administrative charge of the contractor.

Costs incurred for operating expenses are of two types: fixed and variable. Fixed costs are not related to sales volume or other business-level considerations. A fixed cost, such as a maintenance contract for cash registers, is a set dollar amount. Variable costs change in direct relation to sales volume. The administrative charge, for example, will go up and down as sales fluctuate.

Some costs have both fixed and variable components; in our example, repair & maintenance and miscellaneous charges are such items.

Figure 5.9 is a sample Operating Expense Schedule for our case. The costs shown are average for this type of operation.

To use the Operating Expense Schedule:

Step 1: Categorize all variable expenses and enter the percentage amount under the Variable % column.

Step 2: Figure all of the fixed expenses categories and enter the dollar amount under the Fixed $ column.

Step 3: Total the Variable % column to get total variable percentage.

Step 4: Total the Fixed $ column to get total dollar expense.

Step 5: Convert the variable expenses percentage to a dollar figure—multiply the variable expenses percentage by the projected dollar amount of annual sales. For this case, that is 13 percent of $1,375,000, or $178,750.

Step 6: Add both variable and fixed dollar amounts to get a total for annual estimated costs. For this case, that is $178,750 + $23,200, or $201,950.

Projecting an Annual Budget Summary

Our Period/Annual Statement, Figure 5.1, can now be used to enter all of the data prepared in related forms to summarize the projected annual budget. These will reflect all areas of sales and costs for our case history. Figure 5.10 shows that summary.

All figures shown for revenue (sales) and expenses (costs) have been obtained from the survey support forms in Figures 5.1 to 5.9. Standard accounting practice has been used to evaluate gross profit, net operating profit or (loss), and net profit or (loss).

Summary: Urban Office Building

Remember that part of the client's financial objective is "to recover all operating costs from operational revenue ... and ... subsidize the management fee."

Operating Expense Schedule
Urban Office Building

Projected Annual Sales: $1,387,000

Category	Variable %	Fixed $	Total $
Paper Goods	0.5		6,937
Cleaning Supplies	0.5		6,938
Linen and Laundry	2.0		27,750
Replacements	2.0		27,750
Insurance	1.0		13,875
Repair & Maintenance	1.0	2,000	15,875
Exterminator Service		1,200	1,200
Administrative Charge	5.0		69,375
Other Misc. Charges	1.0	20,000	33,875
Total Variable	13.0%	—	—
Total Costs	$180,375 +	$23,200 =	$203,575

FIGURE 5.9 Completed Operating Expense Schedule for Urban Office Building Example

Annual Budget Forecast
Urban Office Building

I.	SALES			
	Cafeteria		$ 825,000	59.5%
	Service Dining Room		300,000	21.6
	Exec./Guest Dining		150,000	10.8
	Special Functions & Other		112,500	8.1
		TOTAL SALES	$1,387,500	100.0%
II.	FOOD COST		$ 547,750	39.5%
		GROSS PROFIT	$ 839,750	60.5%
III.	LABOR COST			
	Payroll		$ 526,198	
	Payroll Related		113,813	
		TOTAL LABOR COST	$ 640,011	46.1%
IV.	OPERATING EXPENSES			
	Paper Goods		$ 6,937	
	Cleaning Supplies		6,938	
	Linen and Laundry		27,750	
	Replacements		27,750	
	Insurance		13,875	
	Repair & Maintenance		15,875	
	Exterminator		1,200	
	Administrative Charge		69,375	
	Other Misc. Costs		33,875	
		TOTAL OPERATING EXPENSES	$ 203,575	14.7%
V.	TOTAL ALL COSTS		$1,391,336	100.3%
VI.	NET OPERATING PROFIT (OR LOSS)		$ (3,836)	0.3%
VII.	MANAGEMENT FEE		$ 69,375	5.0%
VIII.	NET PROFIT OR (LOSS)		$ (73,211)	(5.3%)

FIGURE 5.10 Example Budget Forecast

A review of Figure 5.10 reveals that there will be an operating loss of $3,636, or .3 percent of sales. This must now be addressed by both the client and the contractor. Do they accept that projected loss as additional subsidy or do they change service objectives (pricing, staffing, or other) to eliminate it? Remember that the company is willing to use vending commissions to offset operating losses from the manual foodservice. This operation is likely to have vending commissions sufficient to achieve that objective. More on this can be found in Chapter 6, "Foodservice Vending."

CASE 2: RURAL MANUFACTURING COMPANY

This case, with some modifications, is the same as that presented in Chapter 3. The location is a manufacturing plant near a midwestern city.

The operation has an employee population of 10,000 working two shifts, five days per week. There are also 100 management and executive personnel. Of the 10,000 workers, 7,000 are on the first shift in the plant, 500 are in the office, and 2,500 work second shift in the plant.

There are three cafeterias located strategically around the plant to service the different work groups. Two are in manufacturing areas, and one is in the office area. The office cafeteria has an adjacent executive dining room that provides the management staff with table service for lunch.

Cafeteria #1, in the manufacturing area, operates on both first and second shift, staying open for arriving second-shift personnel. Cafeteria #2, in the plant, and Cafeteria #3, in the office, operate for first shift only. Breakfast and lunch is served in all three cafeterias.

Refreshment service is available at all times via foodservice vending. Numerous vending banks for full-line service are located throughout the plant and office areas. The foodservice caters all company-sponsored events, such as the annual picnic, retirement luncheons, awards dinners, and others. Some catering is also provided for work groups within the plant when scheduled during plant operating hours.

A main kitchen in Cafeteria #1 functions as a commissary. All foodservice and vending production, baking, and warehousing take place in it. Finished foods are moved between locations using hot and cold food carts.

The entire operation, both manual and vended foodservice, is operated by a contract management company on a profit and loss basis. In addition, the contractor provides commissions to the union welfare fund on all vended operations.

Company policy is to recover all direct operating expenses from cafeteria, dining rooms, and special functions revenue under a profit and loss contract arrangement. The company provides space and utilities; all vending equipment is provided by the contractor.

Cafeteria menu prices and vending machine prices are set in the trade union contract and may not be increased without union permission. These are reviewed annually and adjusted only when union wage rates are also adjusted (cost of living and/or wage increases).

The contractor uses a 4-4-5 week quarter with an accounting calendar compatible with the client.

Figure 5.11 is an organizational chart of the contractor's food and vending services. Note that one general manager is responsible for both operations; this has become a common practice in the industry.

Forecasting Revenue

There is one difference in the sales forecast for this case as opposed to Case 1: the design of the form. Whereas Case 1 had a single shift, this case has two shifts, three outlets, and extra meal periods.

The form for this case (Figure 5.12) is used in the same way as the comparable Sales Forecast Planning Form shown in Figure 5.2. Some consideration must be given to the complexity of the case; then adjustments can be made in evaluating potential customer count, check averages, and resultant sales forecasts.

The following assumptions will be used to evaluate estimated annual sales.

MEAL PERIOD	PARTICIPATION PERCENTAGE	CHECK AVERAGE
MANUFACTURING		
Breakfast	10%	$1.25
Lunch	40	3.00
Pre-Shift	10	1.25
Dinner	30	4.00

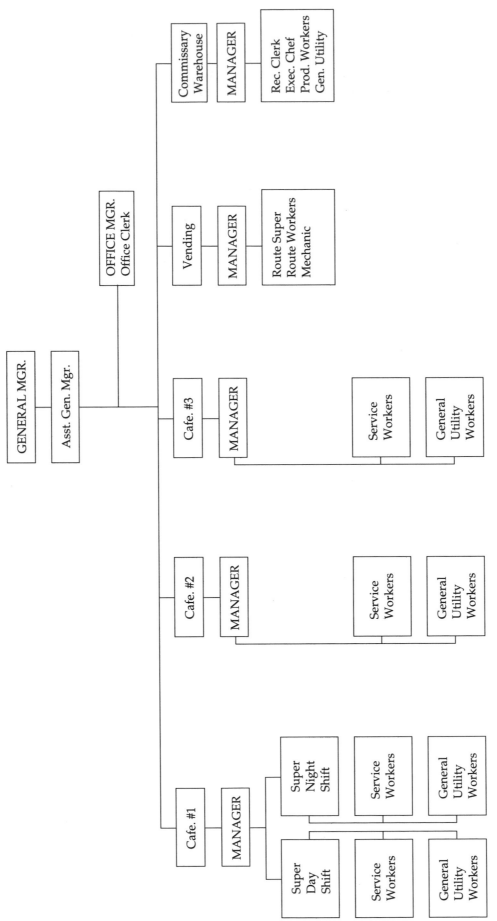

FIGURE 5.11 Organizational Structure for Case 2: Rural Manufacturing Company

Sales Forecast Planning Form
Rural Manufacturing Company

Manufacturing Population Shift #1: _____
Manufacturing Population Shift #2: _____
Office Population: _____
Executive Population: _____

(1)	(2)	(3)	(4)	(5)	(6)
Meal Period	Part. (%)	Average Daily Customers	Estimated Check Average ($)	Estimated Daily Sales ($)	Estimated Annual Sales ($)
MANUFACTURING Shift #1 Breakfast Lunch					
Shift #2 Pre-Shift Dinner					
OFFICE Breakfast Lunch					
EXECUTIVE Lunch					
SPECIAL FUNCTIONS					
TOTAL ESTIMATED DAILY/ANNUAL SALES				$	$

FIGURE 5.12 Typical Sales Forecast Planning Form for a Multishift, Multifacility Manufacturing Plant

MEAL PERIOD	PARTICIPATION PERCENTAGE	CHECK AVERAGE
OFFICE		
Breakfast	10%	$1.00
Lunch	50	2.50
EXECUTIVE		
Lunch	80	6.00
SPECIAL FUNCTIONS		
(Average 25 per day)		6.00

There are numerous variations possible in a case such as this. The manufacturing plant can run six days a week, the office only five. Some parts of the plant can operate only five days, or irregularly. For this example, we'll use a 5-day week and a 250-day operating year.

Based on these assumptions, $3,473,250 is the estimated annual sales forecast, as shown in Figure 5.13.

Forecasting Cost of Sales (Food Cost)

Figure 5.4 was used to forecast sales mix/cost mix for the urban office building. That same format, adjusted to accommodate the sales categories of the rural manufacturer, can be used. Those categories would be:

Sales Forecast Planning Form
Rural Manufacturing Company

Manufacturing Population Shift #1:   7,000
Manufacturing Population Shift #2:   2,500
Office Population: 500
Executive Population: 100

(1)	(2)	(3)	(4)	(5)	(6)
Meal Period	Part. (%)	Average Daily Customers	Estimated Check Average ($)	Estimated Daily Sales ($)	Estimated Annual Sales ($)
MANUFACTURING Shift #1					
Breakfast	10	700	1.25	875	218,750
Lunch	40	2,800	3.00	8,400	2,100,000
Shift #2					
Pre-Shift	10	250	1.25	313	78,250
Dinner	30	750	4.00	3,000	750,000
OFFICE					
Breakfast	10	50	1.00	50	12,500
Lunch	50	250	2.50	625	156,250
EXECUTIVE					
Lunch	80	80	6.00	480	120,000
SPECIAL FUNCTIONS	Est.	25	6.00	150	37,500
TOTAL ESTIMATED DAILY/ANNUAL SALES				$13,893	$3,473,250

FIGURE 5.13   Completed Sales Forecast for Case 2: Rural Manufacturing Company

- Cafeteria breakfast
- Cafeteria lunch
- Cafeteria pre-shift
- Cafeteria dinner
- Executive lunch
- Special functions

A summary of projected annual sales, food cost ratios per category of sales, and resulting estimated annual food cost in both dollars and percentages for this case would look like Figure 5.14. Cost percentages for category sales are estimates made for this case study. An analysis of the menu, pricing structure, and purchase prices for the specific location would be necessary for the analysis.

Note that the projected food cost percentage ratios for each category indicate a menu-pricing structure lower than average commercial equivalents. The overall average of 39.8 percent is also somewhat higher than a commercial equivalent of 33–35 percent. This is in keeping with policy, which says that the foodservice is an employee benefit.

This study also provides standards for use in designing and implementing a cost control system. This is discussed further in Chapter 9, "Cost Control Management."

Sales Mix/Cost Mix Analysis
Rural Manufacturing Company

(1)	(2)	(3)	(4)	(5)
Meal Period or Shift	Projected Annual Sales	Projected Food Cost (%)	Projected Food Cost ($)	Manager's Comments
CAFETERIA				
Breakfast	231,250	35	80,938	
Lunch	2,256,250	40	902,500	
Pre-Shift	78,250	35	27,388	
Dinner	750,000	40	300,000	
EXEC. LUNCH	120,000	50	60,000	
FUNCTIONS	37,500	35	13,125	
TOTALS	(A) 3,473,250	(C) B ÷ A = 39.8%	(B) $1,383,951	

FIGURE 5.14   Completed Sales Mix/Cost Mix Analysis for Rural Manufacturing Company

Forecasting Labor Costs

The same basic personnel categories are employed here as in Case 1: management and administrative, production, service and sanitation, and maintenance. The form in Figure 5.5 can again be used as a planning and evaluation tool. For the rural manufacturer, it must be prepared and summarized for each outlet. One survey would be required for each of the three cafeterias, the production center, and the dining room. These are then combined for an annual payroll projection.

The organizational chart, Figure 5.11, can also be used as a guide. Regardless of the method used, the concept of summarizing salaried and hourly personnel costs to an annual projected payroll cost is universal.

Payroll-Related Costs

The schedule in Figure 5.7 is valid for use with this, or any, case study. Mandated costs and employee benefit categories are unchanged.

While the specifics of the cost basis may change, the concept remains constant. A forecast of projected payroll-related costs can be prepared as was done in Case 1.

Operating Expenses

Operating expenses for this example will be slightly different from those shown in Figure 5.8. That example included an administrative charge for the management fee operation; this example is a profit and loss account and does not exact that charge. Many contractors, however, levy corporate charges with names like "support services," "training and development," or "working capital." These charges may be included as operating expenses or elsewhere on the annual projection.

Statement Format

A typical period statement for a contractor-operated profit and loss account is shown in Figure 5.15. This is a computer-generated period statement that reports sales for the current and two previous periods, as well as year-to-date and budget comparisons. This will be discussed in greater detail in Chapter 9. Suffice it to say at this point that the financial (budget) plan must match the reporting format.

Summarizing the Budget

The summary budget for the rural manufacturer is assembled in the same fashion as that for the urban office building:

Step 1: Estimate sales using Figure 5.12.
Step 2: Estimate cost of sales using Figure 5.14.
Step 3: Estimate labor cost using a form similar to Figure 5.5. Use the organizational chart (Figure 5.11) for details.
Step 4: Estimate payroll-related costs using Figure 5.8 for a model.
Step 5: Estimate operating expenses using a form similar to Figure 5.9.
Step 6: Summarize an estimated annual budget forecast using Figure 5.10 as a model.

Remember, the urban office building and rural manufacturing plant differ only in complexity. The basic method of designing and completing budget forms is the same.

CASE 3: CAMPUS UNIVERSITY

This case is the same as that in Chapter 2, with some additions.

The case involves a moderately large university with an annual enrollment of 8,000 full- and part-time students. It operates on a semester basis; two 15-week terms per year, plus a shorter 10-week summer session having an enrollment of 4,000. The faculty consists of 500 full- and part-time professors. There is a support staff of 1,000 full- and part-time employees.

The service outlets consist of a 500-seat boarding cafeteria, a 400-seat cash cafeteria, a student union building with a food court of specialty food shops, a faculty club dining room, and catering service to all areas of campus.

The production facility consists of a main kitchen adjacent to the cash cafeteria, office and administrative services at the main kitchen, a support kitchen at the boarding cafeteria, and several pantry operations adjacent to meeting rooms around campus.

The facility is operated by the campus dining division of a contract management company. A branch of their vending division runs the vending operation, which has numerous banks of vending machines for cold drinks, hot drinks, snacks, and cold foods as well as some single machine locations for cold drinks.

Under a profit and loss agreement, the contractor must provide three board plans—15-, 19-, and 21-meals per week—for fixed weekly amounts and operate the cash cafeteria and food court at menu prices below that of adjacent commercial operations.

Meal plan board rates were specified in the request for proposal (RFP), the governing agreement, and usually may not be increased during the year in which

FIGURE 5.15 Typical Contractor Period Profit and Loss Statement

		PERIOD ENDING										YEAR TO DATE					
		THIS PERIOD LAST YEAR		PREVIOUS PERIOD		LAST PERIOD		THIS PERIOD		PROFIT PLAN		PROFIT PLAN		THIS YEAR		LAST YEAR	
SUPPORTING SCHEDULE		AMOUNT	%	AMOUNT	%	AMOUNT	%	AMOUNT	%	AMOUNT	%	AMOUNT	%	AMOUNT	%	AMOUNT	%
A	SALES	32.499	100.0	39.809	100.0	52.446	100.0	37.067	100.0	34.100	100.0	80.450	100.0	89.514	100.0	76.633	100.0
	COSTS & EXPENSES																
B	FOOD	31.966	98.2	36.937	92.9	48.704	92.9	40.565	109.5	34.750	101.9	82.025	102.0	89.271	99.7	75.987	99.2
C	PAYROLL AND RELATED COSTS	21.298	65.5	36.583	92.0	46.306	88.1	38.097	102.5	42.560	124.8	95.574	118.8	83.471	93.4	65.456	85.6
	PAPER	2.239	6.9	1.018	2.6	.488	.9	.282	.8	1.810	5.3	4.265	5.3	.770	.9	4.847	6.3
	CLEANING SUPPLIES	.572	1.8							.340	1.0	.805	1.0			.746	1.0
	LAUNDRY & UNIFORMS	2.394	7.4	2.881	7.2	4.067	7.8	3.240	8.7	2.720	8.0	6.420	8.0	7.306	8.2	6.022	7.9
	REPLACEMENTS	.040	.1	.020	.1	.060	.1	.032	.1	.070	.2	.170	.2	.092	.1	.092	.1
	REPAIRS & MAINTENANCE	.195	.6	.159	.4	.187	.3	.157	.4					.343	.4	.075	.1
	INSURANCE									.255	.7	.575	.7			.441	.6
D	DEPRECIATION																
E	OTHER OPERATING COSTS	.438	1.3	.181	.4	.263	.5	.077	.2	.200	.6	.475	.6	.340	.2	.587	.8
	TOTAL COSTS AND EXPENSES	59.142	181.9	77.779	195.3	100.075	190.8	82.450	222.4	82.705	242.5	190.309	236.5	181.593	202.8	154.253	201.2
	OPERATING GAIN OR LOSS (–)	26.643–	81.9	37.970–	95.3	47.629–	90.8	45.383–	122.4	48.605–	142.5	109.859–	136.5	92.079–	102.8	77.620–	101.2
F	OTHER INCOME			.019		.006		.006						.012			
	NET INCOME LOSS (–) FROM OPERATIONS	26.643–	81.9	37.951–	95.3	47.623–	90.8	45.377–	122.4	48.605–	142.5	109.859–	136.5	92.067–	102.8	77.620–	101.2
	DUE FROM OR TO (–) CLIENT	29.718	91.4	41.932	105.3	52.866	100.8	49.084	132.4	52.015	152.5	117.904	146.6	101.018	112.9	84.712	110.5
	AVAILABLE TO IUC FOR OVERHEAD AND PROFIT	3.075	9.4	3.981	10.0	5.243	10.0	3.707	10.0	3.410	10.0	8.045	10.0	8.951	10.0	7.092	9.2

the RFP bid is presented. Increases for subsequent years must be negotiated with the administration.

Vending machine prices have also been established as part of the RFP and may not be increased during a school year. Vending price increases, too, must be negotiated with the administration.

The cash and board cafeterias are open for each of the two 15-week semesters and the 10-week summer session. Minimum services—primarily the cash cafeteria and some food court operations—are provided during down times to meet the needs of those on campus.

The contractor has agreed to pay the university an 8 percent commission on cash sales and a variable commission rate on vending machine sales and will provide a capital investment of $500,000 to improve the physical plant. The contract term is five years. In addition, the contractor agrees to pay for trash removal and utilities for the facilities operated. The university will provide the physical facility, maintain university-owned equipment, and provide other custodial and maintenance services.

The contractor uses the 4-4-5 weeks per quarter accounting period format for their reports. Note that Figure 5.16 can be used for any time period; the form is also used for client commission payment audits.

Forecasting Revenue (Sales)

For this example, we have cash sales, club sales, catering sales, and board rate sales. The cash, catering, and club sales can be forecast utilizing the customer count/check average method. The board rate portion of the income requires a different approach.

Board rates are usually termed *contract sales*. For this case there are 15-meal, 19-meal, and 21-meal contracts offered. Each plan has a different one-time cost and will produce different levels of sales. They also provide different services for the customer (student) and have a variable effect on the cost of sales (food cost).

Forecasting sales revenue also requires the preparation of an annual review of active and inactive periods. The forecast must reflect the fact that students are only on campus during a semester. Figure 5.17 is a format that can be used to assess sales for each month and total sales for the year by category of service. While the format utilizes a calendar month, these can be converted to the chosen accounting periods as necessary.

Using a format of this type provides the manager with the ability to evaluate the effects of the two 15-week semesters and the 10-week summer session. This format also allows an evaluation of cash sales between semesters and is used later to schedule labor and calculate labor/hours.

Each location requires a separate sales forecast. The sum total of all forecasts becomes the annual sales forecast. For this example we will summarize the total sales forecast using the following details:

Contract Prices
    15-meal plan @ $60.00/week
    19-meal plan @ $75.00/week
    21-meal plan @ $80.00/week

Cash Sales (Average of breakfast-lunch-dinner)
    Students: $3.00 check average
    Staff: $2.50 check average

Period/Annual Operating Statement
Campus University

I. SALES		
Contract Sales	$_____	____.__%
Cash Cafeteria	_____	____.__
Faculty Club	_____	____.__
Student Union Food Court	_____	____.__
Catering	_____	____.__
TOTAL SALES	$_____	100.0%
II. FOOD COST	$_____	____.__%
III. GROSS PROFIT	$_____	____.__%
IV. LABOR COST		
Management	$_____	____.__%
Hourly	_____	____.__
TOTAL PAYROLL	_____	____.__
Payroll-Related Costs	_____	____.__
TOTAL LABOR COST	$_____	____.__%
V. OPERATING EXPENSES		
Paper Goods	$_____	
Laundry	_____	
Cleaning Supplies	_____	
Insurance	_____	
Office Expenses	_____	
Maintenance and Repairs		
Trash Removal/Utilities	_____	
Misc. Charges	_____	
TOTAL OPERATING EXPENSES	$_____	____.__%
NET OPERATING PROFIT	$_____	____.__%
VI. OTHER CHARGES		
Commissions/Rent	$_____	____.__%
Depreciation	_____	____.__
Amortization	_____	____.__
Other Charges	_____	____.__
TOTAL OTHER CHARGES	$_____	____.__%
NET PROFIT (LOSS)	$_____	____.__%

FIGURE 5.16 Typical Accounting Period or Annual Profit and Loss Statement Format for a Contractor-Operated Campus Dining Account

Faculty Club
   Lunch: $5.00 check average

Catering
   Fall/Spring: $20.00 check average
   Summer: $10.00 check average

Food Court
   Estimated based on last year's sales

Sales Forecast Planning Form
Campus University

Fall/Spring Student Population: 8,000
Summer Student Population: 4,000
Staff Population: 1,000
Faculty Count: 500

(1)	(2)	(3)	(4)	(5)	(6)	(7)	(8)
Sales Category	Potential Customers	Participation ($)	Average Weekly Customers	Check Average ($)	Est. Weekly Sales ($)	No. Weeks	Annual Sales ($)
CONTRACTS							
Fall/Spr.	8,000						
15 meal	"	22	1,760	60.00	105,600	30	3,168,000
19 meal	"	5	400	75.00	30,000	30	900,000
21 meal	"	3	240	80.00	19,200	30	576,000
Summer	4,000						
15 meal	"	22	880	60.00	52,800	10	528,000
19 meal	"	5	200	75.00	15,000	10	150,000
21 meal	"	3	120	80.00	9,600	10	96,000
CASH							
Fall/Spr.							
Student	5,600	40	15,680	3.00	47,040	30	1,411,200
Staff	1,000	40	2,000	2.50	5,000	30	150,000
Summer							
Students	2,800	40	7,840	3.00	23,520	10	235,200
Staff	800	40	1,600	2.50	4,000	10	40,000
FAC. CLUB							
Fall/Spr.	500	40	1,000	5.00	5,000	30	150,000
FOOD CT.							
Fall/Spr.	6,600	40	18,480	2.00	36,960	30	1,108,800
Summer	3,600	40	10,080	2.00	20,160	30	604,800
CATERING	Previous						
Fall/Spr	Year's	—	1,000	20.00	20,000	30	600,000
Summer	Estimate	—	200	10.00	2,000	10	20,000
TOTAL	—	—	—	—	—	—	9,738,000

FIGURE 5.17 Example of a Specially Designed Sales Forecast Planning Form for a Campus Dining Facility

Utilizing this data a budget sales forecast can now be prepared. A form similar to Figure 5.2, with adjusted meal period categories, can be used. Figure 5.17 is such a form. The contract prices and check average figures used for this case are estimates. To analyze a specific operation, that location's actual (last year) figures should be used.

Both the number of potential customers and the average weekly customer count must be estimated. This is somewhat tougher than forecasting the single-shift, five-day urban office case.

To prepare the Sales Forecast Planning Form:

Step 1: Enter all sales categories in column 1.

Step 2: Enter the population figures for each category in column 1 under column 2. Note that the population for "Contracts" is the same as student population. The population for "Cash" is the basic population minus the number of students purchasing a contract.

Example:

Fall Population.. 8,000
Fall Contracts .... − 2,400*
Fall Cash Sales Population.................................... 5,600

*15 meals @ 1,760 / 19 meals @ 400 / 21 meals @ 240

The same calculation is made for each other student cash sales category.

Step 3: Enter the percentage of population, for each category, expected to participate in the sales category under column 3.

Step 4: Estimate the average weekly customer count for each category in column 4.

(Note that there are seven days for each student cash sales category, five days for each staff and faculty cash category, and one contract for each contract category.)

Step 5: Enter either the board rate or the potential check average projected for each sales category under column 5.

Step 6: Figure estimated weekly sales by category. Multiply the average weekly customer figures from column 4 by the check average or board rate figures under column 5. Enter each result in column 6.

Step 7: Enter the number of weeks for each category of sales under column 7. Note that the Fall/Spring number is 30, and the Summer number is 10.

Step 8: Multiply each sales figure under column 6 by each number of weeks figure under column 7 and enter the result under column 8.

Step 9: Sum column 8 to arrive at the Total, which should be entered at the bottom line. For this case, that amount is $9,738,000.

This analysis provides:

■ Estimated annual sales projection
■ Sales breakdown by type of sale (sales mix)
■ Potential number of customers to be serviced at each sales location

This information can be used to:

■ Plan staffing schedules
■ Plan production schedules
■ Establish a cost control system
■ Forecast gross profit amounts

Forecasting Cost of Sales

Figure 5.4 was used to forecast cost of sales for a B&I segment, an urban office building. It presented each category of sales and each cost percentage by category and evaluated a sales mix/cost mix to arrive at an overall average cost of sales (food cost) for the location.

That same method can be used for the university by altering the sales categories, establishing a target food cost percentage for each sales category, and making the same sales mix/cost mix evaluation. Make the following assumptions regarding sales categories and food cost percentage by category and use Figure 5.4 to evaluate a sales mix/cost mix for the university.

Student contracts	50% food cost
Cash sales (cafeteria)	38% food cost
Cash sales (food court)	35% food cost
Faculty club sales	45% food cost
Catering sales	30% food cost

The results will show a projected overall food cost of 43.75 percent, as shown in Figure 5.18.

Forecasting Labor Costs

As with our last case, forecasting labor costs requires an organizational chart, a listing of personnel, a salary and wage structure, and the number of labor hours needed for each position. Another practical, shorter method can be used. For this method:

■ Project fixed payroll costs. Prepare a summary of salaried and full-time hourly staff. Come up with a dollar amount.
■ Project variable payroll costs. Establish an acceptable percentage for each outlet.

The organizational chart for the university is shown in Figure 5.19. Note that the food service director reports to a corporate district manager, who in turn reports to a division vice-president. That division also provides the necessary staff services required by the location. Staff services, as previously mentioned, include accounting, human resources and training, purchasing, and more.

Sales Mix/Cost Mix Analysis
Campus University

(1)	(2)	(3)	(4)
Sales Category	Projected Annual Sales	Projected Food Cost (%)	Projected Food Cost ($)
Student Contracts	5,418,000	50	2,709,000
Cafeteria Cash Sales	1,836,400	38	697,832
Food Court Cash Sales	1,713,600	35	599,760
Faculty Club	150,000	45	67,500
Catering	620,000	30	186,000
TOTALS	9,738,000	43.75%	$4,260,092

FIGURE 5.18 Example of a Sales Mix/Cost Mix Analysis Form for a Campus Dining Facility

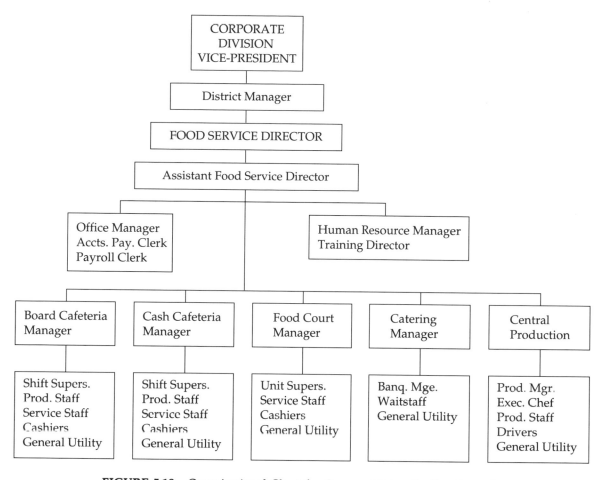

FIGURE 5.19 Organizational Chart for Campus Dining Facility Example

To prepare a labor cost forecast for this case history, we'll modify Figure 5.6, the Labor Cost Planning Form. It's possible to either prepare a complete breakdown of the total required staff as shown or use a short version of this method. For this example we will use the short version, as follows:

■ Forecast expected management and administrative staff salaries, fixed and hourly, on an annual basis. This will be the fixed labor cost.
■ Evaluate hourly staff requirements on a ratio-to-sales basis for each operating area. Projected sales is always the denominator.

Figure 5.20 is an example of this method of payroll budget forecasting. Project management and administrative payroll as $327,080, hourly wages are forecast at $2,571,460, and total annual payroll is $2,898,540.

Note that the forecast for management and administrative personnel utilizes the listing method (number of staff at a salaried or hourly rate). The forecast for hourly personnel uses a percentage method (a budgeted variable percentage for each area of sales). Support staff uses 100 percent of sales as the denominator; other categories use each segment of sales as a denominator.

Example: Projected food court sales is $1,713,600. Projected variable percentage labor cost is 20 percent, so projected food court labor cost is $342,720.

Labor Cost Planning Form
Campus University

(1)	(2)	(3)	(4)	(5)
Category	Number of Employees	Pay Rate ($)	Number of Weeks	Annual Forecast ($)
MANAGEMENT & ADMINISTRATION				
Fd. Svc. Director	1	$1150/wk.	52	59,800
Asst. F.S.D	1	750/wk.	52	39,000
Office Manager	1	500/wk.	52	26,000
HRD Director	1	500/wk.	52	26,000
Exec. Chef	1	750/wk.	52	39,000
Accts. Pay. Cl.	1	8.00/hr.	40 hrs./52	16,640
Payroll Clerk	1	8.00/hr.	40 hrs./52	16,640
Catering Mgr.	1	500/wk.	52	26,000
Foodservice Mgrs	3	500/wk.	52	78,000
TOTAL MAN. & ADM.	11	—	—	$327,080

Hourly Staff	Labor Percentage		Sales ($)	Payroll ($)
Central Kitchen	3		9,738,000	292,140
Faculty Club	20		150,000	30,000
Catering	15		620,000	93,000
CAFETERIAS				
Cash & Board	25		7,254,400	1,813,600
Food Court	20		1,713,600	342,720
			TOTAL HOURLY PAYROLL	$2,571,460
			TOTAL ALL PAYROLL	$2,898,540

FIGURE 5.20 Completed Labor Cost Planning Form for Campus Dining Example

Payroll-Related Costs

Payroll-related costs can be projected using Figure 5.8, the Payroll-Related Costs Planning Form. For this example the projections are shown in Figure 5.21. Note the following differences:

■ Only 11 employees receive management benefits.
■ This is a nonunion shop.
■ There is no employee welfare plan.

This is an example and does not detail the specifics of a particular facility. It is quite likely that some of the hourly personnel are students and do not receive a benefit package, while other hourly staffers would be professionals with a benefit package.

The resulting payroll-related cost for both mandated and employee benefits for this example is $473,771, or 16.35 percent of total payroll.

Payroll-Related Costs Planning Form
Campus University

PROJECTED ANNUAL PAYROLL COST
  Management and Administrative $ 327,090
  Hourly Wages   2,571,460
TOTAL SALARIES AND WAGES $2,898,540

PROJECTED NUMBER OF EMPLOYEES
  Salaried: 11
  Hourly: Varied
TOTAL EMPLOYEES: Varied

(1) Cost Category	(2) % of Payroll Cost	(3) Fixed Cost per Employee ($)	(4) Total Cost ($)
FICA	7.5		217,391
State Unemployment	3.0		86,956
Federal Unemployment	0.6		17,391
Workers Compensation	4.0		115,942
State Disability	0.6		17,391
Health Insurance		1,000	11,000
Life Insurance		200	2,200
Pension Plan		500	5,500
Union Welfare Plan		N/A	N/A
		TOTAL DOLLAR COSTS	$473,771
		Ratio to Payroll	16.35%

FIGURE 5.21 Completed Payroll-Related Costs Planning Form for Campus Dining Example

Operating Expenses

We can use Figure 5.9, the Operating Expense Schedule, for our purposes here. Each area of expense that would be expected from the university can be listed under the first column, "Category." These may differ somewhat from earlier examples. The resulting forecast for this case is shown in Figure 5.22.

Note that the administrative charge, part of the contract for the urban office building, has been omitted. An additional item—trash removal—has been added per the contract. The total amount for operating expenses is $901,730.

Other Charges

This case involves a P&L contract where the contractor agreed to invest $500,000 and pay a rent/commission of 8 percent of all cash sales. In addition, this particular contractor charges amortization of capital investment (the cost of providing the $500,000) and a 2 percent corporate administrative fee to all operating locations. This adds an additional item, other charges, to the operating statement; a summary of these is shown in Figure 5.23. These will be carried forward to the projected annual budget forecast.

All the necessary evaluations to prepare an annual forecasted budget are now complete. Figure 5.24 details the annual budget forecast for the university based on the evaluations presented.

Operating Expense Schedule
Campus University

	Projected Annual Sales: $9,738,000		
Category	*Variable %*	*Fixed $*	*Total $*
Paper Goods	2.0%		194,760
Cleaning Supplies	0.5%		48,690
Linen and Laundry	1.0%		97,380
Replacements	1.0%		97,380
Insurance	1.0%		97,380
Repair & Maintenance	1.0%		97,380
Trash Removal		24,000	24,000
Other Misc. Charges	2.0%	50,000	244,760
TOTAL VARIABLE	8.5%	—	—
TOTAL DOLLARS	$827,730 +	$74,000 =	$901,730

FIGURE 5.22   Completed Operating Expense Schedule for Campus Dining Example

Summary: Campus University

In most ways, a budget forecast for a college or university is similar to that for a B&I account (the urban office building, for example). Some significant differences are:

■ Board rates must be considered.
■ Other charges (for a P&L account) must be considered. These include rent and corporate charges.
■ Seasonal services must be considered.
■ The summary statement must be altered to suit the new account categories.

The six steps to the preparation of a budget shown earlier are still valid. They must be followed, though, keeping in mind the conditions unique to a college or university.

Operating Expense Schedule
Campus University

Projected Annual Sales: $9,738,000	
OTHER CHARGES	
Rent Cash Sales	$284,000
Depreciation	100,000
Amortization	20,000
Corporate Administrative Charge	194,760
TOTAL OTHER CHARGES	$598,760

FIGURE 5.23   Completed Other Charges Expense Schedule for Campus Dining Example

Annual Budget Forecast
Campus University

I. SALES			
Contract Sales		$5,418,000	55.6%
Cash Cafeteria		1,836,400	18.8
Faculty Club		150,000	1.5
Student Union Food Court		1,713,600	17.7
Catering		620,000	6.4
	TOTAL SALES	$9,738,000	100.0%
II. FOOD COST		$4,260,092	43.7%
	GROSS PROFIT	$5,477,908	56.3%
III. LABOR COST			
Management		$ 327,080	
Hourly		2,571,460	
Total Payroll		2,898,540	
Payroll-Related Costs		473,771	
	TOTAL LABOR COST	$3,372,311	34.6%
IV. OPERATING EXPENSES			
Paper Goods		$ 194,760	
Cleaning Supplies		48,690	
Linen and Laundry		97,380	
Replacements		97,380	
Insurance		97,380	
Repair and Maintenance		97,380	
Trash Removal		24,000	
Other Misc. Charges		244,760	
	TOTAL OPERATING EXPENSES	$ 901,730	9.3%
	NET OPERATING PROFIT	$1,203,867	12.4%
V. OTHER CHARGES			
Commissions/Rent		$ 284,000	
Depreciation		100,000	
Amortization		20,000	
Other Charges		194,600	
	TOTAL OTHER CHARGES	$ 598,760	6.1%
	NET PROFIT (LOSS)	$ 605,107	6.2%

FIGURE 5.24 Completed Annual Budget Forecast for Campus Dining Example

CASE 4: COMMUNITY HOSPITAL

Financial planning for hospitals differs between facilities. Also, contracted hospitals do their planning differently than self-operated hospitals.

The American Hospital Association (AHA), through its Hospital Administrative Services (HAS), has developed a uniform system of accounts. Many self-operated hospitals and their dietary departments now use this guideline to develop their annual financial plans.

The various contractors each have their own methods of developing financial plans. While their forms may differ from those used by HAS, they provide the necessary data and are compatible with the HAS reporting system.

Conditions governing a hospital's financial plan are different from those governing a B&I or college financial plan, but the basic idea of establishing a format and forecasting all areas of revenue and expense within that format remains the same.

The six steps of budget forecasting are still valid, though the second step—forecasting sales—is not always relevant to a hospital. Still, the key is to establish a set of planning forms to gather income and cost data.

Most hospitals and health care facilities rely heavily on reimbursement of operating costs from various insurance sources for their major source of income. Medicare is the primary reimburser, and private insurance carriers follow Medicare's reimbursement policies.

Medicare is one of the payroll-related costs discussed earlier; it's a payroll tax paid by both employees and employers and administered under federal law. Medicare and the related program Medicaid, a state-operated plan, were established by the U.S. Congress. Their policies may change as the Congress amends or changes laws applicable to Medicare.

Medicare and Medicaid use Diagnostic Related Groups (DRGs) as the basis for reimbursement. Each individual hospital admission has a specific DRG. That identification allows the hospital to charge only a specified amount regardless of the patient's length of stay in the hospital. If the hospital incurs a cost higher than that allowed for the DRG claim, it must absorb the loss. If a hospital incurs a cost lower than the allowed DRG claim, it may keep the difference. As a result of this Medicare DRG policy, all hospital administrators have a strong cost-containment orientation. This orientation filters down to the nutritional services department.

Most hospitals have an employee cafeteria that is sometimes open to visitors. Those sales are forecast in the same way as those for a B&I employee cafeteria. Many hospitals also receive revenue from catering or other special function services. These potential revenues must also be projected.

Budgeting patient foodservice costs requires forecasting in three areas: food cost, labor cost, and direct operating expenses. These may be evaluated on a cost-per-patient-day or a cost-per-meal-served basis.

In a cost-per-patient-day system, operating costs are evaluated on patient census only. A cost-per-meal-served system must include cafeteria and other meals served in addition to patient meals.

HAS uses a cost-per-meal-served system combining patient, employee, and other meals as part of total dietary department costs. Those costs are compared to total hospital costs, from which is derived the total dietary expenses percentage. That figure is used to compare the operating costs of the dietary department of one hospital to similar hospitals. Since there are no real sales (that second step of budget forecasting) in patient foodservice, there is no forecast for that category.

The primary function of HAS is to provide comparative cost data to hospital administrators. HAS uses eight monthly statistical indicators to compare hospital dietary departments of similar sizes and types. Hospitals pay a fee for this monthly report service. They also submit their department's statistical data to HAS. Figure 5.25 is a listing of the eight categories of indicators used by HAS.

Since HAS influences dietary department accounting procedures, its uniform system of accounts influences financial planning formats also. A hospital utilizing HAS will prepare its annual financial plan using the HAS system of accounts.

While hospitals that follow HAS use a cost-per-meal-served basis, most contractors use the cost-per-patient day system to evaluate and forecast operating costs. They project the occupancy rate of the hospital, food cost of the patient menu, cost of a labor hours plan, and direct expenses to arrive at a cost per patient day. This method is used both to prepare their bid to the hospital and to project their operating costs for budget purposes.

FIGURE 5.25

Eight HAS Indicator Categories

ITEM 1. TOTAL DIETARY EXPENSE PERCENT

Calculation: Total dietary expenses divided by total hospital expenses. Usage: Evaluate the proportion of hospital expenses devoted to the dietary department.

ITEM 2. TOTAL MEALS PER PATIENT DAY

Calculation: Total meals served divided by total patient days. Usage: Verify accuracy of meal count statistics.

ITEM 3. TOTAL DIETARY EXPENSES PER MEAL

Calculation: Total dietary expense cost divided by total number of meals served. Usage: Indicate the cost effectiveness of the dietary department.

ITEM 4. TOTAL DIETARY SALARY EXPENSE PER MEAL

Calculation: Total salaries and wages divided by total number of meals served. Usage: Reflect the labor expense component of Item 3, Total Dietary Expenses per Meal.

ITEM 5. TOTAL MEALS SERVED PER LABOR HOUR

Calculation: Total number of meals served divided by total number of labor hours used. Usage: Measure the labor efficiency.

ITEM 6. INPATIENT MEALS SERVED PER DAY

Calculation: A total of inpatient meals served to obstetrical, medical, and surgical patients. Usage: Verify meal count statistics; generally 2.8 meals per patient day.

ITEM 7. CAFETERIA MEAL PERCENTAGE TO TOTAL MEALS

Calculation: Total cafeteria meals served divided by total meals served. Usage: Verify accuracy of total meal count.

ITEM 8. CAFETERIA MEALS PER LABOR HOUR

Calculation: Cafeteria meals served divided by the number of cafeteria labor hours used. Usage: Gauge production for the cafeteria.

SOURCE: *Management of Medical Foodservice*, 2nd ed., Catherine Sullivan, Van Nostrand Reinhold, 1990.

A contractor also evaluates all other potential sources of revenue—the employee cafeteria, the visitors' coffee shop, catering, vending, and any other source—to project a total profit and loss budget. Most contractors now bid for a hospital account on a profit and loss basis and use a P&L-style budget.

This case involves a facility similar to that presented in Chapter 2. It is a voluntary hospital and is operated by a contractor on a profit and loss basis. The contractor has presented a bid based on a cost-per-patient-day system for all patient food service, a special charge for VIP meals, a specific menu pricing structure for the employee cafeteria, a catering package menu and prices, and other sources of revenue.

Services available in this case are:

■ Dietary services for 500 beds.
■ VIP patient dietary services.
■ An employee cafeteria for both medical and administrative staff.
■ Catering service for special functions of the hospital.
■ A public coffee shop for visitors.
■ Vending machines for employees and visitors in lounge areas and waiting rooms. Vending is operated by a subcontractor supervised by the food service director.

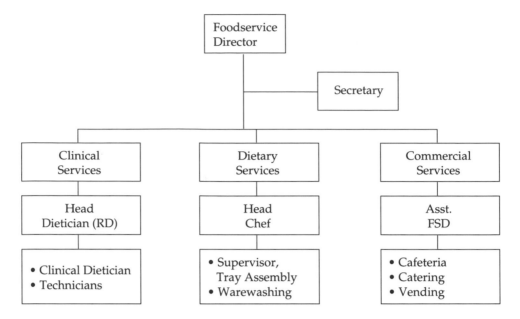

FIGURE 5.26 Organizational Chart for Community Hospital Example

■ The coffee shop is operated by a woman's auxiliary with some production assistance from the main kitchen.

Since the operation is contractor managed, the foodservice director (FSD) reports to a district manager of the contract company as well as to the liaison of the hospital. Figure 5.26 is an example of an organizational chart used by the contractor. Note that the FSD has staff organized into three basic areas—clinical services, dietary services, and catering.

Clinical services is headed by a registered dietician (RD) who provides the technical acumen required to assess patient dietary needs, plan menus, assist patient meal selection, and more. This is a specific requirement not present in other segments of contract foodservice management.

Dietary services (or nutritional services, as many hospitals now call this department) is the department for food production, tray assembly, ware washing, and other related functions. A dietary kitchen differs from a B&I kitchen because of the tray assembly and cart distribution operation—the same sort of work center found in a flight kitchen. Meals are prepared, assembled on trays, shipped to a patient floor, and served by floor personnel. The concept is that of a food factory that processes meals and ships a ready-to-serve tray to a remote location to be served by others. The costs of this sort of food delivery system must be properly assessed for accurate financial planning.

Commercial services are similar to those of a B&I account. These include the cafeteria, catering, and vending.

THE BUDGET FORMAT

The format used by the contractor for this case is similar to the financial plan for a B&I operation, modified for income analysis. There are the same four areas—sales, food cost, labor cost, and direct expenses. Each contractor has its own format for financial planning. Figure 5.27 is a typical format.

In addition, the dietary department prepares a list of statistical information

Hospital Financial Planning Summary Form
Community Hospital

	Bed Capacity	_____ %
	Occupancy Rate	_____
	Projected Annual Number of Patient Days	_____
I.	INCOME	
	Patient Day (meal) Charges	$_____
	VIP Meal Surcharges	_____
	Cafeteria Sales	_____
	ER Trays	_____
	Special Functions	_____
	Nourishments (floor supplies)	_____
	Other Reimbursable Items	_____
	TOTAL INCOME	$_____
II.	FOOD COST	$_____
III.	LABOR COST	
	Management and Administrative Salaries	$_____
	Hourly Wages	_____
	TOTAL SALARIES AND WAGES	$_____
	Payroll-Related Costs	$_____
	TOTAL LABOR COST	$_____
IV.	DIRECT EXPENSES	
	Fixed Expenses	$_____
	Variable Expenses	_____
	TOTAL DIRECT EXPENSES	$_____
	TOTAL ALL OPERATING COSTS	$_____
	OPERATING PROFIT	$_____

FIGURE 5.27 Example Financial Planning Form for a Contractor-Operated, Profit and Loss Hospital Account

for HAS that HAS uses to assess the eight indicators (Figure 5.25) for the analysis provided to member hospitals. Figure 5.28 is an example of such a list.

Forecasting Revenue

Revenue to the contractor is based on the cost-per-patient-day bid, the employee cafeteria, and catering. Some additional income is received from emergency room (ER) meal trays and floor supplies as well as prepared foods sold in the volunteer-operated coffee shop. Use the following process to forecast each area of income:

The Cost-per-Patient-Day Bid

Regular Patient Meals: A specific bid has been made for patient meals using an anticipated occupancy rate for the hospital. Bids vary, but a dollar amount per patient day is set and can be used to calculate income. Use this formula to forecast patient service income:

Occupancy rate percentage × 500 beds × 365 days per year × ($ bid rate) __ . __ = $ income from patient feeding.

HAS Statistical Information

Projected Annual Patient Days	_____
Actual Patient Days	_____
Hospital Census Percentage	_____
Potential Patient Meals	_____
Actual Patient Meals	_____
Nonpatient Meals	_____
TOTAL MEALS SERVED	_____
Productive Labor Hours	_____
Nonproductive Labor Hours	_____
Overtime Hours	_____
Meals per Productive Labor Hour	_____
FTEs	_____
Food Cost per Meal	$ _____
Labor Cost per Meal	$ _____
General Expense Cost per Meal	$ _____
Floor Supply Cost	$ _____
Nourishments Cost Patient/Day	$ _____
Cafeteria Total Sales	$ _____
Cafeteria Customer Count	_____

FIGURE 5.28   Example of Data Used by HAS Statistical Comparisons

Example: If the occupancy rate is 80 percent, the revenue from patient feeding can be figured as follows:

■ 80% × 500 = 400 patients per day × 365 days per year = 91,250 annual patient days.

■ 91,250 patient days × ($ bid rate) = annual projected income from patient meal service.

Patient VIP Meals: In addition to regular patient meals, there is an average of 25 VIP patients per day. There is a VIP per-patient-day surcharge for the more upscale menu. Use this formula to compute additional income:

■ 25 VIP patients per day × ($ bid price) × 365 days per year = $VIP income.

Example: If the bid surcharge was an additional $5.00 per VIP patient day, then 25 × $5.00 × 365 days = $45,625 VIP income.

Employee Cafeteria

Sales in the employee cafeteria can be projected in the same manner as any B&I employee cafeteria. Forecast the number of customers by meal period, multiply by check average, and then total. Figure 5.29 is an example of a forecasting form that can be used to project annual employee cafeteria sales for this case.

These are the steps required to fill out the Cafeteria Sales form:

Cafeteria Sales
Community Hospital

(1)	(2)	(3)	(4)	(5)	(6)
Meal Period	Customer Count	Check Average ($)	Daily Sales ($)	No. Days	Projected Annual Sales ($)
BREAKFAST Mon-Fri. Sat-Sun.					
LUNCH Mon-Fri. Sat-Sun.					
DINNER Mon-Fri. Sat-Sun.					

ANNUAL TOTAL CAFETERIA SALES $_____

FIGURE 5.29 Example Cafeteria Sales Form Used by a Hospital Employee Cafeteria

Step 1: Ascertain the meal periods to be evaluated; consider evaluating weekends as a separate category. Enter the desired categories under "Meal Period."

Step 2: Project customer counts, allowing for differences in weekdays and weekend days. Enter in column 2.

Step 3: Multiply customer count (column 2) by check averages (column 3) and enter the results on each line in column 4.

Step 4: Enter the correct number of annual sales days for each meal period category under column 5.

Step 5: Multiply each daily sales figure (column 4) by each number of days figure (column 5) and enter results in column 6.

Step 6: Total column 6 to evaluate annual total cafeteria sales.

Special Functions (Catering)

It is necessary to prepare a forecast of expected catering income. This is accomplished by an analysis of last year's number of covers (industry jargon for a customer), average selling price per cover, and resulting total sales. A planning form detailing the types of catered events and their potential sales revenue is shown in Figure 5.30.

These are the steps required to complete the Catering Sales Forecast:

Step 1: Evaluate the various types of service offered. Establish categories and enter them in column 1.

Step 2: Review old records and determine the number of events for each category. Enter those amounts in column 2.

Step 3: Review old records and determine the average number of covers at each type of event. Enter those numbers in column 3.

Step 4: Multiply the number of events by average covers for each category. Enter on the appropriate line under column 4.

Step 5: Forecast a check average for each type of event. Enter in column 5.

Catering Sales Forecast
Community Hospital

(1)	(2)	(3)	(4)	(5)	(6)
Type of Service	Number Events	Average Covers	Total Covers	Check Average ($)	Projected Revenue ($)
Coffee Service					
Luncheons					
Dinners					
Holiday Parties					
Other Events					
TOTALS					$ _____

FIGURE 5.30 Example Catering Sales Forecast Form Used by a Contractor at a Profit and Loss Hospital Account

Step 6: Multiply the total covers (column 4) by the projected check averages (column 5) and enter under column 6.
Step 7: Total column 6 to get the forecasted catering income.

Forecasting Cost of Sales

Projected food costs are prepared along the same lines as projected income. This is similar to a sales mix/cost mix method used for a B&I account.

Generally, a specific category of revenue requires an associated category of food cost. Appraising each cost individually and totaling them provides a forecast of annual food costs for the hospital.

Patient Meals

Food costs for patients may be figured on a per-patient-meal or a per-patient-day basis. In either case, a cost analysis of the menu is required.

Where the average patient stay is less than a week, it's usual for a one-week cycle menu to be used. That menu must be costed out to get the average cost per patient day of the one-week cycle. Projected nourishment (between-meal refreshments) costs must be added to the meal costs.

HAS uses an average of 2.8 meals per day for menu costs plus 0.5 meals per day for nourishment costs. This totals 3.3 meals per day per patient. If a cost-per-patient-meal method is used, the formula to evaluate patient meal costs is annual projected patient meals × average meal cost × 3.3.

Example: If annual patients are projected at 91,250 and cost per meal is $1.50, then annual cost for patient meal service can be estimated as:

91,250 × 3.3 = 301,125 projected meals
301,125 meals × $1.50 per meal = $451,688 projected cost
(This is only an example; costs will vary with each different operation.)

Charges for floor supplies (nourishments), ER trays, transfers, and other related costs may either be additional or part of the original bid. The resulting data produces a summary of sales income projected for this case example. This is entered on the Hospital Financial Planning Summary Form, Figure 5.27.

VIP Meal Cost

The additional cost of each VIP meal times the number of VIP meals anticipated gives projected additional VIP meal costs.

Cafeteria Food Cost

The same method used to evaluate projected food costs of an employee cafeteria in the B&I case can be used to project food cost for a hospital. A sales mix/cost mix study, evaluating meal period sales and menu prices, can result in a forecasted cafeteria food cost percentage. That percentage applied to projected cafeteria sales provides an estimate of cafeteria food costs.

Catering and Special Functions

Forecasting the food costs of special functions requires a review of the pricing policy of the hospital. Some locations require that a special function, when sponsored by the hospital, be provided at cost. Others establish a policy that recovers some of the direct expenses or overhead. The pricing policy of the hospital will produce an estimated food cost percentage for special function income. That percentage multiplied by the revenue forecast for special functions will provide an estimated food cost for this category.

Other Food Costs

Nourishments are accounted for in the 3.3 meal estimate used by HAS. Floor supplies may be charged at cost. Other food costs incurred for items particular to a specific hospital must be included in the total projected food costs.

Forecasting Labor Costs

Evaluating projected annual labor costs for the dietary department of a hospital is the same as evaluating labor costs for a B&I operation. It requires an evaluation of necessary department services, a labor hours plan to fulfill the service needs, a wage and salary schedule, an evaluation of payroll-related costs, and a summary of the results.

The organizational chart in Figure 5.26 details the responsibilities of the dietary department. The labor hours plan shown in Chapter 8 (Figure 8.7) is an example of how to forecast the number of FTEs required to fulfil the service requirements.

The Labor Cost Planning Form in Figure 5.31 can be used to project weekly and annual labor costs. The form shows the number of employees required for each work category and the corresponding number of labor hours. Space is provided for wage rates and a summary of expected total weekly costs. These forms can be used to estimate costs annually, by fiscal period, calendar month, or any other desired unit of total labor costs.

The same techniques used for labor hours planning and cost projections for other noncommercial foodservice operations are applicable to the dietary department of a hospital.

Labor Cost Planning Form
Community Hospital

Category	No.	Rate ($)	Hours	Weekly Estimate ($)	Annual Estimate ($)
MANAGEMENT					
Food Service					
Director	1		40		
Asst. FSD	1		40		
Secretary	1		40		
Subtotal	3		120		
CLINICAL SERVICES					
Dieticians	2		80		
Technicians	2		80		
Subtotal	3		160		
DIETARY SERVICES PRODUCTION					
Chef	1		40		
Cooks	4		160		
Aides	4		160		
Pot Washers	2		80		
Sub Total	11		440		
TRAY SERVICE					
Supervisor	2		80		
Tray Aides	10		400		
Dishwashers	4		160		
Subtotal	16		640		
CAFETERIA					
Supervisors	2		80		
Servers	6		240		
Cashiers	2		80		
Subtotal	10		400		
TOTALS	44		1,760		

FIGURE 5.31   Example of a Labor Cost Planning Form Used to Evaluate Projected Annual Labor Cost for a Contractor-Operated, Profit and Loss Hospital Account

Direct Expenses

Direct expenses, called general expense by the HAS uniform system of accounts, can be variable, related to the number of patient days and meals served, or fixed, unrelated to beds occupied or meals served. Figure 5.32 is a sample list of direct expenses. Each area of operations must prepare its own list from charges routinely incurred at that location. The total of projected costs for each item on the list becomes the forecast for direct (general) expenses.

Summarizing the Financial Forecast

After completing an analysis and forecast of all income and expense items, a forecast of the dietary department annual budget can be prepared. Each category

FIGURE 5.32

List of General Expense Items of a Dietary Department

Supplies—Minor Equipment	Supplies—Sanitary
Supplies—General	Cleaning Supplies
Paper Supplies	Uniform Expense
Linen Replacement	Dishes/Silver/Utensils
Office Supplies	Outside Services
Linen Dry Cleaning Services	Repairs—Department
Maintenance Contracts	Travel
Dues and Subscriptions	Recovery of Expenses
Miscellaneous	Telephone Charges
Menus	Bank Charges
Postage	Travel and Lodging

is entered at the appropriate line of Figure 5.27, the Hospital Financial Planning Summary Form, and an annual budget emerges.

This example deals with a profit and loss contract operation. The same method can be used for a self-operator by changing the income category to cost per patient day.

SUMMARY

Financial planning for any type of institutional or noncommercial foodservice operation is carried out using the calendar or fiscal year. The year breaks down into calendar months or multiweek periods. Where a calendar month is used, a three-month period is a quarter; where a weekly period is used, a 4-4-5 week period is used to provide a 13-week accounting quarter.

There is no standard format used to forecast a budget for all types of institutional operations. But there is a five-step procedure useful for all noncommercial foodservices.

A review of four sample budget formats—B&I office building, B&I manufacturing plant, a university, and a hospital—reveals many commonalities.

- Forecasting sales always requires a customer count and check average forecast.
- Forecasting cost of sales always requires a sales mix/cost mix study.
- Forecasting payroll costs always requires an organizational chart and a labor cost planning form.
- Forecasting payroll-related costs always requires a review of mandated costs and employee benefits.
- Forecasting operating expenses always requires a review of fixed and variable costs.

These five similarities always apply; the specifics of given foodservices are different, but the principles of financial planning remain the same.

Every institutional food service director is required to prepare an annual budget. He or she must use a planning method that will achieve the financial objectives of the operation. The financial plan becomes the first step in establishing a cost control system. This is reviewed in Chapter 9.

6

Foodservice Vending

Foodservice vending is an integral part of most noncommercial foodservice operations, both contractor- and self-operated. Under a contractor, vending is usually run through a vending branch that supports the district or regional manual foodservice operations. In a self-op, vending is often the responsibility of the resident foodservice director. If the operation is large enough a separate department is established similar to the vending branch of a contractor.

Vending is part of the service need, whether in a contract- or self-operated unit. Vending machines can be found in office buildings, manufacturing plants, colleges and universities, hospitals, and all areas where traffic indicates a potential market for vended products. Vending machines are also used for coffee break periods, refreshments services, and off-shift service in all segments of institutional foodservice.

This chapter introduces the reader to the field of vended foodservice management, its various markets, and methods of operation.

Upon completion of this chapter, readers should know and understand:

- The history of vending as an industry
- Vending services as they relate to institutional foodservice segments
- Types of vending equipment
- The economics of vending
- The organizational structure of a vending branch
- Basic methods of preparing a vending pro forma forecast of revenue and expense

HISTORY OF VENDING

Vending dates back to 215 B.C., when Hero, a Greek citizen, wrote in *Pneumatika* about a machine that dispensed holy water when five drachmas were inserted. Very little is known about the ultimate disposition of Hero's original work, but a 1587 Italian translation of it contained an illustration of his machine. Figure 6.1 is a reproduction of that illustration. Amazingly enough, the design of the holy water dispenser described in 215 B.C. resembles that of a modern cream dispenser.

Nothing further is known about vending activity until about 1675, when vending turned up in England's taverns. A type of snuff and tobacco box, with a locked lid released by the drop of a coin, was used to sell those products to tavern patrons. Hence the tobacco vending machine, forerunner of the cigarette machine, was born.

In 1822, an Englishman named Richard Carlisle built a book vending machine. It was designed to circumvent local censorship regulations and release him from

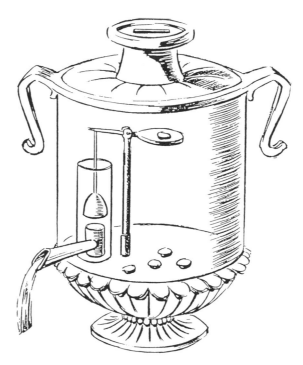

FIGURE 6.1 Hero's Holy Water Dispenser (Courtesy of Rowe International, Inc.)

responsibility for selling blasphemous material. The machine worked, but it didn't save him from prosecution.

Some 35 years later another Englishman, Simeon Dunham, was issued what is thought to be the first patent for an automatic selling device—a postage stamp machine. That patent lay dormant for another 30 years before the automatic sale of stamps began to take hold.

As patents were increasingly used to protect the inventors of other types of new machinery, inventors of vending machines began to protect themselves also. They used the current worldwide patent laws to protect global rights to their inventions.

Vending in the United States

The first financially successful vending business in the United States was founded by Thomas Adams, a chewing gum manufacturer. Adams had machines designed to sell his product for a penny on the platforms of the "el" (the elevated subway) in New York City. He later formed the American Chicle Company, which still exists. Automatic gum machines are still in use and are a thriving business, although the product is now considerably more expensive.

Through the years, vending spread from postage stamps to perfume and even to divorce papers; at one time in Corinne, Utah, divorce papers could be obtained by inserting $2.00 in silver coins into a machine. Of course, they required processing by a local lawyer and a trip through the courts to take effect.

Foodservice Vending

The Horn and Hardart Company was the first to successfully undertake the selling of food in machines. Around 1902, they opened their first Automat, where a customer could slip nickels into a slot in the wall and receive all manner of food from behind glass-front compartments and coffee from the famous lion's-head spigots. These restaurants, where the food was cooked on the premises and dispensed through glass-front compartments, were the forerunners of modern foodservice vending.

Between 1902 and the early 1950s, vending grew from a collection of small sole proprietorships to regional vending concerns and, finally, to large corporations. These larger companies—like Automatic Retailers of America (ARA) and Canteen Corporation—had multiple branches in different cities. Each branch served multiple client locations. A vending contractor branch was often a subcontractor to a manual foodservice prime contractor.

The post-mix soda machine, developed in the mid-1950s, made a cup of soda from metered syrup and refrigerated carbonated water. This was similar to a soda fountain drink without the ice. In the early 1960s, a miniaturized ice flaker was incorporated into the post-mix soda machine. Thus, customers were treated to a cup of soda with ice and vending companies were treated to a dramatic price increase—from five to ten cents per cup.

In 1946, a Chicagoan named Bert Mills developed a machine that dispensed hot coffee into a cup. The coffee was brewed separately, loaded hot, and kept hot in the machine. In 1947, Lloyd Rudd and K.C. Melikian manufactured a refinement of the Mills coffee dispenser that used hot water and liquid coffee concentrate. Then in the 1960s came the most important catalyst to the vending industry: the first true fresh brew machine.

Together, ice-in-the-cup soda machines and fresh brew coffee machines advanced the relationship between foodservice and vending operators. Since vending companies had a stronger cash flow then foodservice companies, they began to purchase foodservice management contractors. The national vending powers acquired regional foodservice companies. In this manner, large national organizations offering both manual foodservice and full-line vending emerged.

VENDING TODAY

Today, vending supports every facet of noncommercial foodservice:

■ Business and industry operations utilize vending for coffee breaks, remote areas, off-shifts, and other services.
■ Colleges and universities utilize vending for dormitory support services, snacks, and general refreshment service.
■ The health care field, especially hospitals, utilizes vending for refreshment services, public services in lounge areas, employee off-shift service, and other services.
■ Elementary and secondary schools utilize vending for support services in many areas.
■ Correctional institutions utilize various vending services for inmates.

Almost everywhere an institutional foodservice exists, there is a support vending service.

Modern vending machines are capable of delivering complete hot and cold meals, hot and cold beverages, dairy products, candy and snacks, and various assorted items. Newer machines will even prepare an order of french fried potatoes and deliver them piping hot. Others deliver nachos and pizza, although these aren't widely used.

The modern institutional vending installation has banks of machines that offer a line of food products similar to that of the employee cafeteria. They are particularly useful for remote areas and off-shifts. Machines may be loaded by operators of the manual foodservice with the same products served in the cafeteria.

VENDING EQUIPMENT AND ITS PROFITABILITY

Different machines have different profit profiles. This is important because employee cafeterias are often subsidized by vending profits; when a manual foodservice operates at a loss, vending profits frequently provide the required subsidy.

Contractors bid many large combined food and vending service locations on a profit and loss basis. The contractor will operate the manual foodservice—at breakeven or loss—in order to obtain the highly profitable vending contract.

In other cases, the client or contractor may want to identify specific costs, so the contract may call for commissions on the vending and a subsidy on the manual food operations.

Hot Beverage Machines

Hot beverage machines primarily dispense coffee but also dispense hot chocolate, instant soup, and tea. Hot drink machines are of two basic types: fresh brew and freeze dried. The fresh brew machine actually brews a cup of regular coffee, decaf coffee, or tea. A freeze dried machine prepares a cup using freeze-dried coffee and hot water.

Both the fresh brew and freeze dried machines offer hot chocolate and dried soup mix beverages from the same mechanisms that prepare the coffee. Recently introduced machines now include two sizes of cappucino and espresso, fresh brewed leaf tea, and varying strengths of low-cal sweetener and whitener. Some operators are now marketing gourmet coffee at locations warranting this item.

Hot drink machines have a low-cost, high–gross profit profile. They can be serviced on an as-needed basis, providing a low labor cost. There is little waste, little loss. Their potential gross and net profits are very high. Figure 6.2 is a picture of a modern hot drink machine.

Cold Drink Machines

Cold drink machines are of two types: post-mix and canned soda. Post-mix machines dispense a fountain drink by mixing syrup and soda in the machine and adding crushed ice to the drink. Canned soda machines deliver a cold can of the selected soda.

Canned soda has become the package of choice, particularly over the 12-ounce cup, even at a higher selling price. Typically, the cost of canned soda is 45–50 percent of sales, compared to 20–25 percent for cups; however, this is usually balanced by lower commissions on the can.

A post-mix soda machine can offer up to eight flavors, with or without ice. It can vend cup sizes from 7 to 18 ounces. This versatility provides the potential to market new flavors and portion sizes without changing equipment. Like its hot drink counterpart, a post-mix soda machine has a low-cost/high–gross profit profile. Figure 6.3 is a picture of a modern post-mix soda machine.

Both soda and can vendors require service on an as-needed basis with a low labor cost.

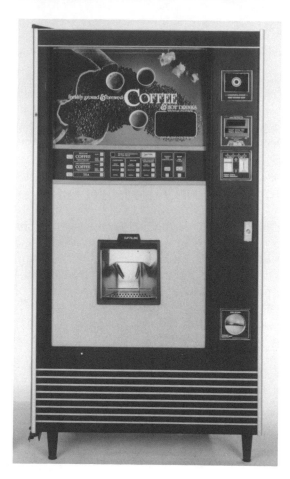

FIGURE 6.2 Hot Drink Vending Machine (Courtesy of Rowe International, Inc.)

FIGURE 6.3 Cold Drink Vending Machine (Courtesy of Rowe International, Inc.)

Change Machines

Machines that provide change for $1, $5, $10, and $20 bills have been available since the 1960s. They've added sales that might have been lost because of lack of coins. The major drawbacks of these machines are expense of investment in the machines, availability of money to stock them, exposure to theft and break-ins, and the use of the coins for nonvending purposes (e.g., local transportation, home poker games, and coin-operated laundries). Figure 6.4 is a picture of a change machine.

The bill validator, introduced in the early 1980s, worked much the same way as previous change machines. Bill validators individually mounted on each vending machine accepted a bill, delivered the chosen product, and returned the correct change. As selling prices rose, validators minimized the need for the deposit of multiple coins, confusion about the amount deposited, and mechanical problems associated with the transaction.

The latest advance in transaction financing is the debit card. These are the size of a credit card and have magnetic strips on the back like credit cards. When the card is inserted into a specifically equipped vending machine, the current value of the card is displayed in a small window, a purchase is made, the product is dispensed, the new value (original less purchase price) is displayed, and the card is returned. Initial applications focused on locations where cash was unavailable (e.g., correctional locations, institutions, government mints, and others), but the debit card's technological flexibility is rapidly developing new uses. The card machines are expanding into university campuses, hospitals, schools, and corporations (in conjunction with their security programs, credit unions, and other internal controls).

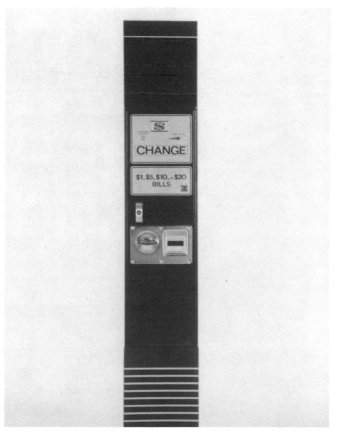

FIGURE 6.4 Change Machine (Courtesy of Rowe Intrernational, Inc.)

Snack Machines

Modern glass-front snack machines have replaced the older candy and pastry machines. A single machine now merchandises candy, pastry, chips, and more. Most foodservice operators utilize them for candy and snacks, but their flexibility also allows them to merchandise audio tapes, toothpaste, pantyhose, plastic raincoats, and more.

Snack machines come in various sizes. Two popular ones are made by the Rowe Company with capacities of 840 products and 1,062 products. They are available with bill acceptors and coin-only models. Figure 6.5 is a photo of the larger one. Note the glass front and full display of all products offered; this makes for excellent merchandising.

Snack machines are moderately profitable. While their gross profit is lower than beverage machines, they add considerably to the overall profit margin. Depending on the products offered, they require a minimum of service and maintenance and have a low-waste, low-loss profile.

Food Machines

Cold food machines are used for both hot and cold food items. Cold food is packaged for customer use. Hot food is packaged for microwave use by the customer. The most common machine used, made by Rowe, is shown in Figure 6.6. Food machines are a necessity where a complete manual foodservice has been replaced by vending. They are labor intensive and wasteful of food product. A

FIGURE 6.5   Snack Machine (Courtesy of Rowe International, Inc.)

FIGURE 6.6   Cold Food Machine (Courtesy of Rowe International, Inc.)

food machine requires heavy periodic service for product rotation and replacement, sanitation, and other work. This means high labor cost.

Cold food merchandisers are often used in conjunction with a microwave oven, a condiment stand, and a service area. Where a full-line vending service replaces a manual operation, several machines and ovens are usually necessary to fulfill the service need. This adds to the capital investment and often eliminates potential gross profit.

Where refrigerated food is sold, the vendor frequently provides free cups, straws, napkins, portion-pack condiments (salt, pepper, mustard, ketchup, mayonnaise, relish, artificial sweetener, and similar items), and plastic utensils. These items are also used by the "brown baggers" who bring their lunch from home, an added expense to the vendor. The hope is that brown-baggers will still purchase a vended beverage.

While food machines generally don't provide a satisfactory gross profit, they are often required by the client to go with the more profitable beverage machines.

Dairy Machines: Milk and Ice Cream

Milk and ice cream machines are usually single-product dispensers, with some exceptions. A milk machine can vend ½-pint, ⅓-quart, and one-pint sizes. It can also vend tetra-pak juice drinks, popular in some locations, and some machines include provisions for canned soda, water, and juices.

Some operators provide small containers of milk and cold packaged beverages from cold food merchandisers, eliminating the need for separate milk machines. If there is heavy demand for milk, a separate machine is almost always used. Ice

FIGURE 6.7 Ice Cream Machine (Courtesy of Rowe International, Inc.)

cream is sold from a freezer machine and is never combined with any other product type. Even with strong consumer demand, ice cream is rarely profitable.

Dairy machines are low–gross profit generators but are often required by the client. Figure 6.7 is a picture of a modern ice cream machine.

Other Equipment

A vending operator often provides additional equipment. This may include a microwave oven, a bill changer, and a condiment stand.

A microwave oven is usually part of a setup including a condiment stand and the various items—utensils, napkins, and more—mentioned above.

Where a bill changer is provided, additional working capital is necessary to maintain a par level of change in the machine. This is investment that has no return.

These extras affect the profitability of a vending installation; they increase the capital investment and depreciation cost, and they lessen the potential commission rate payable to the client.

Cigarette Machines

Cigarette (tobacco) vending machines are still placed at many locations but are becoming less and less common. Most noncommercial locations make every effort to minimize smoking in the work place; some even have incentive programs to encourage smokers to quit. While cigarette vending is still a highly profitable endeavor, fewer and fewer institutional locations provide the product through on-premises vending.

Capital Investment and Gross Profit Margins

Figure 6.8 is a table of vending machine and support equipment items and their current average purchase cost. Machine purchase prices vary with size of purchase and contractual arrangements between the national vending contractors and the machine suppliers.

Figure 6.9 is a table of product lines, average selling prices, and average product cost percentages taken from a national survey. These are overall national averages; specific price and cost structures will vary regionally and with each client's contract arrangements.

Remember that a vending machine installation is a mix of winners and losers:

- Hot and cold beverage machines are high-profit winners.
- Snack and candy merchandisers are moderate-profit winners.
- Dairy machines are low-profit winners.
- Food machines, both hot and cold, are low- to no-profit losers.
- Cigarette machines are high-profit winners but are rapidly going out of fashion.
- Other equipment needs are capital intensive and produce no cash sale or profit.

FIGURE 6.8

Vending Machine and Support Equipment—Average Cost

Machine Type	Average Cost
Hot Drink Machines	
Freeze Dried Coffee	$2,700
Fresh Brew Coffee	3,200
Cold Drink Machines	
Canned Soda	2,200
Post-Mix Soda	5,000
Glass Front Snack Machines	
30-Selection Merchandiser	2,200
35-Selection Merchandiser	2,400
40-Selection Merchandiser	2,600
Food Machines	
Large Cold Food Merchandiser	5,500
Small Cold Food Merchandiser	2,000
Dairy Machines	
Milk (and Cold Drink Package)	3,400
Ice Cream	4,000
Tobacco	
Cigarette Machine	2,000
Other Equipment	
Bill Changer	2,500
Condiment Stand	2,000
Microwave Oven	300
Bill Validator	300

NOTE: Equipment prices will vary by manufacturer. Large contractors will negotiate price discounts on volume purchases.

Typical Product Lines, Selling Prices, Cost Ratios

Machine Type	Average Selling Prices ($)	Average Cost Percentage Ratios
Fresh Brew Coffee		
7 oz.	.30	
9 oz.	.40	22–24% average
12 oz.	.50	
Freeze Dried Coffee		
7 oz.	.30	
9 oz.	.35	20–22% average
12 oz.	.40	
OVERALL HOT DRINK MACHINE COST		20–24% average
Post-Mix Soda Drinks		
9 oz.	.35	
12 oz.	.45	
18 oz.	.55	
OVERALL POST-MIX SODA MACHINE COST		24–28% average
Canned Soda		
12 oz. can	.60	45–50% average
Merchandiser Snack Machines		
Candy, regular size	.55	
King size	.60	
Gum/mints/rolls	.40	
Pastries	.70	40–50% average
Cookies, bagged	.55	
Cookies, jumbo pack	.60	
Micro popcorn	.70	
Sandwiches	1.40–1.60	
Entrees	1.75	
Breakfast items	1.10	45–60% average
Casseroles	1.60	
Pies	.75	
OVERALL MACHINE PRODUCT COST MIX		50–55% average
Milk Machines		
1/2 pt. milk	.50	
1/3 qt. milk	.60	
Pint milk	.65	
Tetra-pak cold drink	.50	
OVERALL MACHINE PRODUCT COST MIX		50–60% average
Ice Cream Machines		
Various products	.60	50–60% average
Cigarette Machines		
Brand name	2.20	
Generic	1.85	70% average

NOTE: The total overall cost of sales (COS) percentage will depend on the sales mix and machine product mix of the location. (See Form F: Summary Pro Forma Budget, page 123.)

FIGURE 6.9 Proprietary National Survey by a Vending Contractor

ORGANIZING THE VENDING BRANCH

A vending organization or the vending department of a foodservice is called a vending branch. Initially all vending branches were separate locations that supported warehousing, production, distribution, and route operations. When foodservice contractors added vending operations to their services (around 1960), the vending branch often became part of a foodservice operation. This was especially true in large manufacturing plants and other major B&I locations.

A vending branch has a distinct and separate organizational structure within the corporation or foodservice organization. It is designed to achieve the financial and service objectives of the branch. The service objectives are the foodservice vending needs of the client. The financial objective is a satisfactory return on investment of the capital required to establish and operate the vending branch. In some cases, the financial objective is also to achieve a net operating profit sufficient to offset a manual cafeteria loss.

A typical branch is a free-standing facility with warehouse space, commissary space, a money room, loading docks, office space, a repair and maintenance facility, and other support services. Figure 6.10 is an example of a typical independent vending branch organization. Where the branch is also part of a major foodservice contract, the commissary would be the kitchen of the manual service.

Note that some branches do not offer a commissary service. In that case, they may subcontract or purchase packaged foods to fulfill the necessary service needs.

Details of Branch Organization

A successful vending branch averages annual gross sales between $3 million and $6 million. It operates multiple routes and services at 20 to 100 separate client locations. The sales volume and number of accounts would determine the size of the staff.

Specific responsibilities of the management staff are as follows:

- *Branch manager:* Responsible for complete operation of the branch—internal production, maintenance, and control; external service; and sales and marketing growth.
- *Assistant branch manager or operations manager:* Supports the branch manager and is responsible in the manager's absence. Specific operating responsibility depends upon need (e.g., warehouse and commissary, route supervision, and mechanic and service workers).
- *Office manager:* Provides administrative and accounting support for the branch.
- *Money room:* Provides handling and control of the cash from the vending routes. The money (cash) room operates as a separate entity directly responsible to the branch manager.
- *Warehouse manager:* The warehouse is responsible for all ordering, receiving, issuing, and controlling of goods and materials used by the branch.
- *Commissary manager:* When a commissary is present, this is a foodservice management position. There is little difference in a vending commissary and the main kitchen of a foodservice—just that all items produced are packaged for a vending machine rather than placed at service points in cold food display counters. In some cases a working chef is also the commissary manager. Gross sales and production volume would determine this.

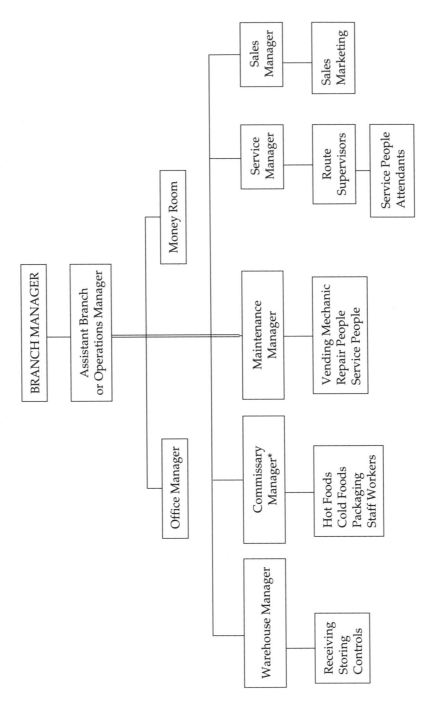

FIGURE 6.10 Typical Vending Branch Organizational Chart

* Not all vending branches have a commissary.

- *Service manager:* Plans the vending route operations, directs the efforts of the route supervisors, and coordinates the route needs with the other departments of the branch operation.
- *Maintenance manager:* Responsible for the operation and maintenance of the machines. Equipment that does not operate will not produce a sale, but it will alienate the customer and decrease future sales potential. The maintenance manager of a vending branch directs the efforts of machine maintenance personnel who may be called by a route worker at a location. These individuals work from radio-equipped support vehicles and respond to calls from the branch to assist a route worker with a mechanical problem.
- *Sales manager:* Where a branch is an independent operation, the sales manager is responsible for the growth of the branch. He or she maintains customer relations with existing clients, conducts efforts to sell new clients, and develops marketing strategies to improve profit potential of the branch. Vending is a highly competitive business, and a good sales manager is key.

A resident branch is part of a major institutional foodservice contract account. It exists solely to service the needs of a single client, such as those described in the urban office building and rural manufacturing company cases. Such branches generally have the same organization as shown in Figure 6.10, but without the sales manager and the commissary manager. A sales manager is not necessary because there's only one client to be serviced. A commissary manager isn't required as long as the main kitchen produces food for vending. A separate vending warehouse is also not required. Both manual and vending often share the same warehouse.

In general, as far as a single operator—contract or self-op—is concerned, it's common to utilize a central facility (such as a food production center) to handle hot and cold food production needs. A vending organization embedded in a resident foodservice must provide service equal to that of an independent vending branch.

THE VENDING PRO FORMA BUDGET

Like a manual foodservice, a vending installation must have a forecast to establish and achieve financial objectives. This is the vending pro forma budget. The pro forma is also used to evaluate the potential sales commissions that can be paid or the amount of profit available to support a subsidy for a profit and loss foodservice contract.

Preparing the vending pro forma budget is similar to preparing the financial forecast (budget) for a manual foodservice. It requires a projection of revenues and expenses or sales and costs.

All contract management companies have a system to prepare a pro forma budget. One company uses six support forms, as follows:

A. Sales and Merchandise Cost Analysis
B. Labor and Related Costs Analysis
C. Direct and Indirect Expense Analysis
D. Capital Investment and Depreciation Schedule
E. Proposed Commission Schedule
F. Summary Pro Forma Budget

A. Sales and Merchandise Cost Analysis

Figure 6.11 is used to forecast sales and merchandise costs for a vending operation. This form allows for projection of sales based on the potential client population and the projection of a sales mix/cost mix to ascertain overall product cost (cost of sales). It's also used to determine the potential gross profit of the operation.

B. Labor and Related Costs Analysis

Figure 6.12 is used to forecast the number of personnel required to support a location and the anticipated total labor cost.

C. Direct and Indirect Expense Analysis

Figure 6.13 is used to forecast direct and indirect expenses incurred by a vending account.

D. Capital Investment and Depreciation Schedule

This form is different from what's been covered for a manual foodservice. Vending is always an investment by the contractor and almost always involves a profit and loss contract. As a result, a vending company must evaluate the capital investment required, develop a depreciation schedule for that investment, evaluate a return on investment (ROI) to support the decision to make the investment, and establish a potential commission structure. Figure 6.14 is an example of a suitable form.

E. Proposed Commission Schedule

Almost all vending operations pay the host organization a commission. The specific amount is evaluated—by product line—at the time the pro forma budget is prepared. Figure 6.15 can be used to figure the amount.

F. Summary Pro Forma Budget

These six forms are usually summarized in a pro forma budget (Figure 6.16). This is, in effect, a projected profit and loss statement for the potential or existing account.

All six forms are similar in nature and purpose to those presented in Chapter 5, "Financial Planning." They are often used in conjunction with the manual financial forecast to prepare a combined pro forma budget. Forms differ among the major contractors, but all use some variation of this concept.

FORM A: Sales and Merchandise Cost Analysis

(A) Population: _____

(1) Machine Type	(2) Vend Price ($)	(3) Weekly per Cap Sales ($)	(4) No. Weeks Gross Sales ($)	(5) Merchandise Cost (%)	(6) Annual Merchandise Cost ($)
Giveaways			‖	‖	
(B) TOTALS		$ _____	$ _____	(C) _____ %	$ _____

FIGURE 6.11 Support Form: Sales and Merchandise Cost Analysis

To complete Form A, the Sales and Merchandise Cost Analysis, follow these steps:

Step 1: Enter machine types in column 1.
Step 2: Enter vend/selling price in column 2.
Step 3: Enter population at Line A.
Step 4: Enter weekly forecast of per capita spending by machine type in column 3.
Step 5: Multiply column 3 × line A × number of weeks of projected operation. Enter the result in column 4.
Step 6: Forecast merchandise cost percentage by product line. Enter in column 5.
Step 7: Evaluate merchandise cost by product line. Enter each total under column 6.
Step 8: Total columns 3, 4, and 6. Enter at line B.
Step 9: Evaluate annual merchandise cost percentage (divide sum of column 6 by sum of column 4). Place result in box C.
Enter results on the summary pro forma budget.

FORM B: Labor and Related Costs Analysis

(1)	(2)	(3)	(4)	(5)	(6)
Position	Number	Wage Rate	Hours per Day ($)	Projected Weekly Cost ($)	Projected Annual Cost ($)
Manager					
Supervisor					
Mechanic					
Routeperson					
Host/Hostess					
Allocations					
Delivery					
Others					
(A) TOTALS				$	$

(B) % Payroll-related costs: _____

(C) TOTAL forecast annual labor cost $

FIGURE 6.12 Support Form: Labor and Related Costs Analysis

To complete Form B, the Labor and Related Costs Analysis, follow these steps:

Step 1: Enter all positions under column 1. Add necessary positions if not listed.

Step 2: Enter the number of workers in each category under column 2.

Step 3: Enter wage rates (hourly or salaried) under column 3.

Step 4: Enter total number of hours per day by worker category under column 4.

Step 5: Evaluate estimated weekly payroll for each category; enter under column 5.

Step 6: Evaluate estimated annual payroll for each category (multiply weekly payroll by 52). Enter at appropriate lines under column 6.

Step 7: Summarize columns 5 and 6 to line A.

Step 8: Enter the percentage amount of payroll-related costs, including vacations, and evaluate annual dollar amount on line B.

Step 9: Evaluate annual estimated total forecast labor cost and enter on line C.

Enter results on the summary pro forma budget.

FORM C: Direct and Indirect Expense Analysis

(A) Projected Annual Gross Sales from Form A: _____

(1)	(2)	(3)	(4)	(5)
Item of Cost	Variable Cost (%)	Variable Cost ($)	Fixed Cost ($)	Total Cost ($)
Vehicle Expense				
Retail Sales Tax				
Licenses/Permits				
Mte. & Repairs				
Sales Commission				
Utilities				
Others (List)				
(B) TOTALS	___ %	$ ___ + $ ___ = $ ___		

FIGURE 6.13 Support Form: Direct and Indirect Expense Analysis

To complete Form C, the Direct and Indirect Expense Analysis follow these steps:

Step 1: Complete the list of expense categories, column 1.
Step 2: Enter annual sales forecast at line A.
Step 3: Estimate and enter variable cost percentages under column 2.
Step 4: Enter fixed cost dollar amounts under column 4.
Step 5: Summarize total percentage amount of column 2 and enter on line B.
Step 6: Multiply total percentage amount of variable costs by projected annual sales from line A. Enter result under column 3, line B.
Step 7: Sum fixed cost dollar amount of column 4.
Step 8: Complete line B and evaluate total estimated direct and indirect expenses. Enter results on Form F.

FORM D: Capital Investment and Depreciation Schedule

(1)	(2)	(3)	(4)	(5)	(6)	(7)
Machine Type	Number of Machines	Unit Cost ($)	Total Machine Cost ($)	Freight Cost ($)	Sales Tax ($)	Total Investment ($)
Hot Drink						
Cup Soda						
Can Soda						
Snacks						
Cold Food						
Milk						
Ice Cream						
Cigarettes						
Bill Chge.						
Validators						
Debit Cards						
Cond. Stand						
Microwaves						
Others (List)						
TOTALS			$	+$	+$	=$

(A) DEPRECIATION ÷ _____ years $ _____

(B) _____ Vehicles @ $ _____ = $_____ ÷ _____ years $ _____

(C) Office Equipment @ $ _____ ÷ _____years $ _____

(D) TOTAL ANNUAL DEPRECIATION $ _____

FIGURE 6.14 Summary Form: Capital Investment and Depreciation Schedule

To complete Form D, Capital Investment and Depreciation Schedule, follow these steps:

Step 1: Enter number of each machine type under column 2.
Step 2: Enter unit cost of each machine type under column 3.
Step 3: Figure total machine cost for each type and enter under column 4.
Step 4: Enter freight cost for each machine type under column 5.
Step 5: Enter sales tax based on column 4 under column 6.
Step 6: Sum each row and enter results under column 7.
Step 7: Sum columns 4, 5, 6, and 7 down to totals.
Step 8: Calculate machine depreciation on line A.
Step 9: Calculate vehicle depreciation line B.
Step 10: Calculate office equipment depreciation on line C.
Step 11: Sum annual depreciation to line D.
Move result to pro forma budget.

FORM E: Proposed Commission Schedule

(1) Product Type	(2) Annual Sales ($)	(3) Commission Rate (%)	(4) Annual Commissions ($)
Hot Drinks			
Cold Drinks			
Can Soda			
Snacks			
Cold Food			
Milk			
Ice Cream			
Cigarettes		per pack	
Others (List)			
TOTALS	(A) $	(B) %	(C) $

FIGURE 6.15   Support Form: Proposed Commission Schedule

To complete Form E, Proposed Commission Schedule, follow these steps:

Step 1: Enter annual sales by product line (from Form A) under column 2.
Step 2: Enter proposed commission rate by product line under column 3.
Step 3: Multiply amounts from column 2 by commission rates from column 3. Enter results in column 4.
Step 4: Summarize column 2 and enter total at box A.
Step 5: Summarize column 4 and enter total at box C.

FORM F: Summary Pro Forma Budget

Projected Annual Gross Sales		$_____	100.0%
Estimated Product Cost		$_____	___._%
Gross Profit		$_____	___._%
OPERATING EXPENSES			
Labor and Related Costs		$_____	___._%
Other Costs: Fixed	$_____		
Variable	$_____		
TOTAL Other Costs		$_____	___._%
Depreciation		$_____	___._%
_____ % Branch Charges		$_____	___._%
TOTAL OPERATING EXPENSES		$_____	___._%
OPERATING PROFIT		$_____	___._%
(Commissions)		$_____	___._%
NET AVAILABLE		$_____	___._%
TOTAL INVESTMENT		$_____	
RETURN ON INVESTMENT		$_____%	

FIGURE 6.16   Support Form: Summary Pro Forma Budget

Step 6: Evaluate average commission rate (C ÷ A). Enter result at box B. Enter results on Form F.

Note: A commission doesn't necessarily have to be a percentage; here, for instance, commission is paid for cigarettes on a per pack basis.

Evaluating the Pro Forma Budget

Each of the major contract management companies has its own method of evaluating the result of the vending pro forma budget and the required capital investment. Much depends on the financial goals of the company and its chief financial officer (CFO).

Three methods are used:

1. Return on Investment (ROI)
2. Return on Assets (ROA)
3. Internal Rate of Return (IRR)

The method selected can vary with the corporation's debt and equity ratios, the present need for short-term cash flow to reduce corporate debt, and other financial considerations. No single method works all the time. If a recent leveraged buy out has created the need for a strong cash flow, the IRR method may be used. If the CFO is a believer in asset management, the ROA method may be used. If the company philosophy favors capital investment, the ROI method may be used. The three may also be combined.

A company may change its CFO and as a result change the method of evaluating a pro forma budget. That same company may change its CFO again and return to the original method. There is no one best method.

This discussion will focus on the return on investment concept. Many organizations try to achieve a 50–75 percent ROI at the location level. Some couple this with a requirement to achieve no less than a 12–15 percent net on sales before corporate overhead, taxes, and profit.

EXAMPLE CASE: RURAL MANUFACTURING COMPANY

An illustrative pro forma budget will be prepared for the rural manufacturing company. Recall that the company has 10,000 employees working two shifts, five days per week. The plant is open 50 weeks per year, closing for group vacations. Vending service is a supplemental refreshment service for the three manual cafeterias.

The criteria for the installation and number of machines and other equipment and capital investment required might resemble the following. (Actual circumstances would depend on client/operator negotiations.)

LOCATION: Rural manufacturing company
TYPE: Heavy manufacturing
POPULATION: 10,000 total
SHIFTS: Days—7,500 population; 2nd shift—2,500 population
NUMBER OF DAYS: 5 days per week, 50 weeks per year
MANUAL SERVICE: Three full-line cafeterias for first shift; one for the second shift
VENDING SERVICES REQUIRED: Refreshment service with adjunct meal service

Ten full-line vending locations, each with:

- Two fresh brew coffee and hot drink machines
- Post-mix cold drink machine
- Snack merchandiser
- Cold food merchandiser
- Milk
- Ice cream
- Microwave oven
- Condiment stand
- Bill changer

Ten refreshment locations, each with:

- Fresh brew coffee and hot drink machine
- Can soda machine
- Snack merchandiser

Canned soda

- Twelve additional machines located in areas adjacent to heavy manufacturing processes

Cigarette vending

- Six machines located adjacent to rest room areas

All drink and canned soda machines equipped with bill validators.
Vending uses a separate on-premises warehouse.

Staffing Requirements and Labor Cost

1. The resident foodservice general manager has overall responsibility for vending.
2. The resident vending branch is directed by a department head as a supervisor/manager, with assistance from the administrative staff of the foodservice operation.
3. Three vending routes are needed to service the equipment: two on the first shift and one on the second shift. A resident mechanic assists in warehouse operations.
4. The warehouse also maintains the money room.
5. Payroll-related costs are projected as 15 percent for FICA, FUTA, workers compensation, and state disability. An additional 10 percent is projected for employee benefits including two weeks vacation pay per employee. Total related costs are projected as 25 percent of payroll.

Direct and Indirect Expenses

- Annual $5,000 vehicle expense
- 5 percent Retail Sales Tax
- $20 per machine annual licensing fee
- 1 percent annual maintenance and repair forecast
- 1 percent annual forecast miscellaneous expenses

Note: Utilities are supplied by the plant.

Corporate Charges

This contractor charges all locations an annual 2 percent of sales as a corporate charge for staff services.

Capital Investment Schedule

Fresh brew coffee machines...$3,500 each
Post-mix soda machines...$5,000 each
Snack merchandiser..$2,300 each
Cold food merchandiser..$5,500 each
Milk machines...$3,400 each
Ice cream machines ....$4,000 each
Cigarette machines ....$2,000 each
Canned soda .... To be provided by the local bottler
Microwave ovens..$300 each
Condiment stands...$2,000 each
Three delivery scooters ....$5,000 each
Various office equipment..$5,000 total

Add freight and sales tax to prices. Freight charges are $100 per machine and $50 per microwave oven, condiment stand, and bill changer. Sales tax is 5 percent on all items.

Chapter 5, "Financial Planning," reviewed six steps required to prepare a budget forecast for a manual foodservice. They are also applicable to a vending pro forma budget. They are:

Step 1: Prepare a set of working forms for financial planning.
Step 2: Forecast all areas of revenue.
Step 3: Forecast cost of sales.
Step 4: Forecast labor and payroll-related costs.
Step 5a: Forecast all operating expenses.
Step 5b: Capital Investment and Depreciation.
Step 6: Summarize all areas of revenue and expense as an annual budget.

Step 1: Prepare a Set of Working Forms

The forms are those in Figures 6.11 to 6.16. There some differences from working forms for a manual foodservice, but they are basically the same format. Two additions are a Capital Investment and Depreciation Schedule (Form D) and a Proposed Commission Schedule (Form E).

Steps 2 and 3: Forecasting Sales and Cost of Sales

Figure 6.11 provides a format to combine forecasting of annual sales and cost of sales on a single form.

Sales for a vending operation are expressed per capita (per person), or "per cap." The per cap is similar to a check average for a manual foodservice—sales per person—but evaluated on a different basis. In vending, per cap is the average *weekly* spending per employee of the population.

Example:
POPULATION 1,000
AVERAGE WEEKLY SALES....................................$3,500
Per cap = $3,500/1000, or $3.50

All vending operators use the weekly per cap as the basis for forecasting and evaluating sales of a vending operation. All of the major contractors maintain excellent database files of average per caps that can be expected from various types of locations.

The per cap for any location can vary based on industry type, average wage of the employees in the operation, geographic location, male/female ratios of the population, and other variables. For the same reasons, the breakdown of the per cap, called sales mix, will also vary. For example, a per cap for hot drinks in a four-season location will vary from the hot beverage per cap in a Sunbelt location. The per cap for cold and hot food items will vary based on the availability of other sources of service. Experienced operators and contractors have an ability to forecast and achieve realistic per caps by each product line.

The per cap is forecast in total and by sales mix using past experience or industry norms. The rural manufacturing company has rounded numbers for illustrative purposes. A per cap of $3.50 per week has been established with the sales mix breakdown as shown in Figure 6.17.

Note that fresh brew coffee machines are used and recall that there are three manual cafeterias available. Also note that there are ten full-line vending locations and ten refreshment centers. This configuration will have a bearing on both the per cap and the sales mix.

The cost basis of each product line has been derived from averages shown in Figure 6.9. These have been added to the analysis of Figure 6.11 to provide:

- Total per cap
- Per cap by product line
- Cost of sales by product line
- Total annual gross sales forecast
- Total annual cost of sales forecast

Figure 6.17 details these items completed as steps 2 and 3, forecasting sales and cost of sales, of the pro forma budget procedure.

FORM A: Sales and Merchandise Cost Analysis
Rural Manufacturing Company
Population: 10,000

(1)	(2)	(3)	(4)	(5)	(6)
Machine Type	Vend Price ($)	Weekly per Cap Sales ($)	Annual Gross Sales ($)	Merchandise Cost (%)	Annual Merchandise Cost ($)
Hot Drink	.30	1.20	600,000	22	$132,000
Cold Drink	.30	.30	150,000	24	36,000
Can Soda	.60	.70	350,000	45	157,500
Snack Mach.	.60–.75	.50	250,000	40	100,000
Cold Food	.75–1.75	.50	250,000	45	112,500
Milk	.50	.10	50,000	50	25,000
Ice Cream	.50	.10	50,000	50	25,000
Cigarettes	2.25	.10	50,000	60	30,000
(B) TOTALS	—	$3.50	$1,750,000	35.3%	$618,000

FIGURE 6.17 Completed Example of Sales and Merchandise Cost Analysis for Rural Manufacturing Company

Sales are forecast as $1,750,000. Cost of sales is $618,000, or 35.3 percent of sales. Sales of packs of cigarettes are forecast as approximately 22,200.

Step 4: Forecast Labor and Payroll-Related Costs

Route structure is crucial to forecasting labor costs. The location and accessibility of machines, the capacity of each machine, the number of food machines with perishable products, and other considerations all have an effect on route structure. Each machine is evaluated on the number of services (refills, change replenishments, etc.) required in a week. A competent vending manager is skilled at structuring routes and scheduling route personnel. This example has three route workers.

The general manager will provide managerial direction to a working manager/supervisor for the vending operation, obviating the need for a vending branch manager.

Payroll-related costs, including all mandated taxes, employee benefits, and vacation pay, are estimated as 25 percent of total payroll.

Use the format of Figure 6.12. Staff requirements, related wage and salary costs, daily hours worked, and resulting weekly costs are entered; the result is Figure 6.18.

The result shows that labor costs are projected as $213,200 including payroll-related costs (mandated taxes, benefits, and vacation accrual).

Step 5a: Forecast All Operating Expenses

This category is the same as that used for the manual foodservice. A list of costs is compiled, they are judged either fixed or variable, and an estimate and summary table is prepared. Two items appear on this list that are unique to vending: sales tax and machine licenses ($20 per machine per year).

The original forecast of $3.50 per week per cap is a total of all revenue from vending machines including sales tax. For forecasting purposes, the sales tax component of the per cap is evaluated as an operating expense. The example uses a sales tax of 5 percent. Later accounting reports will adjust sales to reflect the sales tax.

FORM B: Labor and Related Costs Analysis
Rural Manufacturing Company

(1)	(2)	(3)	(4)	(5)	(6)
Position	Number	Wage Rate ($)	Hours per Day	Projected Weekly Cost ($)	Projected Annual Cost ($)
Mgr/ Supervisor	1	800/wk	8	800	41,600
Mechanic	1	15/hr	8	600	31,200
Route Workers	3	10/hr	24	1,200	62,400
Office	1	8/hr	8	320	16,640
Warehouse	1	9/hr	8	360	18,720
(A) TOTALS	7	—	56 hours	$3,280	$170,560
(B) 25% Payroll-related costs					$ 42,640
(C) TOTAL forecast annual labor cost					$213,200

FIGURE 6.18 Completed Example of Labor and Related Costs Analysis for Rural Manufacturing Company

FORM C: Direct and Indirect Expense Analysis
Rural Manufacturing Company

Projected Annual Gross Sales: $1,750,000

(1)	(2)	(3)	(4)	(5)
Item of Cost	Variable Cost (%)	Variable Cost ($)	Fixed Cost ($)	Total Cost ($)
Vehicle Expense			$5,000	$ 5,000
Retail Sales Tax	5%	87,500		87,500
Licenses/Permits			2,600	2,600
Mte. & Repairs	1%	17,500		17,500
Sales Commission				
Utilities				
Other (List)	1%	17,500		17,500
(B) TOTALS	7.0%	$122,500	$7,600	$130,100

FIGURE 6.19 Completed Example of Direct and Indirect Expense Analysis for Rural Manufacturing Company

Depending on company policy, other costs not shown in this example may appear as direct or indirect expenses. Although accounting and company policy may vary, the method of evaluation remains the same.

Figure 6.13 can be used, with modifications, to evaluate direct and indirect expenses. Using the data provided for this case, the results shown in Figure 6.19 can be anticipated.

Step 5b: Capital Investment and Depreciation

Capital investment consists of machine cost, freight cost, and sales tax on a machine or piece of equipment. Some operators also include the initial installation cost as a capital investment; some do not.

Different pieces of equipment have different life spans and depreciation schedules. Most of the major vending companies use a simplified format for forecasting depreciation costs. Machines are generally depreciated over five years. Some companies use a longer life to improve the pro forma budget results. Vehicles and office equipment have varying schedules.

Keep in mind that a vending operator can usually recover 100 percent of the investment if an account is lost. All equipment, vehicles, and office furniture are easily removed and relocated. Unless an investment has been made in leasehold improvements, there is little risk of having to write off a capital loss if the account is terminated prior to the end of the depreciation schedule.

Figure 6.14 can be used to summarize the capital investment and evaluate the necessary annual depreciation charges. The example assumes a simplified five-year depreciation schedule for all investments. The results, using the data from the example, are shown in Figure 6.20.

The total capital investment is $430,050. The annual depreciation charge is $90,010.

**FORM D: Capital Investment and Depreciation Schedule
Rural Manufacturing Company**

(1)	(2)	(3)	(4)	(5)	(6)	(7)
Machine Type	Number of Machines ($)	Unit Cost ($)	Total Machine Cost ($)	Freight Cost ($)	Sales Tax ($)	Total Investment ($)
Hot Drink	30	3,600	108,000	3,000	5,400	—
Cold Drink	10	5,000	50,000	1,000	2,500	—
Canned Soda*	22					
Snack (Dry)	20	2,600	52,000	2,000	2,600	—
Cold Food	10	5,500	55,000	1,000	2,750	—
Milk	10	3,400	34,000	1,000	1,700	—
Ice Cream	10	4,000	40,000	1,000	2,000	—
Microwave	10	300	3,000	500	150	—
Condiments	10	2,000	20,000	500	1,000	—
Bill Chge.	10	2,500	25,000	500	1,250	—
Cigarette	6	2,000	12,000	600	600	—
Other (List)						—
TOTALS	126	—	$399,000	$11,100	$19,950	$430,050

(A)	DEPRECIATION ÷ five years	$ 86,010
(B)	Three Vehicles @ $5,000 = $15,000 ÷ five years	$ 3,000
(C)	Office Equipment @ $5,000 ÷ five years	$ 1,000
(D)	TOTAL ANNUAL DEPRECIATION	$ 90,010

*NOTE: 22 canned soda machines are to be provided by the supplier (bottler).

FIGURE 6.20   Completed Example of Capital Investment and Depreciation Schedule for Rural Manufacturing Company

Step 6: Summarize to a Pro Forma Budget

Figure 6.16 uses data from Figures 6.11 to 6.15 to provide a summary pro forma budget. The revised pro forma budget for the rural manufacturing company is shown in Figure 6.21.

Note that the net operating profit, before paying a commission to the client or using it to subsidize the manual foodservice, is estimated as $663,690. This is well in excess of the profit required to provide a 75 percent return on investment.

Evaluating a Commission Structure

Prior to evaluating a commission structure, an estimate of the dollar amount of commissions that can be paid to a client is required. The operating profit projected

FORM F: Summary Pro Forma Budget
Rural Manufacturing Company

Projected Annual Gross Sales		$1,750,000	100.0%
Estimated Product Cost		618,000	35.3
Gross Profit		$1,132,000	64.7%
OPERATING EXPENSES			
Labor and Related Costs		$ 213,200	12.2%
Other Costs: Fixed	$ 7,600		
Variable	122,500		
TOTAL Other Costs		130,100	7.4
Depreciation		90,010	5.1
2% Branch Charges		35,000	2.0
TOTAL OPERATING EXPENSES		$ 468,310	26.7%
OPERATING PROFIT		$ 663,690	37.9%
(Commissions)		$_____	___.__%
NET AVAILABLE		$_____	___.__%
	TOTAL INVESTMENT	$ 450,050	
	RETURN ON INVESTMENT	161.6%	

FIGURE 6.21 Completed Example of Summary Pro Forma Budget for Rural Manufacturing Company, Without Commissions

for the vending installation at the rural manufacturing company is $663,690. How much of the operating profit can the company pay as commissions and still have a fair return on investment (75 percent)? Examine the following:

The capital investment is $450,050.
A desired ROI might be 75 percent, or $337,538. The calculation is performed like so:
$663,690 (operating profit)
less $337,538 (desired 75 percent ROI)
equals $326,152 (available for commissions and food sudsidy).
$326,152 can be paid as commissions and subsidy and still allow a potential 75 percent ROI.

In a case such as the rural manufacturing company, the manual foodservice may be operating at a loss and require a subsidy from the vending operation. Figure 5.13 indicated that the company's gross food sales would be $3,473,250. Figure 5.14 indicated that cost of sales would be $1,383,951, or 39.8 percent. If labor and other costs exceed 60.2 percent of gross sales, the manual foodservice would operate at a loss. Considering the company operates three cafeterias and two shifts, that could well be the case.
If the analysis indicated that the manual foodservice required a $100,000 subsidy and the vending operation required a 75 percent ROI, then the following equation would result:

$663,390 (operating profit) less $337,538 (desired net available from vending)
less $100,000 (required manual operations subsidy)
equals $226,152 (potential commissions available).

FORM E: Proposed Commission Schedule
Rural Manufacturing Company

(1)	(2)	(3)	(4)
Product Type	Annual Sales ($)	Commission Rate (%)	Annual Commissions ($)
Hot Drinks	600,000	22	132,000
Cold Drinks	150,000	20	30,000
Can Soda	350,000	9	31,500
Snack Machines	250,000	9	22,500
Cold Food	250,000	0	—
Milk	50,000	5	2,500
Ice Cream	50,000	5	2,500
Cigarettes	50,000	25¢/pack	5,550
TOTALS	$1,750,000	12.9%	$226,550

FIGURE 6.22 Completed Example of Proposed Commission Schedule for Rural Manufacturing Company

FORM F: Summary Pro Forma Budget
Rural Manufacturing Company

Projected Annual Gross Sales		$1,750,000	100.0%
Estimated Product Cost		618,000	35.3
Gross Profit		$1,132,000	64.7%
OPERATING EXPENSES			
Labor and Related Costs		$ 213,200	12.2%
Other Costs: Fixed	$ 7,600		
Variable	122,500		
TOTAL Other Costs		130,100	7.4
Depreciation		90,010	5.1
2% Branch Charges		35,000	2.0
TOTAL OPERATING EXPENSES		$ 468,310	26.7%
OPERATING PROFIT		$ 663,690	37.9%
Commissions and subsidy		$ 326,550	18.7%
NET AVAILABLE		$ 337,140	19.3%
TOTAL INVESTMENT		$ 450,050	
RETURN ON INVESTMENT		75.9%	

FIGURE 6.23 Completed Example of Summary Pro Forma Budget for Rural Manufacturing Company, Without Commissions

Under this scenario,

- A $100,000 subsidy can be provided to the manual operations.
- A $226,153 commission can be paid to the client.
- A 75 percent ROI can be achieved by the contractor.

Developing a Commission Structure

Once the potential commission amount has been decided, a commission structure can be formulated. Commissions are usually paid as a percentage of sales by product line, except for cigarettes, which are usually on a cents-per-pack basis.

High–gross profit machines (cold beverage, for instance) can pay higher commissions than low–gross profit machines (like food and dairy). A good commission structure balances these types, allowing the client a high enough return and the contractor a sufficient profit margin against a population change.

Numerous commission configurations that total approximately $226,153 are possible. Usually, a good configuration is high rates on hot and cold drink machine sales, moderate rates on canned soda and snacks, low rates on dairy products, and no commission on food products. Figure 6.22 is a proposed commission structure for the rural manufacturing company.

This follows these principles, with a high rate of 22 percent on hot drinks and 20 percent on cold soda. Canned soda and snacks are bid as 9 percent, with dairy products at 5 percent. Cigarettes are bid at 25 cents per pack. The proposed structure will provide the client with a projected commission of $226,550. It will also provide the operator with a net available of $437,140, or 24.9 percent, on sales. This will allow for the necessary $100,000 subsidy to the manual food operation and leave $337,140, or 19.3 percent, on sales for the contractor. The results are a satisfactory ROI and an equally satisfactory net percentage to sales.

Figure 6.23 is a completed pro forma budget with commissions and subsidy added, indicating the potential resulting net available to the contractor.

SUMMARY

Foodservice vending is an integral part of most institutional and noncommercial foodservice operations. The responsibility for the vending operation is often given to the foodservice director.

When vending is contracted, it is usually operated as part of a vending branch. When vending is self-operated, it's almost always part of the foodservice director's responsibility.

Vending dates back to Hero, a citizen of ancient Greece, who invented a machine to dispense holy water around 215 B.C. Foodservice vending in the United States began with the Horn and Hardart Company around 1902.

Vending today is in every facet of the institutional foodservice industry. All segments have vending to support the manual services provided.

The economics of vending are such that an installation with a large population (i.e. manufacturing plant) can provide sufficient net profit to offset manual food-service losses and still pay a commission to the client. This is often the case for a contractor in a large installation.

Foodservice directors in the noncommercial segments require a good working knowledge of foodservice vending operations, economics, and management.

7

Menu Management

A menu is a list of products served by a foodservice operation. Every foodservice, commercial or noncommercial, has but one true purpose: to prepare and serve its customers the items on the menu.

In Chapter 2, management was defined as the accomplishment of objectives through others. Those objectives had two components: service needs and financial goals. In a foodservice, the menu is the vehicle used to achieve both.

Remember that planning is the essence of management; if the plan is sound, success is possible. Planning and managing the menu well makes achievement of all other foodservice objectives possible.

The different financial and service objectives for the various segments of noncommercial foodservice mean menus are planned with different operational requirements. In the commercial segment, an operator plans a menu to satisfy a specific market niche. In the noncommercial segment, that market niche is pre-established: the menu is planned to suit an existing situation.

This chapter provides the reader with an understanding of the fundamentals of menu management and how to apply them to the various institutional foodservice industry segments.

Upon completion of this chapter readers should know and understand:

- The fundamentals of menu management
- Constraints on menu planning
- Concepts of menu cycling
- Menu management in
  business and industry foodservice
  college and university foodservice
  health care foodservice
  contractor operations
- The menu and cost controls

THE FUNDAMENTALS OF MENU MANAGEMENT

If planning is the essence of management, menu planning is the essence of menu management. If the menu is well planned, operational objectives are attainable; if the menu is poorly planned, the reverse is often true.

The following are four basic concepts of menu management:

1. Establish customer (and client) preferences. Who are the customers? What are their wants and needs?

2. Establish menu objectives. What service and financial goals must the menu achieve?
3. Consider menu constraints. What *Skills, Equipment* and *Time* (SET) constraints are present in the operation?
4. Execute the menu plan to achieve menu objectives.

All menus should be managed with these four concepts in mind.

Establishing Customer Preferences and Menu Objectives

The objective of any menu is to satisfy patron needs and produce a satisfactory financial result. In a noncommercial foodservice operation, the need is established by the host facility. That client or company makes the decision regarding what services will be offered, during what periods, and under what conditions.

In a cash facility such as a B&I operation, satisfactory financial results can be achieved with menu pricing structure. The menu and its pricing must produce a satisfactory dollar amount of gross profit to meet all other operating expenses and, where necessary, the desired net profit goals. In a noncash outlet, (health care and correctional, for example) the menu must meet the necessary budgetary constraints regarding cost per meal.

Consider these examples:

■ A business and industry location with a heavily subsidized foodservice and correspondingly low menu prices will have a different financial objective than one with a profit and loss orientation. This affects the menu.
■ A contract-managed profit and loss university foodservice, with low participation of boarding students at fixed rates, will have a different financial objective than a self-operated college with a high number of boarding students.
■ A voluntary hospital with a short average patient stay will have a different service need than a long-term care, profit-oriented operation.
■ A school lunch operation, using federal subsidies, will have a different financial structure than one not using the National School Lunch Program incentives.

Each case has its own special menu objectives. While there are similarities in menu management techniques, there are also different service and financial goals.

The fundamentals of menu management remain the same. The application of those management principles changes with the type of facility, nature of contractual obligations, and location.

SET CONSTRAINTS

Three constraints, skill, equipment, and time, were mentioned. These are called the SET constraints. They exist in all foodservice operations and must be considered when planning any menu.

Skill Constraints

Skill constraints are limits imposed by the food preparataion abilities of the production staff. A location with a skilled chef, a baker, and other expert staff may plan menus that utilize their talents. If the facility has a cook with the title "chef" but not the training, menus must be planned around that fact. This includes the cold foods section, hot foods, baked goods, and desserts. The same is true of all other production personnel. A menu must reflect the true skill level of the staff.

Skill constraints may be unavoidable when the location of a foodservice dictates them. Some geographic locations have few skilled culinary workers available. And many correctional operations utilize an inmate work staff. Whatever the reason, a skilled staff simply may not be available.

Where staff culinary skills are insufficient to produce the desired menu, other means of production are available. These include the purchase of prepared or semi-prepared foods and an emphasis on freezer merchandise. Such a decision has a bearing on equipment, another constraint.

Equipment Constraints

Equipment constraints can affect functional areas including receiving, refrigerated and frozen storage, dry storage, and production. If a product cannot be properly received, stored, and produced, it should not be on the menu.

Capacity of production equipment is another consideration. If fryers, ovens, stove tops, steamers, and so on aren't sized to meet production needs, this imposes an equipment constraint. A menu must be planned to suit the existing equipment and its capacity. If the equipment won't let the operator produce the desired menu, the menu must be reformulated.

Equipment constraints may be unavoidable. Noncommercial foodservice operations are usually designed and installed by consultants, not operators of the facility. As a result, the physical plant is often designed without a specific menu in mind. While this is contrary to sound design principles, it is the rule rather than the exception.

Time Constraints

Time constraints chiefly involve the number of labor hours available at scheduled times to meet all production needs. If the budget allows 40 labor hours per day for production personnel, then the menu should be producible in those 40 labor hours.

Also, some office building and manufacturing locations will accept deliveries for the foodservice only at specific times, and equipment may be available only during certain times.

Taken together, the three SET constraints are an important facet of menu planning. The institutional foodservice director is always responsible for customer satisfaction and financial objectives and is always dealing with these constraints.

MENU CYCLING

A cycle menu, used by almost all institutional foodservices, is planned for a specific period of time—based on the operation's requirements—and repeated.

Menu cycles often run four to six weeks. In the case of a college or university, they may cover an entire semester. The length of the menu cycle is planned to suit the individual operation.

Many contractors using a four-week accounting period use a four-week cycle menu. This coincides with the cost control plan and allows evaluation of the menu in conjunction with the financial cycle.

Some health care facilities use a single-week cycle. This is especially true in a hospital where the average length of patient stay is seven days or less. It's less prevalent in facilities where patient stay is longer.

The length of the cycle also depends on the manager's menu philosophy. If a manager wants to limit the time required for menu planning, a cycle concept is advantageous. If a manager is desirous of a changing, creative menu, the cycle concept has less value.

Advantages and Disadvantages of Menu Cycling

Menu cycling has both advantages and disadvantages. Advantages include:

- Less time required for menu planning
- Advance knowledge of purchasing requirements
- Greater control over cost estimates
- Less training time for culinary personnel
- Easier review of past sales records and forecasting

Disadvantages include:

- Patron boredom
- Less menu creativity
- Menu items may be limited to fresh ingredients that are always available

To overcome the disadvantages, managers often plan periodic special merchandising days within the cycle. These are marketed as theme promotions and add a little zest to the ordinary. They are discussed in greater detail in Chapter 10, Sales and Marketing.

Another method of overcoming menu cycling's disadvantages is to allow for seasonal change. This variation uses two or four sets of cycles to suit the season. A two-set cycle might have a fall/winter and spring/summer pattern; a four-set cycle, summer/fall/winter/spring. Other combinations are used by creative managers.

The reason for menu cycling is to establish an operating menu plan that is predictable, pleases the customer, and produces the desired financial results. Properly used, cycling greatly helps manage the institutional foodservice menu.

MENU MANAGEMENT EXAMPLES

Following is a review of menu management principles as they apply to the four case examples discussed in Chapters 2 and 5. This will provide a concrete review of menu management in the various segments of the institutional foodservice industry.

Business and Industry: Urban Office Building

Two previously reviewed business and industry example cases, the urban office building and the rural manufacturing company, are both classified as B&I but have different operational plans and menu management needs.

Following is a review of the urban office building's menu needs and a plan to manage those needs.

The urban office building has 2,000 employees, 100 executives, and these service needs:

- An employee cafeteria
- A service dining room
- Four executive dining rooms
- Special functions
- Coffee break service via vending machines

So there are a minimum of four menus required:

1. A cafeteria menu
2. A service dining room menu
3. Executive dining room menu
4. Catering (special function) menus

Marketing Information and SET Constraints

The cafeteria provides both breakfast and lunch services. Its customers are employees, most of whom commute to work on public transportation.

A marketing survey of the employees indicates many two-income families; the employee eats the main meal of the day in the cafeteria. It further shows that the population is 60 percent female and 40 percent male. The predominant age group is late 30s to mid 40s, but employees range in age from early 20s to early 60s.

The skills of the production staff are high, wage rates are a little higher than average, and working conditions are excellent.

The facility was designed by the contractor as part of the original agreement. As a result, it has the necessary equipment to receive, store, produce, and serve nicely varied, freshly prepared foods.

The building has a separate delivery entrance for the foodservice operation. There are no impediments to deliveries or employee access. The labor budget allows for ample staff to meet almost any need.

Meal service is provided for the 2,000 employee population who break for lunch at 20-minute intervals. The projected customer count over the entire lunch period is 1,200 customers.

The Cafeteria Menu

The proposed cafeteria menu for this operation is a four-week, seasonally changed menu cycle. In addition, numerous special merchandising days are planned throughout the year.

The breakfast menu should be standard and unchanging to allow ease of production and service. A take-out area must be provided for the employee who prefers to eat at the desk.

The lunch menu should have a standard full-line pattern for sandwiches, salads, desserts, and beverages, each with a daily special. The remainder of the lunch menu should be planned as part of the cycle with the daily pattern shown in Figure 7.1.

Pricing Policies

Our case example states that the cafeteria menu should achieve a 35 percent food cost for the breakfast menu and a 45 percent food cost for the lunch menu. This will provide a 65 percent/55 percent gross profit, respectively. Considering the

FIGURE 7.1

Cafeteria Menu Pattern Plan for Urban Office Building

Appetizers	Entrées	Desserts
3 Juices	1 Solid Meat	2 Two-Crust
	1 Fish	Pie
Soups	1 Extended Item	1 Single-Crust
1 Heavy	1 Special	Pie
1 Light		1 Cake
	Vegetables	2 Specials
Salads	2 Potatoes	1 Pudding
1 Large Entrée	1 Starch	1 Gelatin
1 Small Entrée	1 Other	1 Fruit
3 Side Salads		Ice Cream
Self-Serve Bar	Sandwiches	
	2 Wrapped Specials	Beverages
	Various Made-to-Order	Assorted
		Hot & Cold

average menu prices of the commercial sector, this allows the company operation to compete effectively.

Customer Satisfaction

Management desires a 15 percent participation for breakfast and a 60 percent participation for lunch. Further objectives are a $1.00 check average for breakfast and a $2.50 check average for lunch. If both of these goals are achieved, the operator is satisfying customer needs. Both objectives are well within industry norms.

Service Dining Room Menu

The service dining room has 100 seats and is available for lunch to employees and their guests. It is intended to provide an upscale meal for its patrons.

The menu pattern should use the cafeteria menu as a base with additional cooked-to-order items unavailable in the cafeteria. The same two soups, the daily entree salad, daily hot sandwich, and solid meat and fish entrees should be on the menu. Grill and broiler items not available in the cafeteria should also be part of the daily and weekly cycle plan for the dining room. Desserts and beverages from the cafeteria can be better marketed and presented and used as part of the dining room menu cycle. This allows for ease of production of all items. The attention given to merchandising, marketing, and seasonal promotions in the cafeteria should extend to the dining room.

Figure 7.2 details a dining room menu plan.

Note that the primary cafeteria items are the basis for the dining room menu. The difference is in à-la-carte service. In addition, all dining room sandwiches are made to order and properly garnished, and there is a daily Chef's Special hot entrée item and grilled sandwiches.

Pricing Policies

The financial forecast called for a $6.00 check average at a 35 percent food cost. Pricing of the menu should be approximately 20 percent higher than cafeteria prices to attain the goal; menu merchandising will also help.

FIGURE 7.2

Dining Room Menu Plan for Urban Office Building

	Cafeteria	*Dining Room*
Appetizers	3 Juices _____ 2 Other _____	
Soups	1 Heavy _____ 1 Light _____	
Entrée	1 Broiled Meat 1 Fish _____ 1 Extended Item _____	 1 Chef's Special
Vegetables	2 Potatoes _____ 1 Starch _____ 2 Other _____	Plus French Fries
Salads	1 Large Entrée Salad _____ 1 Small Entrée Salad _____	
Sandwiches	....	Various Made-to-Order Grilled, Burgers, etc.
Desserts	Pies _____ Cakes _____ Puddings and Gelatin Desserts ____	
Beverages	Assorted _____	

Customer Satisfaction

If the forecast of 10 percent of population—or 200 customers per day—with a check average of $6.00 or higher is achieved, the patrons will be happy.

Executive Dining Rooms

There are four executive dining rooms available to top management and their corporate guests. This type of operation is usually very personal and reflects the needs and wants of the executive staff.

Menus for executive dining are usually prepared in consultation with the executives in question. Executives' and their guests' health concerns, personal diet preferences, and other factors must be considered. The menu should be custom designed after consultation with each of the executives who use the particular facility and should meet their personal needs. While some of the items available on the daily cafeteria and dining room menus may be offered, additional gourmet items must also be continuously available.

If a corporation has overseas operations—as this one does—catering to international tastes becomes important. Such a service is just another way to fulfill the needs of the executives and their guests. Only a custom-designed menu will meet this objective.

Figure 7.3 is an example of an executive dining room menu prepared by the contractor in consultation with the client liaison. It is an example of the special attention paid to an executive and guest menu.

Wednesday
Luncheon Fare

Appetizers
Crepe Stuffed with Chicken

Fresh Fruit Salad

Mixed Greens   Melon in Season

* * *

Soup of the Day
Broccoli and Spinach Soup

Consomme
Chicken or Beef

* * *

Entrees
*Fish of the Day

*Pasta Primavera

Tenderloin of Beef Wellington

* * *

Desserts
Seasonal Fresh Fruit

Ice Cream or Sherbet

Selection of Pastry

Coffee   Decaffeinated   Variety of Tea

*Lower Cholesterol Entree   W 2

Available Everyday...
* * *

New York Cut Sirloin Steak

Chopped Sirloin Hamburger Steak
served with Fresh Bermuda onion and French fries

*Grilled Breast of Chicken Sandwich
on croissant or kaiser roll

Broiled Filet of Sole

The Presidential Club Sandwich

The 270 Chef Salad
mixed greens topped with assorted meats & cheese

*Fresh Seasonal Fruit Platter
served with cottage cheese or sherbet

*Assorted Steamed Vegetable Platter
plain or with butter sauce

Caesar Salad
with julienned grilled chicken

**Omelettes
cheese, mushroom, or western

**can be ordered with egg white only

FIGURE 7.3 Executive Dining Room Menu, Chemical Bank, New York City

Pricing Policies

Chapter 2 detailed the pricing policy to recover the cost of food and direct labor only. This requires an evaluation of those costs to establish the menu prices.

Customer Satisfaction

Customer satisfaction in an executive dining room can only be measured by continuous communication with the individuals serviced. Many executives, if unhappy, are quick to express displeasure. This makes gauging customer satisfaction somewhat easier than it might be in other areas of the foodservice.

Menu Planning

Menu planning requires certain tools. Each operation should design a set of planning forms for the menu like the planning forms for the financial forecast. Usually some sort of wide-column spreadsheet detailing the categories of the menu is used. Figure 7.4 is one example; remember, though, there are as many planning sheets as there are managers and locations. The design of the sheet is not important as long as it works for the manager using it.

In addition to a planning form, the menu planner requires the following:

■ A set of standard recipes
■ A listing of all menu items under consideration
■ Past production records
■ Past sales records

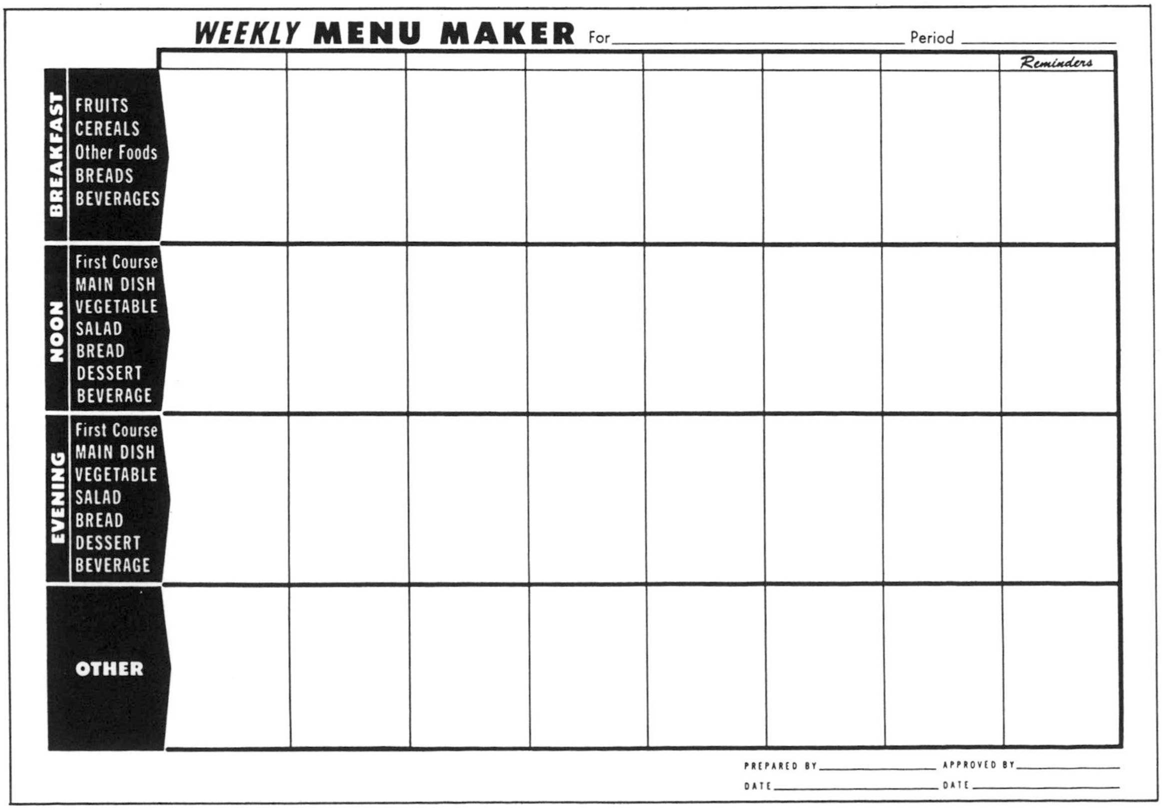

FIGURE 7.4 Example of a Menu Planning Form

The standard recipes are used to assess menu ingredients, the availability of fresh, seasonal foods, and the cost of each item.

The listing of all menu items under consideration is usually available from an operations manual, a menu manual, or other files established by the foodservice director.

The production records detail previous methods of production. This allows the menu planner to ensure that there are no equipment constraints for a planned menu.

Sales records provide the menu planner with a history of customer satisfaction gauged by the sales figures.

All prior records are used when planning a menu. If the records have been kept properly, they will be effective for planning. If record keeping was poor, the mistakes made on previous menus can be made again.

Business and Industry: Rural Manufacturing Company

Let's take our rural manufacturing example and apply the same menu management principles as above. The plant, remember, had the following numbers and needs:

■ 10,000 employees, including administrative and executive personnel
■ Two operating shifts, five days per week
■ Three employee cafeterias—one main and two satellite facilities
■ Meal service for breakfast, lunch, dinner, pre-shift, and post-shift service
■ An executive dining room service for 100 executives—lunch only
■ Refreshment and work break service by vending machines
■ Catering service for company-sponsored events, special awards dinners, company picnics, and other

There are four menu requirements for this facility:

1. A cafeteria menu for three meals per day
2. An executive dining room lunch menu
3. Vending menus for the food merchandisers
4. Catering (special function) menus

Marketing Information and SET Constraints

A marketing survey has provided some information regarding the population: Plant employees are primarily male; ages range from 25 to 55 with the majority between 35 and 50. They are a mixed group of blue collar, semiskilled, and skilled workers.

The office population is 70 percent female; they are mostly data processing and clerical semiprofessionals.

The skill qualities of the food production staff are just satisfactory. On site at the main kitchen is a baker, a good cook/chef, and semiskilled hot and cold food production personnel. Satellite cafeterias have semiskilled personnel only.

The equipment in the main kitchen supports a full bakery, hot food production needs, and cold food pantry operation. The satellite kitchens have only minimal preparation equipment; most food comes from the main kitchen and is reheated.

Service areas in the main cafeteria support a full line of foods—hot, cold, grilled—and beverages. The two satellite cafeterias have limited hot and cold food service space, small grill stations, and small beverage areas.

The main kitchen has ample receiving, storing, and refrigerated space, with adjacent office space and equipment.

There are few time constraints at the main kitchen; workers have 24-hour access with no restrictions. The two satellite kitchens have limited time for setup and breakdown of meal service.

The Cafeteria Menu

The breakfast menu should be suitable for heavy industrial workers. The lines and grill stations in all cafeterias serve eggs, meats, potatoes, cereals, rolls, pastries, and other items that commonly comprise a hearty breakfast. The full breakfast menu is available daily, with no changes.

The lunch menu should suit the workers at the main cafeteria, the factory area satellite cafeteria, and the satellite office cafeteria. The lunch and dinner menus use the same patterns.

The daily menu offers made-to-order sandwiches, grill items with french fries, steam table entrees and vegetables, cold foods, desserts, and beverages. Figure 7.5 is a template of the cafeteria menu.

In addition, the office satellite cafeteria offers daily specials tailored to the mostly female population: cold foods, salads, and other light items.

The menu in all locations is a four-week cycle with seasonal variations.

Pricing Policy

The food service is operated by a contractor on a profit and loss basis, but the trade union in the plant has an agreement requiring certain price constraints. This results in the pricing of the cafeteria menu at 40 percent cost of sales with prices approximately 10–15 percent below comparable commercial restaurants.

Customer Satisfaction

Manufacturing companies seldom achieve high participation. Many employees still bring their own lunch and use the vending centers for supplementary services—a soda or dessert, for example. If the projected participation and check average forecasts made for the plant in Chapter 5 are achieved, the customer will be satisfied. The numbers from Chapter 5 are shown in Figure 7.6.

FIGURE 7.5

Cafeteria Menu Plan for Rural Manufacturing Company

Appetizers	Desserts	Vegetables
2 Juices	1 Two-Crust Pie	Mashed Potato
	1 Single-Crust Pie	Alternate Potato
Soups	2 Individual Items	1 Starchy Vegetable
1 Heavy	1 Cake	1 Green Vegetable
1 Light	Pudding	
	Gelatin Dessert	Salads
Grill Station	Fresh Fruit	1 Entrée Salad (Office)
Burgers		Various Side Salads
Other Grill Items	Hot Foods	Self-Serve Salad Bar
French Fries	1 Solid Meat or Fish	
	1 Extended item	Beverages
Sandwich Station	1 Pasta Item	Full-Line Hot and Cold
Full Line of Made-to-Order Sandwiches		

FIGURE 7.6

**Forecast Participation and Check Averages,
Rural Manufacturing Company**

Meal Period	Participation (%)	Projected Check Average ($)
MANUFACTURING		
Shift #1		
Breakfast	10	1.25
Lunch	40	3.00
Shift #2		
Pre-Shift	10	1.25
Dinner	30	4.00
OFFICE		
Breakfast	10	1.00
Lunch	50	2.50

Executive Dining Room

Manufacturing plant executives are from different market groups than their urban office building counterparts. Their eating habits tend to match those of the plant workers and others from their particular region.

For this operation, a menu extracted from the cafeteria menu should suffice. The addition of specific items requested by the executives is all that is needed to achieve customer satisfaction.

Pricing Policy

Menu items in the executive dining room are priced the same as the cafeteria. There is a $1.00 per meal service charge for wait staff service.

Customer Satisfaction

As with the urban office building, customer satisfaction can be measured by participation and comments from the executives.

Vending Menu

Vending machines serve all plant and office personnel. Banks of full-line machines include cold food merchandisers with prepared foods that can be heated in adjacent microwave ovens.

The vending machines should serve primarily as a refreshment center for coffee break periods and secondarily as a meal center for those electing to use them. The menu need is to provide items for the cold food merchandisers that are compatible with these two objectives.

The same cycle concept of menu planning used for the manual operation can be used for the vending service. Some standard items are offered daily; others are offered on a cyclical basis. Standard foods include pastries, bagels, cookies, and other coffee break standbys. The varied offerings include sandwiches, soups, hot casseroles, and other items suitable to a meal service.

The main cafeteria kitchen is a commissary for both the two satellite kitchens and the vending operation. All vending packaged foods must be producible in that facility within its skill and equipment constraints.

Menu Planning

The same methods of menu planning discussed for the urban office building are applicable to the rural manufacturing company. A set of standard recipes, a listing of eligible menu items, past production records, and past sales records are required.

Records for the company would also include a breakdown of sales information by cafeteria location and shift. Each location and shift requires separate data to allow accurate analysis.

College and University: Campus University

The case of the campus university can use the same principles of menu management followed thus far. The university has the following statistics and service needs:

- 8,000 annual enrollment of full- and part-time students
- 4,000 ten-week summer session enrollment
- 500 full-time faculty
- 1,000 staff employees
- 500-seat boarding cafeteria
- 400-seat cash cafeteria
- Food court in student union building
- Faculty club dining room
- Catering to all areas of the campus
- Support vending service in all areas of the campus
- Management company operated on a profit and loss contract
- 8 percent commission rate on cash sales
- Variable commission rate on vending sales
- $500,000 capital investment

There are four menu requirements for this facility:

1. Board rate menus for 15-, 19-, and 21-meal per week plans
2. Cash cafeteria menu
3. Faculty club menu (lunch only)
4. Catering menus

In addition, the food court requires various menus to suit the needs of the product lines offered. Vending provides a standard refreshment service without cycle merchandising.

Marketing Information and SET Constraints

No two campuses are alike, so marketing information is vital for the campus dining service to fulfill customer expectations. This would include:

- Gender/ethnic mix of the student body
- Age groups of students and staff participating in board rate and cash cafeterias
- Geographic breakdown of student body
- Religious composition of student body; is there a predominance of Catholics, Protestants, Jews, Muslims, or other groups?
- Special needs, like "training tables" for athletes

Most campus dining facilities have some equipment constraints at the different locations. The main kitchen may have ample equipment to receive, store, and produce the necessary menu items, but the satellites may be short on space or equipment.

Skill constraints in this example concern the abilities of the professional full-time production staff and student part-time employees utilized in the kitchen.

Meal periods are established by university policy and student needs. Between meal setup time may be insufficient. Staffing plans must be coordinated with menus to provide for smooth transition between mandated meal services.

The Board Rate Menu

Figure 7.7 is an example of a board rate menu for a college or university.

The Cash Cafeteria Menu

The cash cafeteria provides service to nonboard students and the university staff. The menu must serve both groups.

Generally, the board rate menu provides the basis for cash cafeteria entrée selection. The cash menu is filled out with other offerings that meet patron needs. Figure 7.8 is an example of a menu pattern for a cash cafeteria.

While the location may dictate additional menu needs, this pattern is typical for a facility of this type.

Faculty Club Menu

Faculty clubs are similar to executive dining rooms in a B&I foodservice. The faculty of a college or university are usually a diverse, multifaceted group.

Not all faculty join the club and utilize the lunch service. Some days, like Fridays, many campuses have limited classes and limited faculty on campus, so participation is difficult to project.

Many faculty clubs have a daily buffet menu with wait staff service for desserts and beverages. Some offer both a buffet and a short à-la-carte menu.

The menu pattern for a faculty club features the same items available from the cash and board cafeterias. The service area(s) of a club may or may not have production equipment. Most have simple satellite catering kitchens with ware-washing facilities. All foods are prepared in the main kitchen. The menu planner must work within these constraints and still satisfy patrons.

Catering Menus

Some universities do an extensive catering business and have many catering menus. The catering market includes students, special groups, staff, faculty, and administration. Each group has different needs.

Cornell University has a catering package typical for a large university. Figure 7.9 is an example of a catered dinner menu.

Pricing Policies

Pricing policies for campus dining vary but must provide the college or university with sufficient income to cover all operating costs. Most colleges hope to achieve a return from vending commissions that can be used for other purposes.

The basic student board rate is assessed annually and adjusted to suit cost projections. Where a contractor operates the college foodservice, they charge a weekly board rate to the school. The school adds its own overhead and charges the students a semester board rate, payable to the university.

LUNCH MENU DINNER
MARCH 8-14

M

LUNCH:
GRILLED CHEESE SANDWICH(327,11.3,18.3,29.2)
TACOS(278,11.3,16.0,24.5)
VEGETARIAN TACOS
PASTA WITH TURKEY & VEGETABLES(273,14.0,11.1,29.7)

DINNER:
CHICKEN NUGGETS(270,1.4,1.6,1.6)
LENTIL RICE LOAF(170,6.0,9.0,15.0)
GRILLED PORK CHOP(135,17.3,6.8,0.0)
 SPAGHETTI & MARINARA SAUCE(236,7.8,6.3,38.3)

T

LUNCH:
FOOTLONG HOT DOG(467,14.6,25.2,44.4)
VEGETARIAN REUBEN(485,20.2,27.6,43.4)
TOFU FRIED RICE(180,6.4,6.8,24.3)
SHRIMP EGG ROLLS(320,11.4,5.7,45.7)

DINNER:
HAMBURGER(330,19.4,15.9,26.3)
BLACKEYED PEA JAMBALAYA(570,21.4,11.1,96.9)
SWISS CHEESE CROQUETTES(572,28.9,30.2,45.0)
HERBED BAKED CHICKEN(221,26.0,10.5,1.4)

W

LUNCH:
CHEESE PIZZA(371,19.7,14.8,40.1)
VEGETARIAN BEAN CASSEROLE(332,13.1,7.9,52.9)
BLT(273,11.3,11.2,31.2)

DINNER:
PASTA BAR
FRIED SHRIIMP(377,31.0,17.5,24.4)
PAELLA(466,30.0,18.9,42.9)
BAKED RED SNAPPER

T

LUNCH:
VEGETABLES LO MEIN(307,10.1,12.1,39.9)
GARDEN PATTY SANDWICH(294,19.9,8.2,37.9)
CHICKEN PATTY SANDWICH(452,18.6,24.8,38.6)

DINNER:
BEAN BURRITO(417,15.3,19.7,45.6)
SPINACH LASAGNA(225,17.9,7.7,21.9)
ROAST TURKEY(182,29.5,5.1,2.6)

F

LUNCH:
VEGETARIAN PASTA(175,4.9,4.0,30.5)
MEATBALL SANDWICH(347,14.1,11.2,47.1)
MUSHROOM SPINACH QUICHE(395,14.8,27.1,23.3)

DINNER:
FRIED CHICKEN(277,32.7,9.4,13.2)
CHEESE RAVIOLI(226,8.7,4.1,37.3)
ITALIAN STYLE RICE & BEANS(229,9.1,5.6,36.6)
CHICKEN PAPRIKA(246,29.2,9.4,10.1)

S

BRUNCH

DINNER:
CHEESE PIZZA(371,19.7,14.8,40.1)
STIR FRIED VEGETABLES W/BROWN RICE(303,7.5,12.3,43.3)

S

CLOSED FOR SPRING BREAK

DINING HALLS REOPEN MONDAY, MARCH 22

Wellness & You Entrees are denoted by this symbol

NUTRITIONAL INFORMATION:
Calories, Protein(gm), Fat(gm),
Carbohydrates(gm) RESPECTIVELY.

hurricane dining

health stanford dining

mahoney/pearson dining

FIGURE 7.7 Sample One-Week Board Rate Menu as Used for College and University Example

FIGURE 7.8

Example of a Cafeteria Menu at Campus University

Breakfast		
Full-Line Breakfast	Breads, Toast	Pancakes and Waffles
Menu	Eggs and Meats	Hot and Cold Beverages
Fruits and Juices	Pastries and Muffins	
Cereals		

Lunch and Dinner		
Soups	Entrées	Sandwich Station
1 Heavy	2 Daily for Lunch	Various Made-to-Order
1 Light	2 Daily for Dinner	
		Desserts
Salads	Grill Station	2 Two-Crust Pies
Salad Bar	Various Grill Items	1 Single-Crust Pie
	Specialty Sandwiches	Various Individual Items
	French Fries	Cookies
		Fresh Fruit

Students seldom eat all the meals they've contracted for in their board plan. Contractors maintain excellent records of these absentee rate percentages (or missed-meal factors) for each different board plan and each meal. When they bid for a new client, they use this information to establish a competitive but realistic board rate.

Menu prices in the cash cafeteria are usually established 5–10 percent below comparable commercial operations. Much depends on the type of contract a management company has, the rate of commission paid, and the annual sales volume.

Menu prices and operator's costs are affected by the services the college does or doesn't provide (e.g. trash removal, maintenance). Generally, though, 5–10 percent below commercial prices is the target.

The food court on a college or university campus will duplicate the menu patterns and prices of nearby commercial operations. Some large universities offer "branded" items at their food courts, which are really on-campus franchises of the major fast food chains. (This concept is described in detail in Chapter 10, "Sales and Marketing.")

Customer Satisfaction

Customer satisfaction with a campus dining operation can be difficult to measure. There are three factions to satisfy: students, staff, and faculty, and there are different dining possibilities: board, catering, vending, cash, and food court.

For students, satisfaction with the foodservice is often a function of the time of the semester. Students tend to be satisfied at the beginning of a semester and become less so with the arrival of midterm exam period. As final exam week approaches, they often become even more dissatisfied. The foodservice director must anticipate these natural academic rhythms and make the necessary adjustments. For example, a number of foodservice directors schedule midnight study breaks with cider and doughnuts or similar exam week stress relievers.

Requirements for staff satisfaction are similar to those of B&I employees. The difficulty is satisfying staff foodservice needs with a cafeteria menu designed primarily for students. Again, the foodservice director must ensure that the menu is satisfactory to the staff as well as the students.

Faculty eat in the cash cafeteria when not lunching at their club. They are

Cornell Catering

COMPLETE SERVICE DINNERS

Complete Service Dinners

Number One
Cream of Asparagus Soup
Bremans Salad
Haddock Dore
Broccoli au Gratin, Broiled Tomato Parmesan
Rolls and Butter
Almond Cake
Coffee, Tea

Number Two
Gazpacho
Caesar Salad
Fresh Broiled Scrod with Lemon Butter
Rice with Mushrooms, Vegetable Medley
Rolls and Butter
Strawberry Parfait
Coffee, Tea

Number Three
Truffles Tomato Soup
Regency Salad
Grilled Swordfish, Caper Butter
Rice with Mushrooms, Green Beans Bremans
French Baguettes and Butter
Lemon Tart
Coffee, Tea

Number Four
Cream of Fresh Herb Soup
Spinach, Romaine, and Mushroom Salad
    Homemade Dressing
Poached Salmon Beurre Blanc
Fresh Broccoli with Pine Nuts, Tomato Florentine
Sour Dough Baguettes and Butter
Fresh Fruit Sayabon
Coffee, Tea

Number Five
Spinach and Pear Soup
Romaine, Mandarin Oranges, Artichoke Hearts, Vinaigrette
Scallop and Shrimp Brochette
Rice with Mushrooms, Vegetable Jardiniere
Rolls and Butter
Grasshopper Pie
Coffee, Tea

Number Six
Vichyssoise
Romaine and Mushroom Salad, Homemade Dressing
Breast of Duck Bourguignon
Rice Pilaf, Vegetable Jardiniere
Rolls and Butter
Lemon Honey Mousse
Coffee, Tea

Number Seven
Fresh Fruit Cup
Romaine, Mandarin Oranges, Artichoke Hearts, Vinaigrette
Stuffed Boneless Breast of Chicken
Vegetable Melange
Rolls and Butter
Old Fashioned Chocolate Cake
Coffee, Tea

Number Eight
Curried Eggplant Soup
Citronade Salad
Chicken Cordon Bleu
Tomato Stuffed with Broccoli, Rice with Mushrooms
Rolls and Butter
Cheesecake with Fruit Puree
Coffee, Tea

Cornell Catering

Number Nine
Fresh Fruit Cup
Bremans Salad
Roasted, Sliced Leg of Lamb with Mint Jelly
Dilled Potatoes Anthony, Stuffed Zucchini
Rolls and Butter
Custard Fruit Tarte
Coffee, Tea

Number Ten
Honeydew Melon Wedge
Arnauds Salad
Broiled Shish Kabob
Rice Pilaf, Broccoli with Lemon Butter
Rolls and Butter
Hot Apple Pie with Cinnamon Ice Cream
Coffee, Tea

Number Eleven
Chilled Melon Wedge
Romaine and Mushroom Salad, Homemade Dressing
New York Strip Steak
Baked Potato, Zucchini with Onions
French Baguettes and Butter
Cheesecake with Fruit Puree
Coffee, Tea

Number Twelve
Mushroom and Clam Veloute
Caesar Salad
Tenderloin of Beef Bordelaise
Vegetable Melange, Alsacienne Potatoes
Sour Dough Baguettes and Butter
Chocolate Decadence
Coffee, Tea

Number Thirteen
Fresh Tomato Soup Truffles
Regency Salad
Prime Rib of Beef au Jus
Alsacienne Potatoes, Vegetable Melange
Rolls and Butter
Chocolate Bavarian
Coffee, Tea

Number Fourteen
Fresh Fruit Cup
Romaine and Mushroom Salad
Roast Round of Beef au Poivre
Green Beans Bremans, Rice with Mushrooms
French Baguettes and Butter
Chocolate Mousse
Coffee, Tea

Number Fifteen
Switzerland Cheese Soup
Romaine and Mushroom Salad, House Dressing
Scallopini of Veal Marsala
Fettucini Bremans, Broiled Tomato Parmesan
Rolls and Butter
Chocolate Mousse
Coffee, Tea

Number Sixteen
Cream of Leek Chantilly Soup
Regency Salad
Veal Oscar
Rice Pilaf, Tomato Florentine
Rolls and Butter
Fresh Fruit Sabayon
Coffee, Tea

FIGURE 7.9 Example of a Catering Menu (Courtesy of Margaret Lacey, Cornell University)

similar in many ways to business executives and often voice their opinions if dissatisfied.

The foodservice director of a campus dining operation listens to all three cash cafeteria patron groups to assure customer satisfaction. The director also uses the food court with its varied menu to merchandise items that are not available in the cash cafeteria. This outlet can be a major asset to the FSD in helping to combat menu fatigue.

Health Care: Community Hospital

The basic principles of menu management can also apply to a hospital.

Community Hospital has the following statistics and service needs:

■ 500-bed voluntary (nonprofit) hospital with an outpatient center, an MRI center, and an emergency room
■ Sufficient staff and medical personnel to support the mentioned services and capacity
■ A centralized kitchen and tray assembly service for the patients
■ Employee cafeteria with three meals per day and an overnight meal for shift workers
■ A doctors' dining room serving a lunch buffet
■ A visitors' coffee shop operating from 7:00 A.M. to 7:00 P.M.
■ A catering service for special functions
■ Vending snack service in all areas

The foodservice must maintain per-patient-day dietary service costs within strict guidelines.

There are five menu requirements for this facility:

1. Dietary menu for patients
2. Employee cafeteria menu for breakfast, lunch, dinner, and an overnight shift meal
3. Doctor's dining room lunch buffet menu
4. Coffee shop menu for breakfast and remainder of the day
5. Catering service menu

In addition, cold food items are needed for the vending machines. These are prepared by the main kitchen and provided to the vending subcontractor.

Marketing and SET Constraints

Every hospital has its own built-in foodservice market. The patient population can be as varied as that of the surrounding area. In a major metropolitan area, this can mean a mixture of ages, sexes, ethnic backgrounds, and other qualities. The foodservice director must assess the dominant market forces of the area.

Patients are not the prime customers of a hospital; doctors are. Patients are at a given hospital because a doctor decided to admit them. Further, most doctors are on staff at more than one hospital and can admit patients to any of them. Hospital administrators make every effort to have their hospitals selected, including the offer of a quality, subsidized foodservice.

Employees of a hospital are a mix of medical staff, nursing staff, environmental employees, housekeeping staff, and others. This market encompasses many age and ethnic groups, which means the foodservice director must try to satisfy many different patrons.

Visitors to a hospital are a market for the coffee shop. They are usually of the same market mix as the patients and share their demographics.

Skill levels in a hospital are often affected by wage scales and working conditions. The health care industry in general has difficulty attracting highly skilled culinary personnel to its kitchens. The working hours are one constraint. The seven-day, two-and-a-half–shift operation creates the same problems as experienced in the hotel industry but without the prestige of a hotel job. In most cases a skilled worker would rather say "I work at the XYZ hotel" than "I work at the XYZ hospital."

Many hospitals have old equipment, installed earlier for entirely different menus, production requirements, and delivery systems. Some modern kitchens are specifically designed for menu production, patient tray makeup, and distribution characteristic of hospital foodservice, but improvisation by the FSD is not unusual.

Lack of proper equipment causes time constraints in a hospital. Tray assembly also squeezes available time; 500 patient trays take a definite number of minutes to assemble and distribute. This must be considered when production is planned.

Taken in total, the SET constraints of a hospital are often more stringent than for other types of institutional foodservice. This has an effect on menu planning and management.

The Dietary Menu

The primary menu in a hospital facility is the dietary menu prepared for the patients. That menu must satisfy the patient, the prescribing doctor, and the nutritionist (registered dietician) planning and preparing it.

Dietary menus come in six types called *modified diets*. Each is a specific diet required by the patient's physician or condition and planned by the dietician. There are six separate diets that must be part of every dietary menu:

1. Regular diet
2. Restricted calorie diet
3. Restricted sodium diet
4. Restricted fat diet
5. Restricted fiber diet
6. Full liquid diet

Patients may be given a selective or nonselective menu. A selective menu allows patients a meal choice from foods allowed on their prescribed diets. A nonselective menu is prepared by the dietary staff without patient input.

Proponents of a selective menu system give the following reasons for its use:

1. *Less expensive.* Patient selection allows the listing of inexpensive food items that are popular with many patients.
2. *Limited leftovers.* Since patients select their own menu they are more prone to eat what they select.
3. *Increased patient acceptance.* If patients select their own meals they are more likely to be happy with them.

Using a selective menu places the burden of monitoring the selection on the professional staff of the foodservice. Patients must pick an adequately nutritious meal while staying within a prescribed diet.

Proponents of a nonselective system give the following reasons for its use:

1. *Less expensive.* There are fewer food items to purchase, store, produce, and serve.
2. *Less personnel.* Fewer personnel, with less culinary skill, are required to prepare a nonselective menu.
3. *Diet control.* It's easier for the dietary staff to control a patient's food intake by not offering a selection.
4. *Less management.* It's easier to manage a nonselective menu than a selective one (less inventory and easier production).

Generally the selective menu is preferred where SET constraints (sufficient skill, equipment, and time) allow its use. Both selective and nonselective menus have their place. The foodservice director and hospital administration choose which type of menu is best suited to their financial and service objectives.

Dietary Menu Cycling

Cycling of a patient menu is less difficult than that of an employee menu. The length of the cycle need only be a day or two longer than the average length of patient stay. If the average length of stay is 7 days, a 10-day cycle will easily fill the need. It's best not to utilize an exact 7-day menu cycle; that would repeat the same menu items on the same day every week. If a 10-day cycle is used, menu items will repeat on different days in alternate weeks.

Figure 7.10 is an example of a 10-day menu cycle over a 7-day week.

Special holiday menus must be planned for Christmas, New Year's, Easter, Thanksgiving, and other holidays at appropriate times. Friday menus must have non-meat entrées for those who desire them.

Dietary Menu Management

As with directors of other institutional operations, the foodservice director requires some tools to assist in menu management. These include standard recipes, recipe cost sheets, purchasing specifications, menu planning forms, and the same administrative aids required for other foodservices.

Dietary menus, considering the six potential diet modifications, require a system that ensures patients receive the proper menu for ordering. This is usually handled by preparing six separate menus, each with a color-coded heading denoting a specific diet.

FIGURE 7.10

Typical Calendar Pattern for a 10-Day Menu Cycle

JUNE 1992						
Sunday	*Monday*	*Tuesday*	*Wednesday*	*Thursday*	*Friday*	*Saturday*
	1 #1	2 #2	3 #3	4 #4	5 #5	6 #6
7 #7	8 #8	9 #9	10 #10	11 #1	12 #2	13 #3
14 #4	15 #5	16 #6	17 #7	18 #8	19 #9	20 #10
21 #1	22 #2	23 #3	24 #4	25 #5	26 #6	27 #7
28 #8	29 #9	30 #10				

Diet menu planning is the function of the staff therapeutic dietician(s). The diet menus must meet all general nutritional standards as well as the particular guidelines of the prescribed diet.

The recommended daily allowance (RDA)—first published by the Food and Nutrition Board of the National Research Council, National Academy of Sciences, in 1943—is a general guideline. The current listing, accepted by most authorities, is the *Daily Food Guide* published by the U.S. Department of Agriculture.

The RDA information is a frame of reference. It does not meet the need to provide special diets for certain patients. RDA listings are meant to provide healthy persons with guidelines for their nutritional maintenance.

The goal of the menu plan is to provide adequate nutrition within each modified diet. The therapeutic dietician must ensure this, but it's up to the foodservice director to see that the dietary menu meets all other constraints and requirements.

Figure 7.11 is an example of one day's selective menu for a location such as a community hospital. This is for the regular diet. Figure 7.12 is an example of using that regular diet base to prepare one of the required five modified diets. Note that most food items on the regular diet menu are used in one form or another on the modified diet menus.

Steps in Planning the Dietary Menu

Catherine Sullivan, in her book *Management of Medical Foodservice*, outlines 12 steps for planning the dietary menu. Figure 7.13 lists them; they are useful to health care facilities for successful menu planning.

The Diet Manual

Every hospital foodservice and many other health care facilities require a diet manual to guarantee that standard modified diets are provided. That manual must meet the standards of accrediting boards or agencies governing the operation.

All of the contract management companies active in health care foodservice have their own diet manuals. These usually meet or exceed state and federal agency requirements. Some smaller self-operated facilities have diet manuals that have been developed by a consulting dietician. Others use published manuals accepted by the relevant agencies. The Iowa Dietetic Association and the American Dietetic Association each publish popular manuals. The Iowa manual is less complex than the ADA manual.

The Joint Commission on Accreditation of Hospitals requires that a dietician develop, or adopt, a manual with the cooperation of the medical staff and other appropriate dietary personnel. It is easier to adapt an existing manual (such as one of those mentioned above) than to develop a new one. More and more health care locations, other than hospitals, are being required by either state or federal regulation to provide both a diet manual and supervision by a registered dietician. It's likely that all health care locations will require diet manuals and appropriate supervision of their use in the future.

The Menu Review Committee

One way to ensure a well-planned menu is with a menu review committee. That committee should be chaired by the foodservice director and include all interested parties, i.e., an officer of the hospital (sometimes the hospital administrator or assistant), the clinical dietician, the chef or head cook, and production and service supervisors. At a self-op, the committee may also include the purchasing manager.

The menu review committee should meet initially to establish basic guidelines and prepare a working agenda for the clinical dietician who prepares the detailed menu. The committee should meet again to review the results and finalize the

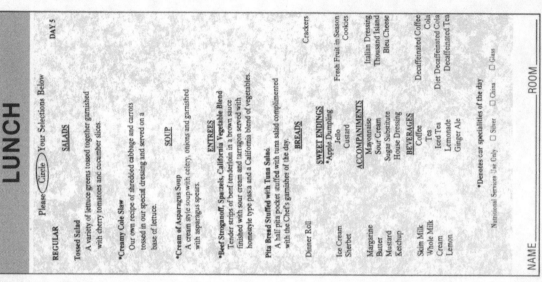
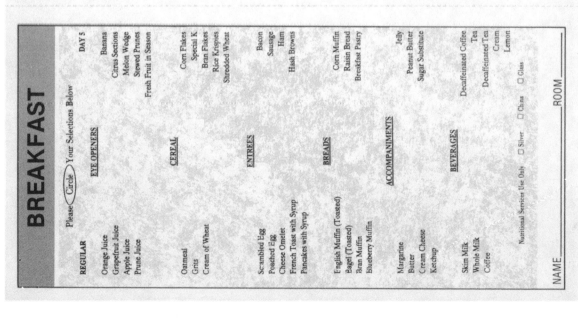

FIGURE 7.11 Selective Hospital Menu, Shands Hospital (Courtesy of Ruby B. Puckett, MA, RD, LD, Shands Hospital, Gainesville, FL)

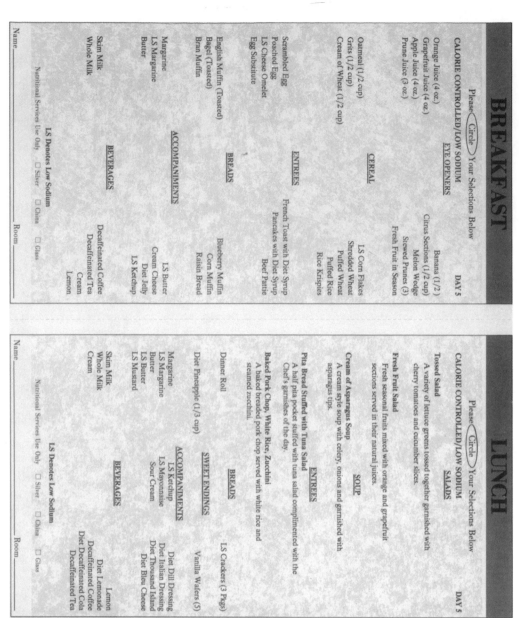

FIGURE 7.12 Example of a Low-Sodium, Calorie-Controlled Diet Menu (Courtesy of Ruby B. Puckett, MA, RD, LD, Shands Hospital, Gainesville, FL)

FIGURE 7.13

12 Steps in Dietary Menu Planning

1. Plan the lunch and dinner entrée(s) for the entire week/cycle. Plan the rest of the meal around the main entrée(s) selection.
2. Plan the vegetable and potato categories to accompany the entrées. Give consideration to variety in color, texture, flavor, form or shape, and consistency.
3. Plan salads to accompany the rest of the meal. Use fruits or vegetables rather than high-protein foods such as eggs, cheese, or seafood. Consider variety and avoid using foods that are already on the menu.
4. Plan bread category. The use of at least one hot bread per day will add variety and appeal.
5. Plan appetizer. If soup is used, do not repeat items such as chicken noodle along with baked chicken as an entrée. If fruit or juice is used, it should be different from the salad or dessert category.
6. Plan a dessert to complement the meal. Do not repeat items in other categories. Seek variety in temperature, texture, and other factors that will add interest. Limit "empty calorie" desserts as much as possible.
7. Plan the breakfast entrée. Offer eggs at least four times per week.
8. Plan the fruit or juice for the breakfast meal. Consider a good source of vitamin C.
9. Plan cereal category. For a selective menu, plan one hot and one cold cereal.
10. Plan the breakfast bread. In addition to toast, plan for a hot bread, pancakes, or French toast for interest.
11. Insert beverages such as coffee, tea, milk and standard items as well as condiments.
12. Plan the bedtime nourishment if it is served on a daily basis for all patients.

SOURCE: Management of Medical Foodservice, 2nd ed. Catherine Sullivan, Van Nostrand Reinhold, 1990.

menu and should meet each time major changes in the original menu are planned. This should not be too time consuming if the proper menu plan is developed initially.

Pricing Policies

There are no pricing policies for the dietary department menu. There are just cost constraints. The measure of control for a dietary menu is food cost per patient-day—the total amount of money spent for food divided by the number of patient-days served.

Example:
Time period.. One month
Average daily patients..450 per day
Number of patient-days..30 × 450 = 13,500
Expenditures for food...$94,500
Average food cost per patient day:
$94,500/13,500 = $7.00 per patient day

The average food cost per patient-day for the month is $7.00. If that's within the budgetary allowance for the hospital, great. If it exceeds budget, not so great. The point is that the pricing policy is really a budget policy. The menu must be managed to keep food cost per patient-day within the budget.

Customer Satisfaction

Hospital foodservice seldom satisfies a majority of its "customers." Hospital patients are not there by choice and would usually prefer to be elsewhere. Nonetheless, every effort must be made to evaluate that patient's foodservice wants and needs and fulfill them.

Patients are often put on special diets by physicians, resulting in food selections they don't like. This is difficult to overcome. Sometimes the menu selections and meal times don't suit patients. Or medication can dull patients' palates or distort their moods. Each of these situations creates an unhappy client.

Many management devices exist to counter these problems. The two most common are the food preference survey and the patient record card (now generally computerized). Each of the contract management companies use these, as do many well-managed self-operators. Figure 7.14 is a food preference survey form used at Shands Hospital.

Patient satisfaction does not come easily; it requires dedication. Unfortunately, the pressures of everyday production and budgetary constraints almost guarantee that total patient satisfaction will not be achieved.

The Cafeteria Menu

The cafeteria in a hospital is similar to its counterpart in a B&I location. The difference is in the nature of the employees and the hours of operation.

A hospital employee cafeteria caters to employees of varied market groups: medical staff, nursing staff, housekeeping employees, and others. Therefore, the menu must be planned to suit different tastes. In some hospitals, visitors are also allowed to use the cafeteria.

The cafeteria should use a B&I-style cycle menu. The most popular cycle is four weeks. The basis for the cycle should be the dietary menu's regular diet.

Preparing a four-week cycle menu with the regular diet menu as a base can be a challenge. The objective is to use the same production labor for the dietary menu to prepare a satisfactory employee cafeteria menu without additional labor hours. Depending on the menu pattern of the cafeteria, the regular dietary menu can provide several entrees, all of the soups, salads, and desserts, and the beverages. The addition of a salad bar, sandwich station, and grill station can turn the dietary menu into a very acceptable employee cafeteria menu.

Cafeteria Menu Constraints

The same SET constraints must be considered for this cafeteria as for any other foodservice: skill levels, equipment capacity, and production time.

Skills of culinary employees can't ordinarily be improved on demand. If a manager desires a menu item beyond the skill level of the kitchen staff, he or she might consider purchasing a semi-prepared item. Baked goods and many other prepared foods are available from suppliers. These provide excellent menu diversity without requiring excess skill from the production staff.

The equipment in a hospital kitchen and the service area(s) of the cafeteria can place major constraints on the menu. Equipment may be suitable for dietary kitchen production but not for a cafeteria.

The cafeteria service area might not be equipped to serve a modern menu. Salad bars, sandwich stations, and similar set-ups are not possible in older cafeterias that were constructed for straight-line service and not the food court system popular today.

The time constraint in a hospital is affected by the equipment's capacity to produce and hold food items, the hospital's ability to attract and schedule workers to produce the menu, and the budgetary constraints on supporting sufficient staff.

An employee cafeteria in a hospital must usually recover the operating cost in the menu price. Operating costs usually include the cost of food, supplies, and additional labor required to staff the cafeteria—the servers and cashier. All other

Food and Nutrition Services Patient Questionnaire

1. My diet order was:
   Regular _____ Modified _____ Don't know _____

2. The meal I enjoyed the most was:
   Breakfast _____ Lunch _____ Dinner _____

   Key: 5—Strongly Agree   4—Agree   3—Neutral
   2—Disagree   1—Strongly Disagree

3. My meals were:

Appetizing	5	4	3	2	
Served at the correct temperature	5	4	3	2	
Served by a courteous staff	5	4	3	2	

4. Which meal was served most courteously?
   Breakfast _____ Lunch _____ Dinner _____ All _____

5. Do you have any comments you would like to share about your meals? _____
   _____

6. The Nutrition Services personnel who provided menu service were:

Courteous	5	4	3	2
Responsive	5	4	3	2
Helpful	5	4	3	2

7. The Nutrition Services personnel who provided counseling and education were:

Knowledgeable	5	4	3	2
Helpful	5	4	3	2
Responsive	5	4	3	2

8. Do you have any comments you would like to share about the Food and Nutrition Services staff? _____
   _____

THANK YOU FOR YOUR HELP! Optional:

Name _____

Room Number _____ Date _____

FIGURE 7.14 Example of a Survey Form for Patients

Welcome!

The entire staff of Shands Hospital joins in saying "Welcome" and in wishing you a pleasant stay and a successful recovery. As a patient and guest you are the most important person here.

Your physician has written an order for your diet as well as other orders that make up your complete care. Your diet order is translated into menu choices. When possible we will provide you with a selective menu tailored for your special diet needs.

The Food and Nutrition Services staff is composed of over 160 employees and serves meals and snacks to over 6,000 people per day. Tons of fresh eggs, meats, vegetables, fruits, bread and dairy products are purchased and prepared fresh daily for your individual meal.

The staff includes Registered Dietitians, Dietetic Technicians, Cooks, Bakers, Aides, Assistants, Managers, Supervisors, Technicians, Secretaries and Patient Nutrition Representatives. The Patient Nutrition Representatives will deliver and pick up your selective menu and answer basic questions about menu selection.

The Dietetic Technicians and Registered Dietitians are educated and trained in nutrition therapy and may assist you in meeting special nutrition needs by adjusting your physician ordered hospital diet and providing guidance for home nutrition needs.

All of us are here to make your stay pleasant. Please help us to serve you better by filling out this questionnaire and returning it to the Patient Nutrition Representative who picks up your menu.

Thank you,

Department of Food and Nutrition Services

labor can be charged to the dietary service. If well managed, this can be accomplished.

Cafeteria Menu Plan

The menu plan requires a format for breakfast, lunch, dinner, and a night-shift meal. The basic plan should be coordinated with the dietary menu.

The breakfast menu will service the departing night shift, the arriving day shift, and the early meal for the day shift. A standard breakfast menu, using a grill station, steam table, cold foods section, beverage section, and cashier can fill the need. The menu should be as complete as the equipment and staffing constraints allow. There is little need for a cycle menu; most customers will accept the choices available from a standard full-line breakfast menu.

The lunch and dinner menus can be the same since they usually service different shifts. This allows the menu planner to use both the lunch and dinner entrées from the dietary selective menu to plan the cafeteria menu.

The salad bar, grill station, and self-service sandwich station can add variety and excitement to the basic menu. The currently popular salad bar and self-serve sandwich station, with food priced by the ounce, is very effective for customer satisfaction.

The number of appetizers, soups, entrees, vegetables, and desserts can be planned similar to previously shown in Figure 7.1. As before, plan a menu format and then prepare the cycle menu.

The night-shift meal is a major problem for a hospital foodservice. The minimal population and their differing meal preferences create difficulties; some employees prefer lunch or dinner while others want breakfast. The most desirable arrangement is a cook-to-order station with both grill and breakfast items. The steam table can also be used for some hot items.

There are two alternatives to a night-shift meal service: an early opening for breakfast or vending machines in the cafeteria for the off-shift meal. This is identical to a vending satellite in a manufacturing plant.

Pricing Policies

The pricing policy in this facility is to recover the cost of food, supplies, and additional labor required to operate the cafeteria. This is common in hospitals and allows for pricing 40 to 50 percent below average commercial prices.

Considering that direct operating costs for a commercial establishment run 50 to 52 percent of sales, a hospital cafeteria menu priced at around 50 percent of a comparable restaurant will usually meet budget and still provide an excellent employee benefit.

Customer Satisfaction

Customers in a hospital employee cafeteria are varied. Their ethnic, social, and professional backgrounds are mixed. The only common denominator is that they work in the health care industry.

Assessing customer satisfaction here requires an adept foodservice director. He or she must be equally attentive to the employee cafeteria and the patient dietary service. Often the foodservice director is too oriented towards one or the other. They are separate entities, each requiring managerial attention.

The same efforts made to foster customer satisfaction in other industry segments must be made in a hospital cafeteria. Anything less may well fail.

The Doctors Dining Room Menu

A doctors dining room is a hospital's marketing tool designed to get doctors to send their patients there. Some hospitals, as shown in our example case, provide a special doctors dining room for lunch.

The lunch buffet has proved very successful in doctors dining rooms. Complemented by staff service workers at the buffet table and on the dining room floor, a buffet can be satisfying and inexpensive. The menu can be prepared from items on the daily dietary menu and the employee cafeteria menu, supplemented by whatever the chef adds. The addition of beverage and dessert service can make a simple buffet more elegant.

Little extra effort is required to produce the menu for the doctors dining room. What is required is the imagination of the foodservice director and the staff servers to create a desirable atmosphere where the medical staff will feel comfortable and at home.

Pricing Policy

The doctors dining room is a combination of an employee benefit and a marketing tool whose purpose is to satisfy doctors so that they'll continue to send patients to the hospital. The pricing policy should be recovery of cost, or even a bit less.

Customer Satisfaction

A doctors dining room is like a private club. The patrons (doctors) have common interests, a desire to exchange professional conversation, and a need to socialize with their peers. The dining room should satisfy these wants and needs.

It's not difficult for a foodservice director to gauge customer satisfaction; if a sizable number of the medical staff use the facility regularly, all is well. Doctors won't return if they're uncomfortable or unhappy.

Doctors are often quick to evaluate the total service and patient care levels of a hospital and communicate their opinions to the hospital director. This includes the physical plant (operating room, for example), the nursing staff, the custodial staff, the dietary department, and their own services—such as a doctors dining room.

The Coffee Shop Menu

The coffee shop in most hospitals is a profit-making venture. It is often used by an auxiliary organization (such as the ladies auxiliary) to raise funds at the hospital. Many a hospital has obtained a major piece of equipment or paid for improvements via auxiliary efforts.

The coffee shop menu provides a breakfast-lunch-dinner cycle to visitors during visitors' hours. Some are anxious relatives awaiting the results of surgery on a family member. Others have traveled some distance and arrive at the hospital in need of a meal before or after visiting a sick relative or friend.

A carry-out service is always part of a well-managed coffee shop. The potential customers for this service are employees of the hospital and patients via their visitors. Patients often desire "goodies" from an outside source. Foods such as ice cream, a special sandwich, or pastry and coffee are potential sales items.

Some hospital employees also use the coffee shop much the same as an employee at the urban office building uses the service dining room. When they have a guest or desire a change from the cafeteria fare, they will eat in the coffee shop.

A coffee shop menu will include a standard breakfast and short-order grill menu as well as daily specials, soups, entrees, and salads produced by the main kitchen.

Since this is a profit-making venture, the menu must be merchandised in the same manner as any other coffee shop. The quality of the menu itself, the use of menu boards outside to denote a daily special, and other merchandising and marketing techniques of commercial restaurants should be used in the hospital coffee shop.

SET Constraints

All SET constraints apply here in the same way they do at any other foodservice. Employees' skills dictate the limits of the menu, whether produced in the coffee shop or main kitchen; in some locations the workers are volunteers from the charitable organization operating the coffee shop. Where that is the case, the employees, and thus the skill level, may change periodically. This must be considered when designing the menu.

The equipment in the coffee shop is usually limited. The menu must reflect the potential of the equipment to handle the type and number of menu offerings.

Time is not usually a constraint in a coffee shop. There is usually enough time to pre-prepare the necessary items as long as there is culinary support from the main kitchen. Since the labor costs are subsidized by the use of volunteer workers, labor hour requirements are usually minimal.

Pricing Policies

The coffee shop is a profit-making commercial operation. It must compete with neighboring restaurants regarding quality, service, and price. The menu should be priced somewhat below prices in adjacent operations to provide a marketing advantage, but that's not always necessary. If the perceived value is sufficiently high, normal commercial menu prices can prevail.

Customer Satisfaction

How are sales, check averages, and customer counts? How are customer comments running? Use the same indicators here as in any commercial operation.

Franchise Operations

In some locations, the coffee shop has a sales potential exceeding $1 million per year. As a result, fast food chains are acquiring coffee shops as franchise outlets. While this has meant changing their standard menus to suit the hospital's therapeutic dietitians, they've done so. Pioneered by McDonald's, several fast food chains operate hospital branches.

The Catering Menu

Catering is catering. There is little difference between a commercially catered affair and one prepared and served by an institutional foodservice. Every catered function should have a purpose, a plan, and the management to execute it.

Catering events in the institution include:

■ Organizational awards luncheons and dinners
■ Management special events
■ Employee clubs and organizations
■ Trade union meetings and special needs

■ Client luncheons and dinners
■ Fund-raising dinners

Business and Industry

Business and industry locations, in both office buildings and manufacturing plants, have individual catering needs dictated by management and employees. There are generally no standard catering menus; rather, a menu is designed for each occasion.

In some large manufacturing plants, a dinner can be catered for several thousand people. United Food Management served a catered dinner for 20,000 people in the early 1920s. At the time, according to United Foods, it was the largest group of people ever served a sit-down meal in an institutional setting.

Other large catered affairs might include company picnics, the annual stockholders' meeting, special Christmas parties, charitable fund-raising drives, and more.

Campus Dining

Figure 7.9 is the catering menu from Cornell Dining Services. The catering services it offers are typical of a school or college that size.

Catering on campus is now big business. A foodservice director can achieve up to 10 percent of gross sales annually from catering. Between 4 and 6 percent is typical.

Markets for catering on a campus are the students, faculty, and administration. Student organizations—e.g., fraternities or sororities, dining clubs, and athletic teams—are always in need of catering services.

Faculty may need catering for business meetings, the faculty senate, or other such affairs. The administration has the same needs as the B&I segment mentioned previously.

Hospital and Health Care

Most health care facilities have the same catering menu needs as a business and industry location. Some large hospitals have standard menus available for presentation to a prospective client.

Hospitals cater—often at cost or even a loss—to fund-raising groups that support the hospital. This adds an additional constraint to the management of the menu.

SET Constraints

There are many constraints that affect a large catering function by a foodservice whose primary business is not catering.

Equipment constraints are usually overcome by renting any additional necessary equipment as any commercial caterer would. The cost of the rental is added to the sales price of the event.

Time constraints are a different matter. If the foodservice does not have time to cater an event, it can't book the function. In some cases, a foodservice director can subcontract a large catered event. Each situation needs to be addressed individually.

The Contractors

Most contractors provide location foodservice directors with a catering manual that includes menus, skill and equipment requirements, and other related information. When a manager requires additional assistance in planning the catering menu or the catering event, a corporate or division staff specialist is usually available.

The corporate staff department assists in the preparation of a standard catering menu package specifically for the needs of each facility. These are usually duplicative of the same need at another facility.

Marketing Information

Each of the major contractors maintains active computer-based files with marketing information for all industry segments. They are capable of generating data for any segment in any geographic area. These would include per capita spending, menu sales mix, menu costs, gross profit from specific selling prices, and much more.

The top tier, and some of the regional contractors, have food standards and research departments. These departments provide their resident foodservice directors with information necessary to manage their menus. The following are some of the services they provide:

- Research and establish recipes
- Provide standard production systems
- Maintain a database file of ingredient costs
- Have the ability to pre-cost a cycle menu for a client bid
- Have both executive chefs and therapeutic dieticians on staff for specialized conditions
- Have special menu plans for seasonal promotions

In effect, a professional menu management team is available to all clients.

SET Constraints

SET constraints exist in every contracted operation. In most cases these are equipment constraints resulting from the existing configuration of the kitchen. In many cases, the contractor will invest in improvements if the potential return on investment is satisfactory. Some examples are:

- Providing a manufacturing plant an investment for new equipment in exchange for the vending rights on a low or no commission structure
- Remodeling a B&I cafeteria to make it more cost efficient in return for a longer term contract
- Providing a school district with a capital investment it needs (and cannot obtain from the taxpayer) in return for contract concessions
- Providing a college or university with a food court to alleviate the overcrowding in the cash cafeteria

In any case, where a capital investment can reap a satisfactory return on investment, a contractor is likely to provide it. Their primary motives are to increase the service, lower the operating costs, and increase the gross or net profit.

Pricing Policies

Contractors establish most menu prices as a result of proposals made to the client. All requests for proposals (RFPs) require a sample of the anticipated menus, including selling prices. On a college board plan, a weekly price is usually bid. In a hospital, a food cost per patient-day is forecast. In all cases, menu selling prices are established at the time of the bid.

Subsequent menu price increases are usually presented to the client at the annual budget meeting. If operating costs have increased over the past year, a menu price increase is requested. The increased selling price is either established by the client or with client permission. It's rare that the contractor establishes selling prices.

When a union is involved, the menu price is part of the bargaining agreement, and no increase in selling prices is possible. The only way a contractor can obtain a price increase is for the client to bargain for it at the next union negotiation. As an alternative, the contractor can request a subsidy from the client. This is sometimes easier to obtain than an increase in selling prices, particularly in a union shop.

Customer Satisfaction

One of the objectives of all menus is customer satisfaction. Contractors have a number of marketing survey tools to assist them in measuring this objective.

The best method of measuring customer satisfaction is the same for contractors and self-operated foodservices. If the participation percentage of employees, students, and other customers is sufficient and an acceptable check average is maintained, customers are happy. If either the participation or the check average for that meal period is lower than projected, there is work to do.

THE MENU AND COST CONTROLS

In Chapter 2 we said the tasks of management were planning, organizing, staffing, leading, and controlling. Planning was described as making the best use of men and women, money, materials, methods, and machines. Controlling was described as the opposite of planning, one of the methods of the plan.

Menu management is like other types of management. The plan initiates the control process; if, for instance, the plan is to achieve a specific sales and cost mix, the results are reported as part of the control process. If the plan is to achieve a specific participation percentage, those results are similarly reported in the control process.

Preparation of a menu plan includes evaluation of the SET constraints and the design of control methods to evaluate the plan's effectiveness. Specific items of menu management that are part of the cost control mechanism include:

- *Standard recipe preparation.* This establishes both quality control and portion control.
- *Menu cycling.* This sets sales patterns and sales mix/cost mix patterns.
- *Menu selection.* This can change labor requirements and, therefore, payroll costs.
- *Production and service methods.* These can also change labor costs.

When the menu is well managed, the cost control system is in place and activated.

Chapter 9, "Cost Control Management," will review this area in greater detail.

SUMMARY

A menu is a list of products produced and served by a foodservice operation. The menu is the means to achieve the business's financial goals.

If planning is the essence of management, then menu planning is the essence of menu management. Managing a menu should include four basic steps:

1. Establishing customer and client preferences.
2. Establishing menu objectives.
3. Considering menu constraints.
4. Effecting the menu plan.

Customer and client preferences will differ from segment to segment with the type of service, the nature of the client, and the potential customer base. There are differences within each segment that also require analysis for a menu to provide customer satisfaction.

Three basic constraints exist in planning all menus. They are skill, equipment and time. These are called the SET constraints.

Skill constraints concern the culinary arts skills of the production staff.

Equipment constraints are limitations imposed by the physical apparatus available. They exist in the kitchens, service areas, receiving and storage areas, and other foodservice areas.

Time constraints involve the number of labor hours available to produce and serve the menu.

A cycle menu is planned for specific periods and then repeated. Menu cycles may be for a four-, five- or six-week period, a semester, a school year, or any other suitable time period. The length of the cycle is planned to suit the particular location and type of operation.

Managing the menu establishes basic patterns used as part of the cost control system. When a menu is well-managed, the cost control system is well established.

8

Labor Hours Planning

One of the tasks of the manager is to make the best use of the available resources. Perhaps the most important of those resources is people. Scheduling people is called labor hours planning, a building block of the financial planning used to establish the financial goal.

This chapter details the planning of available labor hours to achieve service goals.

Upon completion of this chapter readers should know and understand:

- The basic content and definition of labor hours as a management resource
- Two methods for planning labor hours:
  1. Daily labor hours planning to achieve the service needs
  2. Weekly labor hours costing to achieve the financial objective
- Some standard productivity results expected by different industry segments

LABOR HOURS DEFINED

The task of planning is the essence of management. Labor hours planning guides the use of men and women, the human resource. Staffing is based on the L/H plan developed to achieve the service need. When a manager develops a L/H plan, he or she is laying the groundwork for staffing, leading, and controlling.

Total labor hours is the number of hours scheduled each day, for all staff, to accomplish the work necessary to achieve operational goals. Chapter 5, "Financial Planning," apportioned all work to four categories of employees:

1. Management and supervision
2. Production
3. Service
4. Sanitation and maintenance

Daily labor hours is the result of multiplying the number of workers in each category by the number of hours scheduled for each worker, each day. Figure 8.1 is an example for the production department of a B&I location.

In this example, the production department has seven employees with a total of 56 L/H per day to complete all food production needs (this establishes the time constraint of menu management cited in Chapter 7). The L/H production plan for this work group must match service needs, and the cost of the labor hours scheduled must be compatible with the financial objectives.

L/H planning is the detailed work assignment, for each employee, that has

Labor Hours per Day, Production Department

Position	Number	Daily Hours Scheduled	Total Daily Labor Hours
Chef	1	8	8
Cooks	2	8 Each	16
Kitchen Worker	4	8 Each	32
TOTAL	7	—	56 L/H

FIGURE 8.1 Example of Labor Hours for Production Department of Urban Office Example

been projected as labor cost in the financial plan; in effect it's what each employee will do and when he or she will do it.

A well-operated institutional foodservice uses the minimum number of employees and labor hours possible to achieve the service need. This in turn helps to accomplish the financial goal.

DAILY LABOR HOURS PLANNING METHODS

There are various methods reported in management literature for scheduling labor hours. One that is used by a large number of foodservice managers is an adaptation of the Gantt chart, developed by Henry Gantt in the early 1900s. Gannt's chart first establishes the goal and then identifies and schedules the steps required to achieve that goal.

Gantt, an industrial engineer, developed management methods for manufacturing. He did not conceive of service—as practiced in the hospitality industry, for example—as work. Neither did he envisage his methods adapted to managing in a service industry. Modern managers have adapted the Gantt chart to service industries. It is particularly useful in planning labor hours for an institutional foodservice operation.

Figure 8.2 is a labor hours utilization chart based on Gantt's work. It provides a planning form for development of a work schedule of labor hours in a foodservice operation and offers an efficient method of labor hours planning for foodservice managers.

An institutional foodservice must accomplish three goals by the efficient use of its available labor resource:

1. Produce the necessary menu in the required amounts.
2. Serve the produced menu to the clients of the foodservice.
3. Clean and maintain the facilities where the food is produced, served, and provided.

USING THE LABOR HOURS PLANNING CHART: URBAN OFFICE BUILDING

Let's use the labor hours planning chart to create a daily plan for the production department of the urban office building.

The urban office building has a total of 40 foodservice employees serving breakfast and lunch in the employee cafeteria and lunch in an employee dining room and three executive dining rooms.

Figure 8.3, the Labor Cost Planning Form, is reproduced from Chapter 5.

DEPARTMENT _____

DATE _____

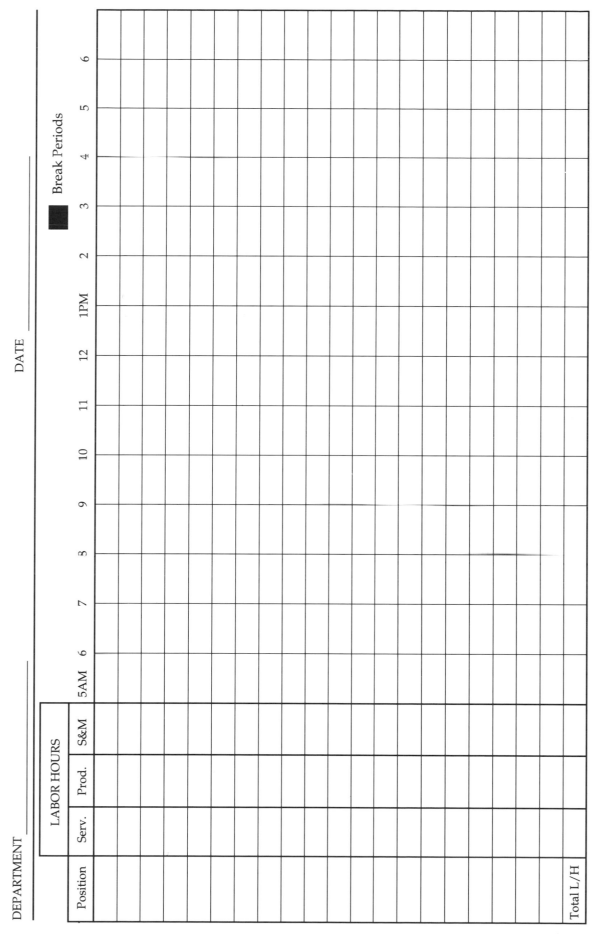

FIGURE 8.2   Example Labor Hours Planning Chart

169

Labor Cost Planning Form,
Urban Office Building

(1)	(2)	(3)	(4)	(5)
Position	No. of Workers	Total Weekly Labor Hours	Wage Rate ($)	Present Weekly Wage Cost ($)
I. MGE./ADMIN.				
General Manager	1	40	650/wk.	650.00
Asst. Gen. Mgr.	1	40	500/wk.	500.00
Bookkeeper	1	40	350/wk.	350.00
Office Clerk	1	40	7.00/hr.	280.00
Subtotal	4	160		1,780.00
II. PRODUCTION				
Executive Chef	1	40	600/wk.	600.00
Cooks	2	80	10.00/hr.	800.00
Kitchen Worker	2	70	8.00/hr.	560.00
Baker	1	40	400/wk.	400.00
Kitch. Utility	2	70	5.00/hr.	350.00
Subtotal	8	300		2,710.00
III. SERVICE				
Cafeteria Sup.	1	40	400/wk.	400.00
Caf. Workers	10	350	5.00/hr.	1,750.00
Cashiers	3	75	6.00/hr.	450.00
Waitstaff	6	120	7.00/hr.	840.00
Subtotal	20	585		3,440.00
IV. SAN. & MTE.				
Head Utility	1	40	10.00/hr.	400.00
General Utility	6	210	5.00/hr.	1,050.00
Porters	2	70	5.00/hr.	350.00
Subtotal	9	320	—	1,800.00
TOTALS	41	1,365	—	$9,730.00

FIGURE 8.3 Completed Labor Cost Planning Form for Urban Office Building

Sample Schedule: Kitchen Worker

The production department has a staff of eight with the following breakdown:

1 Chef @ ....8 hours per day
2 Cooks @ 8 hours each ....16 hours per day
2 Kitchen Workers @ 7 hours each ....14 hours per day
2 Kitchen Utility @ 7 hours each ....14 hours per day
1 Baker @ ....8 hours per day
TOTAL ....60 HOURS PER DAY

Six workers with a total of 46 labor hours per day are scheduled to complete all production and dining room à-la-carte service needs. The remaining two utility workers provide 14 labor hours per day for sanitation and maintenance work. In this case they are both pot washers—one in the kitchen, one in the bakery.

An L/H schedule is required to schedule à-la-carte work station assignments during lunch, meet all production needs, and maintain sanitation and maintenance requirements.

As an example of using the L/H planning chart to plan production, service, sanitation, and maintenance tasks, we will review one employee, Kitchen Worker. Following are specifics for planning the effective use of his eight-hour day.

POSITION:	Kitchen Worker
SHIFT:	6:30 A.M. to 3:30 P.M.
SERVICE:	Lunch at à-la-carte grill station
PRODUCTION:	Hot entrée items as assigned by the chef
CLEANUP:	Grill station and kitchen work station

Filling Out the Planning Chart

There are four steps to planning the labor hours of each employee:

Step 1: List the position.
Step 2: Enter the required service period(s).
Step 3: Enter the employee meal break periods.
Step 4: Complete the schedule. Enter all production and cleanup tasks.

As an example, apply the four steps to the position of Kitchen Worker at the urban office building.

Step 1: List the position.
  Place the position on the labor hours chart at the left column.
Step 2: Enter the required service period(s).
  In this case the production staff serves lunch at all à-la-carte stations. Show a box on the chart that assigns this worker to the à-la-carte grill station from 11:30 to 1:30.
Step 3: Enter the meal break periods of the employee.
  It's typical for full-time foodservice employees to receive two half-hour meal break periods. These breaks must be given. They usually come right after the meal period.

After Step 3, the kitchen worker's schedule looks like Figure 8.4. All service needs and break periods have been charted.

FIGURE 8.4

Preliminary Schedule for Kitchen Worker

6:30 – 9:00	OPEN FOR SCHEDULING
9:00 – 9:30	Breakfast break
9:30 – 11:30	OPEN FOR SCHEDULING
11:30 – 1:30	Serve Lunch on à-la-carte grill station
1:30 – 2:00	Lunch break
2:00 – 3:30	OPEN FOR SCHEDULING

The time available for scheduling other work is:

6:30–9:00	2 ½	hours
9:30–11:30	2	hours
2:00–3:30	1 ½	hours
	6	hours

There are six hours available for production and cleanup work.

Step 4: Complete the schedule. Enter all production and cleanup tasks.
At this point, figure how much production work can be accomplished between 6:30 and 9:00 and between 9:30 and 11:30. Time must be available to set up the grill station prior to 11:30. Also evaluate the amount of cleanup and/or prep work possible for the following day between 1:30 and 3:30.

After step 4, filling in production and cleanup work assignments, the resulting labor hours schedule looks like Figure 8.5.

Figure 8.6 details this schedule as it should be placed on the L/H chart using the four-step procedure.

In summary, the kitchen worker position has the following service, production, and cleanup L/H available:

Production and setup work ....4.5 hours
Service work ....2.0 hours
Sanitation & maintenance work...1.5 hours
TOTAL L/H..8.0 hours

Each position, for each of the four departments, should be scheduled in the same manner. The results will define the total labor hours available for management and supervision, production, service, and sanitation and maintenance work for the location.

ASCERTAINING TOTAL LABOR HOUR REQUIREMENTS

The example for the kitchen worker showed how to schedule a single position but does not show how to establish the total requirements for production, service, and sanitation and maintenance work required of a location.

Service needs are established by the meal periods serviced and the policy of

FIGURE 8.5

Completed Schedule for Kitchen Worker

6:30 – 9:00	Morning production as assigned by the chef
9:00 – 9:30	Breakfast break
9:30 – 11:00	Complete morning production tasks
1:00 – 11:30	Set up à-la-carte grill station
11:30 – 1:30	Serve lunch on à-la-carte grill station
11:30 – 2:00	Lunch break
12:00 – 2:00	Serve on grill station
2:00 – 3:30	Assigned cleaning schedule in kitchen area

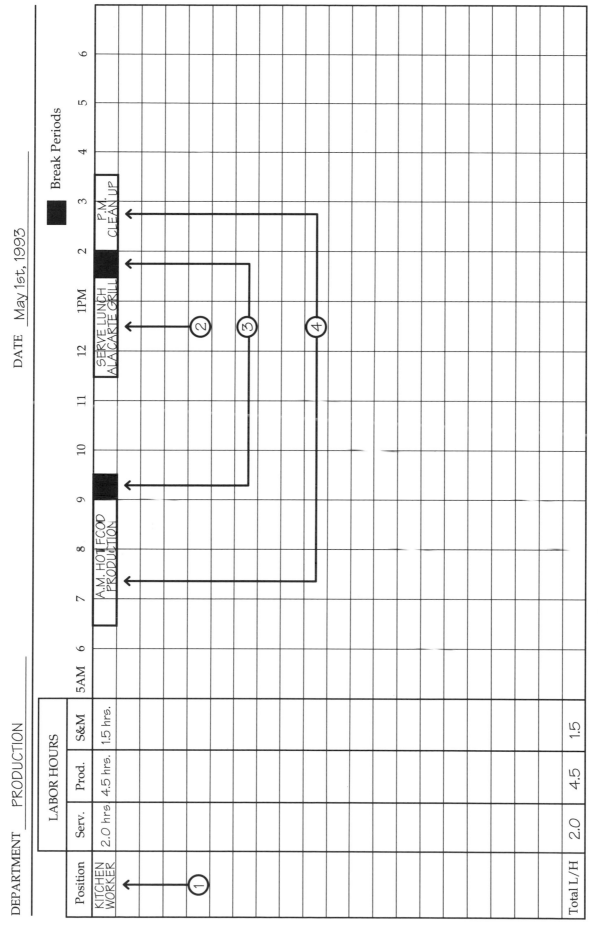

FIGURE 8.6 Example Labor Hours Plan for Kitchen Worker

173

the client or operation, production needs are established by the menu plan, and sanitation and maintenance needs are established by the physical plant. All of these needs must be assessed for the L/H plan to fulfill them.

Service Needs

The first step in projecting the required L/H to staff an operation is to estimate the service needs by finding points of customer contact with the service staff during meal periods. These are the service points that require a server and not self-service by the customer, including production stations that are also service stations, like a made-to-order grill.

Review the following to establish the service points that are required for the urban office building.

BREAKFAST: 7:30–9:00
Cafeteria
1 grill station
1 steam table station
1 cold foods backup station
1 beverage backup station
1 carry out station
1 cashier
TOTAL: 6

Six service workers are required to provide the necessary service for breakfast in the cafeteria. The schedule for breakfast is 7:30 to 9:00. Total service L/H for breakfast is nine hours.

LUNCH 11:30–1:30
Cafeteria
2 grill station
2 steam table
2 made-to-order sandwich station
2 backup cold foods station and salad bar
1 backup for beverage station
1 cafeteria runner to support all areas
2 cashiers

Dining Room
4 wait staff stations
1 cashier

Executive Dining Room
2 wait staff stations

A total of ten cafeteria service stations, six waitstaff stations, and three cashier stations are required for the lunch period from 11:30–1:30. Total L/H for lunch is 38 hours.

Each of the six cafeteria workers who serve both breakfast and lunch have a daily schedule of 3.5 hours at a service point. This would allow 4.5 hours per day for other production and cleanup work.

Each of the four cafeteria workers who serve lunch have only two hours daily scheduled at a service point. If they are full-time employees, they each have six hours per day for other scheduled production and cleanup.

If the waitstaff is part time, which is usual, each would have a two-hour service period and a two-hour setup and breakdown for a total of four hours each.

If the cashiers are part time, which is also usual, there would be one cashier for cafeteria breakfast, two for lunch, and one for the dining room lunch. Time outside of the service periods is usually reserved for administrative chores like register reports, cash counting, and similar tasks.

The resulting L/H schedule for the service workers and cashiers would look like that shown in Figure 8.7. Note that the same pattern used for the example kitchen worker has been used. Each position has its service points established, break periods provided, and the remaining time assigned to routine cafeteria production and cleanup work.

Production Needs

Production needs are dictated by the menu and menu item sales forecast. The menu, in turn, was planned with an eye on the number of available production hours—the time constraint.

In this case, the labor hours available for production are the open hours, prior to the meal periods, that the production staff have on their schedules. In addition, the cafeteria service staff has open hours available for cold food and pantry production work.

The six production and ten cafeteria service workers have a total of 69.5 labor hours available for all areas of production. The menu requirements must be planned to meet this time constraint. Figure 8.8 details the production time planned for this need.

Cashiers

For this example there are three cashiers. Cashiers often combine the tasks of working at a register station during meal periods and performing administrative work at other times. Our example uses this principle, with three cashiers performing 7.5 hours at service points and 6.0 hours of administrative work.

Sanitation and Maintenance Needs

For this example there are two utility workers on the production staff, six on the sanitation and maintenance staff, and two porters scheduled. The total of ten workers at a schedule of 8 hours per day each equals 80 labor hours available for all sanitation and maintenance work not scheduled to the production and service staffs.

The two utility workers on the production staff are pot washers in the bakery and kitchen. The six general utility workers on the sanitation and maintenance staff are dishwashers who operate the dish machine and dish room. The two porters are general area cleaners for the entire facility. Figure 8.9 is a sanitation and maintenance schedule and a cashier's schedule.

Supervision and Management

Supervision and management has not yet been scheduled. The example case provides a staff of:

DEPARTMENT __SERVICE (cafeteria and dining room service)__   DATE __May 1st, 1993__

■ Break Periods

Position	Serv.	Prod.	S&M	Schedule (5AM–6PM)
SUPERVISOR				SET UP / SUPERVISE BKST. / LUNCH SUPERVISION / ADMIN WORK
Cafet. #1	3.0	5.0		SET UP / BKST. GRILL / PRODUCTION SET COLD FOOD UP / LUNCH STATION #1 / PRE-PREP
Cafet. #2	3.0	5.0		SET UP / BKST. / PRODUCTION SET COLD FOOD UP / LUNCH STATION #2 / PRE-PREP
Cafet. #3	3.0	3.5	1.5	SET UP / BKST. COLD FOOD / PRODUCTION SET COLD FOOD UP / LUNCH STATION #3 / CLEAN UP
Cafet. #4	3.0	3.5	1.5	SET UP / BKST. BEV. BACKUP / PRODUCTION SET COLD FOOD UP / LUNCH STATION #4 / CLEAN UP
Cafet. #5	3.0	3.5	1.5	SET UP / BKST. CARRY OUT / PRODUCTION SET COLD FOOD UP / LUNCH STATION #5 / CLEAN UP
Cafet. #6	1.5	3.0	2.5	SALAD PREP / PRODUCTION SET SALAD UP / LUNCH STATION #6 / CLEAN UP
Cafet. #7	1.5	3.0	2.5	SALAD PREP / PRODUCTION SET SALAD UP / LUNCH STATION #7 / CLEAN UP
Cafet. #8	1.5	3.0	2.5	SALAD PREP / PRODUCTION SET SANDWICH UP / LUNCH STATION #8 / CLEAN UP
Cafet. #9	1.5	3.0	2.5	SALAD PREP / PRODUCTION SET SANDWICH UP / LUNCH STATION #9 / CLEAN UP
Cafet. #10	3.0			SALAD PREP / PRODUCTION SET UP / LUNCH STATION #10 / CLEAN UP
Cashier #1	1.5			BREAKFAST CASH STAT. / OFFICE WORK / CASH STATION CAFETERIA / ADMIN WORK
Cashier #2	2.0		1.0	CASH STATION CAFETERIA / ADMIN WORK
Cashier #3				CASH STATION DINING ROOM / CLEAN UP
Waitstaff #1	2.0	1.0	1.0	SET UP / EXECUTIVE / CLEAN UP
Waitstaff #2	2.0	1.0	1.0	SET UP / EXECUTIVE
Waitstaff #3	2.0	1.0	1.0	SET UP / DINING
Waitstaff #4	2.0	1.0	1.0	SET UP / ROOM
Waitstaff #5	2.0	1.0	1.0	SET UP / SERVICE
Waitstaff #6	2.0	1.0	1.0	SET UP / SERVICE
Total L/H	39.5	38.5	21.5	

LABOR HOURS

FIGURE 8.7 Completed Labor Hours Planning Chart for Service Workers

DEPARTMENT PRODUCTION

DATE May 1st, 1993

■ Break Periods

Position	LABOR HOURS Serv.	Prod.	S&M	Schedule
CHEF	2.0	4.0		MORNING PRODUCTION / SUPERVISION & SPECIALS / PRODUCTION PLANNING
Cook #1	2.0	5.5	.5	PRODUCTION / SERVICE STATION #1 / PRE-PREP / CLEAN
Cook #2	2.0	5.5	.5	PRODUCTION / SERVICE STATION #2 / PRE-PREP / CLEAN
K.W. #1	2.5	4.0	1.5	KITCHEN PRODUCTION / SET UP / GRILL SERVICE / CLEAN UP SCHEDULE
K.W. #2	2.5	4.0	1.5	KITCHEN PRODUCTION / SERVICE STATION #3 / CLEAN UP SCHEDULE
BAKER		8.0		MORNING PRODUCTION / PRE-PREP PLANNING
Utility #1			8.0	ASST. BAKERY - POT SINK / ASST. BAKER POT SINK
Utility #2			8.0	KITCHEN POTS / KITCHEN AREA POTS CLEAN / KITCHEN POTS / POTS AREA CLEAN
Total L/H	11.0	31.0	20.0	

Time scale: 5AM 6 7 8 9 10 11 12 1PM 2 3 4 5 6

FIGURE 8.8 Completed Labor Hours Schedule for Production Workers

DEPARTMENT Cashiers, Sanitation & Maintenance

DATE May 1st, 1993

■ Break Periods

Position	LABOR HOURS			Schedule
	Serv.	Prod.	S&M	
Cashier #1	3.5			SET UP / CAFETERIA CASH REGST. → ADMINISTRAT. ASSIGNMENT → CAFETERIA CASH REGISTER → ADMINISTRATV. ASSIGNMENT
Cashier #2	2.0			CAFETERIA CASH REGISTER → ADMIN. WORK
Cashier #3	2.0			DINING ROOM CASH REGISTER → ADMIN. WORK
HEAD UTILITY				SUPERVISION & ADMINISTRATION → SUPERVISION and ASSISTANCE → SUPERVISION & ADMIN
KITCHEN UTILITY			8.0	POTS & PANS IN KITCHEN → POTS & PANS IN KITCHEN → AREA CLEANING
BAKERY UTILITY			8.0	ASSIST. BAKER → POTS & PANS BAKERY → POTS & PANS BAKERY → AREA CLEANING
Gen. Ut. #1			8.0	DISH ROOM → ASSIGNED CLEANING → DISH ROOM STATION #1 → DISH ROOM
Gen. Ut. #2			8.0	DISH ROOM → ASSIGNED CLEANING → STATION #2 → DISH ROOM
Gen. Ut. #3			8.0	DISH ROOM → ASSIGNED CLEANING → STATION #3 → DISH ROOM
Gen. Ut. #4			8.0	CLEAN ASSIGN → ASSIGNED CLEANING → STATION #4 → CLEAN KITCHEN AREA
Gen. Ut. #5			8.0	CLEAN ASSIGN → ASSIGNED CLEANING → STATION #5 → CLEAN KITCHEN AREA
Gen. Ut. #6			8.0	CLEAN ASSIGN → ASSIGNED CLEANING → STATION #6 → CLEAN KITCHEN AREA
Porter #1			8.0	CAFETERIA ASSIGNMENT → CAFETERIA → CAFETERIA → FINISH CAFETERIA
Porter #2			8.0	DINING ROOMS → DINING ROOMS → DINING ROOMS → FINISH DINING ROOM
Total L/H	7.5		8.0	

Time scale: 5AM 6 7 8 9 10 11 12 1PM 2 3 4 5 6

FIGURE 8.9 Completed Labor Hours Schedule for Cashiers and Sanitation and Maintenance Workers

1 general manager
1 assistant general manager
1 cafeteria supervisor
1 head utility supervisor
1 bookkeeper
1 office clerk

Generally there is no L/H plan prepared for these individuals. Their workload varies day to day as need dictates. A summary of their responsibilities is usually contained in their job descriptions. Supervisors and managers generally prepare their own work plans to satisfy each day's needs.

The service, production, cashier, and sanitation and maintenance labor hours are summarized as follows:

	Service	Production	S&M	Total
Service L/H	39.5	38.5	21.5	
Production L/H	11.0	31.0	20.0	
S & M L/H	—	—	80.0	
TOTAL L/H	50.5	69.5	121.5	241.5

A daily labor hours planning form that schedules all the work in a foodservice operation is an invaluable management tool of foodservice directors. It is particularly useful where costs exceeds sales and a subsidy is required.

When operating losses occur, management or the client liaison always request justification. (That same management usually required the service that caused the excess of costs over sales.)

The preparation of an L/H chart allows the foodservice director to show where the labor costs are being incurred. A detailed breakdown of labor hours required for service, production, cashiers, and sanitation and maintenance shows the exact costs of the services demanded. If management wishes to lower labor cost, it must reduce required services.

WEEKLY LABOR HOURS PLANNING

Daily labor hours planning will usually suffice to evaluate the work requirements for service, production, and sanitation and maintenance, but it doesn't provide a manager with an analysis of the projected cost of labor and its ratio to sales.

A manager is often required to calculate the number of labor hours he or she can schedule and still achieve a desired percentage of payroll to sales. For example, a location anticipates a customer count of 1,000, a check average of $2.00, and an average hourly wage of $5.00. The goal for payroll is 25 percent of sales. How many labor hours may be scheduled and still achieve the 25 percent goal?

Forecasted sales are 1,000 × $2.00 ....$2,000 gross sales
Desired payroll is 25 percent of sales...$500 payroll
Labor hours at 500/5.00 may not exceed ....100 L/H

A maximum of 100 labor hours can be scheduled for this example and still achieve the payroll cost objective.

Figure 8.10 is a weekly labor hours planning chart that can be used to forecast the financial results of a weekly work schedule. It is prepared and evaluated before a schedule is put into effect. It allows the planner (the manager or supervisor) to

| JOB TITLE | RATE | HOURS PLANNED | | | | | | | WEEKLY TOTAL | | SUMMARY | |
		SAT.	SUN.	MON.	TUES.	WED.	THURS.	FRI.	HOURS	AMOUNT		
											PROJECTED SALES	$ _____
											ESTIMATED PAYROLL	$ _____
											PAYROLL RELATED	$ _____
											TOTAL PAYROLL	$ _____
											% TO SALES	_____ %
											DATE PREPARED	_____
											PREPARED BY	_____
											APPROVAL	_____
TOTAL HOURS	⨯									⨯		
CUSTOMER COUNT												
CHECK AVERAGE												
ESTIMATED SALES		$	$	$	$	$	$	$				
SALES PER LABOR HOUR		$	$	$	$	$	$	$				

FIGURE 8.10 Weekly Labor Hours and Payroll Cost Planner

forecast a payroll-to-sales ratio derived from a specific customer count, check average, and work schedule.

Requirements for Using the Weekly L/H Planner

Prior to preparing a weekly assessment of the potential labor-to-sales percentage, three items are required:

- A daily forecast of customer count
- A daily forecast of check average
- A completed daily labor hours planning form

The forecast of daily customer count and check averages are used to prepare the daily and weekly sales forecast. The daily L/H plan is used to prepare the overall work schedule.

Potential Results of the Weekly Planner

The weekly planner, when effectively used, will provide the manager with a forecast of sales per labor hour, by day and week, and an expected payroll percentage for the coming week. A manager can project staffing to meet the financial needs of the location. The weekly planner also provides the basis for a daily review to ascertain if the weekly objective will be met. These become part of the cost control system covered in Chapter 9.

Preparing the Weekly Planner

There are ten steps and some calculation required to prepare the planner for a week's operation.

Step 1: Under "Job Title," enter the title of each position to be scheduled for the coming week. Do not enter the worker's name, only the job title.

Step 2: Under "Rate," enter the hourly wage rate for each position shown for each respective job title.

Step 3: Under "Hours Planned," enter the number of hours scheduled for each position for each day of the week. (NOTE: This assumes a Saturday-through-Friday pay week. This can be altered to suit the location's pay schedule). Do not allow for days off. This is not a work schedule but an L/H schedule.

Step 4: Under "Weekly Total," at the "Hours" column, enter the total weekly hours for each position. (Sum left to right to get this). This will provide the total weekly labor hours scheduled for each position for the week, including the day off schedule.

Step 5: Multiply the rate times hours and enter under "Weekly Total." This will provide the total forecasted cost of each position for the week.

Step 6: Total all Saturday through Friday columns and the "Hours" and "Amount" columns, downwards. Enter each column total at the "Total Hours" line. This will provide a daily and weekly total of scheduled labor hours and a weekly total of anticipated payroll cost.

Step 7: Enter the projected daily customer count under the columns for each work day at the "Customer Count" line.

Step 8: Enter the projected daily check average under the columns for each work day at the "Check Average" line.

Step 9: Calculate each day's projected sales (projected check average × projected customer count) and enter under the respective columns. Enter the results at the "Estimated Sales" line. Also enter the total estimated weekly sales.

Step 10: Evaluate each day's projected sales per labor hour and enter at the line with that title, in each day and for the week.

At this point you can evaluate the projected average hourly wage by dividing the total amount by total hours.

You now have all of the information you need to evaluate the results of your work schedule and ascertain if you will meet the budget requirements.

Calculations

At the right side of the form is a space for calculating the results of the ten steps. It is necessary to complete steps 1–5 below to prepare the evaluation.

Step 1: At line A, Projected Sales, enter the amount derived in step 9, above.

Step 2: At line B, Estimated Payroll, enter the amount derived in step 6 above.

Step 3: At line C, Payroll Related, enter the amount of projected payroll-related costs anticipated. (This figure is available from the budget forecast.)

Step 4: At line D, Total Payroll, enter the sum of lines B and C.

Step 5: At line E, % To Sales, enter the labor cost percentage expected—line D divided by line A.

You can now compare the potential results of your planned schedule to the financial objectives of the operation.

Figure 8.11 is an example schedule prepared for one location, the food court in the university. That case projected a financial objective of 20 percent variable cost payroll with 15.7 percent payroll-related costs (total 23.2 percent). The planning chart projects a labor cost of 16.7 percent, which is well within the desired 23.2 percent.

In some cases the originally forecast schedule and payroll will exceed the desired financial objective. For instance, if the example in Figure 8.10 forecast a payroll of 22 percent, that amount would exceed the objective by 2 percent. To evaluate the number of labor hours that must be trimmed from the payroll, do the following:

■ Multiply the excess (2 percent) by projected sales.
■ Divide the result by the average cost per labor hour.

The result is the number of labor hours that must be reduced from the schedule to achieve the desired 20 percent payroll objective.

Example
2% of $8,600.00 = $172.00
$172.00/$6.00 = 28.7 L/H

The $6.00 is the average cost per labor hour. The resulting 28.7 is the number of labor hours that must be cut from the schedule to achieve the desired payroll-to-sales percentage.

A schedule can be reduced across the board by cutting an equal number of hours from each worker, or it can be reduced by rescheduling other work and

FAST FOOD OUTLET: CAMP JS UNIVERSITY

JOB TITLE (1)	RATE (2)	HOURS PLANNED (3)							WEEKLY TOTAL (4)(5) HOURS	AMOUNT
		SAT.	SUN.	MON.	TUES.	WED.	THURS.	FRI.		
A.M. Supervisor	$8.00	6	-	4	4	4	4	6	28	$224
A.M. Service Worker #1	$5.00	6	-	4	4	4	4	6	28	$140
A.M. Service Worker #2	$5.00	6	-	4	4	4	4	6	28	$140
P.M. Supervisor	$8.00	7	7	5	5	5	5	7	41	$328
P.M. Service Worker #3	$5.00	7	7	5	5	5	5	7	41	$205
P.M. Service Worker #4	$5.00	7	7	5	5	5	5	7	41	$205
TOTAL HOURS (6)		39	21	27	27	27	27	39	207	$1,242
CUSTOMER COUNT (7)		500	150	250	250	250	250	500	2150	
CHECK AVERAGE (8)		$4.06	$4.00	$4.00	$4.00	$4.00	$4.00	$4.00	$4.00	
ESTIMATED SALES (9)		$ 2,000	$ 600	$ 1,000	$ 1,000	$ 1,000	$ 1,000	$ 2,000	$ 8,600	
SALES PER LABOR HOUR		$ 51.28	$ 28.37	$ 37.04	$ 37.04	$ 37.04	$ 37.04	$ 57.28	$ 41.55	

SUMMARY

PROJECTED SALES	(A)	$8,600
ESTIMATED PAYROLL	(B)	$1,242
PAYROLL RELATED	(C)	$195
TOTAL PAYROLL	(D)	$1,437
% TO SALES	(E)	16.7%

DATE PREPARED   MAY 15, 1993

PREPARED BY   M.W.

APPROVAL   V.P.

FIGURE 8.11 Completed Weekly Labor Hours Plan for One Location in the Food Court of Campus University Example

eliminating some labor hours. A review of the service, production, and cleanup needs will usually provide the basis for your cuts.

STANDARD PRODUCTIVITY MEASURES

Every foodservice manager desires a yardstick with which to evaluate the productivity of labor hours scheduled. He/she constantly seeks to improve productivity and increase efficiency. In institutional foodservice management, that yardstick is hard to find.

Commercial foodservices compare sales per labor hour for like restaurants to evaluate the efficiency of an operation. Such operations must be identical in style and type for the comparison to be of any value.

A good example of like operations is the fast food industry. Each of the major chains has established sales-per-labor-hour goals to meet financial objectives. In all locations, the operations are the same. They have the same menu, physical plant, pricing structure, and other conditions. All else being equal, the sales-per-labor-hour comparison is practical.

In noncommercial foodservice, there are more differences than similarities; this makes establishing productivity standards difficult. Some areas of difference include:

■ The menu: prepared from scratch or dependent on convenience foods
■ The kitchen: well-equipped or poorly equipped
■ Employee skills
■ Service requirements: the desire of an employer to provide more or less service to employees
■ Number of satellite locations in a manufacturing plant
■ Number of service hours in an office building
■ Ratio of boarders to cash sales in a campus foodservice
■ Number of beds (patients) served in a hospital foodservice
■ Number of units, and their sizes, in a school system foodservice

Contractors and self-operators use a variety of productivity gauges that help them measure standards. These include:

■ Number of meals produced per labor hour, a hospital statistic
■ Number of square feet cleaned by the utility crew per labor hour
■ Number of meals served per labor hour

Contract foodservice corporations use such indices to compare one location to another. Recall that the health care segment has a means, established by the American Hospital Association, to compare labor hours per patient meal and labor hours per patient day.

The various elementary and secondary school systems have standards established to evaluate meals per labor hour (MPLH). Each state or school district has its own; for example, the state of Mississippi has set its standard between 12 and 15 MPLH, depending on the size of the school.

Each segment has a variety of data available, but none is universally applicable. Most managers develop yardsticks that satisfy their needs and then compare their own results to those standards.

SUMMARY

When a manager prepares a labor hours plan, he or she is developing the groundwork for staffing, leading, and controlling.

Labor hours are the total number of hours scheduled for all staff workers each day. The limit on labor hours that can be utilized is established as part of the financial plan.

A version of the Gantt chart is an excellent planning tool to figure the service, production, and cleanup tasks to be assigned to each worker.

Weekly labor cost planning ensures the achievement of financial objectives. When a daily and weekly plan are used together, a manager has a complete picture of the labor resources used at a foodservice.

Establishing standard productivity results for an institutional foodservice is difficult, but possible.

9

Cost Control Management

Cost control management is, simply, controlling operating costs to achieve the desired financial objective.

Cost control applies—is necessary, in fact—to any segment of the noncommercial foodservice industry. Figure 9.1 illustrates the flow of management tasks. The cost control system is part of the financial plan.

Remember these management concepts:

- The plan is rooted in the objective.
- Controlling is a method that is part of the plan.
- A cost control system is rooted in the financial plan.

The foodservice director is responsible for establishing the cost control system, which tracks the cost of food, labor, and direct expenses.

This chapter reviews the basic concepts of control as a management function and relates those concepts to the development of a cost control system for a noncommercial foodservice.

Upon completion of this chapter, readers should know and understand:

- Control as a basic management process
- Elements of a cost control system for a noncommercial foodservice operation
- The weekly operating report (WOR) and its function and use
- The food cost control cycle
- Accounting and its relation to cost control
- Break-even analysis and its use

CONTROL: A BASIC MANAGEMENT PROCESS

Management literature generally defines control as a four-step process:

1. Establish standards.
2. Compare results to the established standards.
3. Identify deviations in performance (results) as compared to standards.
4. Correct the deviations.

This process is as applicable to institutional foodservice as it is to any other area of management, as follows.

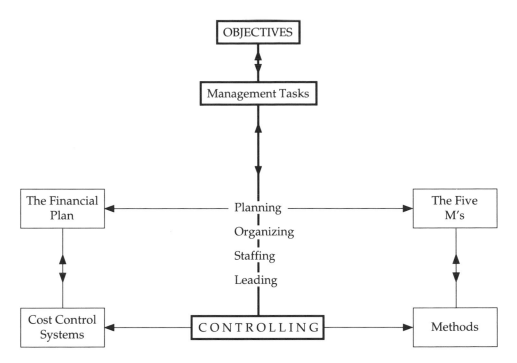

FIGURE 9.1 The Cost Control System

Step 1: Establish Standards. When an institutional foodservice establishes its financial goals, it also establishes standards for sales, cost of sales, labor cost, direct expenses, and profits or losses (subsidy). Taken together, these constitute the operating budget.

Step 2: Compare Results. Results may be compared as necessary on a daily, weekly, or accounting period basis. The comparison method is designed into the cost control system.

Step 3: Identify Deviations. A review of the periodic reports allows for a comparison of all areas of sales and costs to standards and an identification of deviations from standards.

Step 4: Correct Deviations. Depending on the deviation, an action plan is made to increase attendance or check average to correct a problem, alter the menu to correct a food cost problem, or change employee schedules to correct a labor cost problem.

Analyzing the reasons for deviations from standards and taking corrective action is a routine function of management.

The key to effective control is the design of the system. That system must provide the foodservice director with the necessary comparisons on a timely basis and the system must be administratively efficient.

COST CONTROL AS A SYSTEM

A cost control system must, in a timely manner, deliver information needed by a manager. To be effective, it must be designed for the particular foodservice.

Even with that, remember this: Systems don't control, they report. *Managers* control. A manager controls by using the information gathered from the cost reporting system to compare results to standards and develop an action plan to correct deviations from standards.

A control system is a method of achieving a management objective. A foodservice cost control system is a method of reporting detailed results of sales (where applicable), cost of sales or food purchases, labor cost, and direct expenses to achieve foodservice management onjectives. The need for these reports will differ with the objectives of the various institutional foodservices.

■ A business and industry location needs to assess the operating sales and costs of employee cafeterias, dining rooms, and other services. These are evaluated on the basis of a standard accounting income statement, also called the profit and loss statement.
■ A health care operation has a different need. It evaluates operating costs on a cost-per-patient-day basis.
■ A campus dining operation needs to track costs for student board plans, cash costs for other outlets, and cost of sales for catering.
■ A foodservice vending operation needs to measure per capita spending and operating costs.
■ A correctional facility has no cash sales, so managers need a comparison of food, labor, and operating costs per inmate day or per meal.

Each industry segment evaluates its financial results in accordance with its particular objectives. Reporting needs differ from segment to segment.

An effective cost control system identifies the specific needs of the foodservice and develops a system to report on those needs. The needs, remember, are first established by the financial goals.

While the development of a system is important, the system alone will not guarantee cost control. *Systems do not control, they merely report. Managers control.*

ELEMENTS OF COST CONTROL FOR AN INSTITUTIONAL FOODSERVICE

Every noncommercial foodservice manager requires a reporting system that meets the particular needs of the facility in question. Those needs are determined by a review of the previously prepared financial plan.

The following are some examples.

Business and Industry (B&I) Example

Cost reporting needs for a B&I operation fall into the four categories of the profit and loss statement:

■ Sales
■ Food cost
■ Labor cost
■ Direct expenses

Standards for each of the four categories already exist. The accounting period, either 4-4-5 week or calendar month, has also already been established. Now, additional cost control information is gathered on a daily and weekly basis to supplement those two standards. This provides each foodservice director with immediate information for comparison to standards.

Sales

- Sales are simply customer counts multiplied by check averages.
- The standard for a B&I customer count is participation percentage by meal period.
- The standard for check average is set by a review of menu pricing policy and market potential.
- The information needed is a report on daily customer count, participation percentage, and check average. These must be summarized weekly and monthly.

Food Cost

- Food cost percentage is composed of sales mix and cost mix by menu categories and meal periods (see Figure 5.14, Chapter 5).
- The standard for overall food cost is percentage to sales.
- The information needed is the dollar value of food expenditures by menu categories and their percentage relationship to sales.

Labor Cost

- Labor cost is comprised of management salaries, hourly wages, and payroll-related costs.
- The standard for total labor cost is established by the staffing plan for the operating budget. That plan detailed the number of workers in each category, their respective wage or salary schedule, and the number of work hours to be scheduled.
- The information needed is a summary of the number of regular or overtime hours worked and the resulting weekly payroll costs. (Payroll-related costs are automatically controlled when payroll is controlled.)

Direct Expenses

- Direct expenses are made up of fixed and variable costs.
- The standard for direct expenses is a dollar amount for each fixed cost item and a percentage to sales for each variable cost item.
- The information needed is a weekly summary of expenses by fixed cost category and a percentage of sales report for variable costs.

A cost control system that identifies needed information will help fulfill the foodservice's control requirements. Recognize that we've completed step 1 of the cost control process: Establish standards. Such a system of reports will provide the foodservice director with the necessary information to complete steps 2, 3, and 4 of the cost control system.

All other segments of the institutional foodservice field can identify their cost control system needs in a similar manner to this B&I example. Some, such as health care, require specialized reporting. Regardless of the type of institution, an identification of needs is essential to the development of a system.

THE THREE QUESTIONS

There are three questions to be answered when identifying needs for the design of any cost control reporting system for any foodservice:

1. What information is needed?
2. How often is it needed?
3. How will the information be gathered and reported?

The answer to these three questions will identify the needs. It will also identify the type and sequence of reports required to develop the cost control system.

In the previous B&I example, information needs have been established in the four categories of sales, cost of sales, labor costs, and direct expenses. Standards have already been established for each of these categories in the financial plan.

Sales

1. What information is needed?

   The customer count and check average, by meal period, and by area.

   Were budgeted sales met? If not, why not?

2. How often is the information needed?

   Daily, summarized weekly and/or by accounting period, possibly by menu cycle.

3. How will the information be gathered and reported?

   Gather from the daily sales reports and cashiers' reports.

   Summarize weekly on the weekly operating report.

Cost of Sales

1. What information is needed?

   Net expenditures (usage) for various categories of foodstuffs.

   How do they relate, on a percentage basis, to departmental and gross sales?

2. How often is the information needed?

   Weekly, summarized monthly, by accounting period, or by menu cycle.

3. How will the information be reported and gathered?

   Gather inventory information from daily and weekly stock and order sheets.

   Gather purchase information on a daily record of invoices and a weekly summary of purchases and expenses. Report summarized results on the weekly operating report.

Labor Costs

1. What information is needed?

   The labor costs for both salaried and hourly personnel.

   Were payroll-related costs within budget?

2. How often is the information needed?

   Weekly, summarized monthly, or by accounting period.

3. How will the information be gathered and reported?

Gather weekly, hourly, and overtime amounts from time cards of hourly employees.

Gather total weekly payroll costs from the accounting department payroll summary.

Report summarized results on the weekly operating report.

Direct Expenses

1. What information is needed?

   The dollar amounts of all fixed cost operating expenses, the dollar amounts, and ratio-to-sales of all variable cost operating expenses.

2. How often is the information needed?

   Daily, summarized weekly and monthly or by specific accounting period.

3. How will the information be gathered and reported?

   Gather daily costs on a daily record of invoices and a weekly summary of purchases and expenses.

   Report summarized results on the weekly operating report.

REPORTING FORMS

The specific information needs for the four areas of sales and costs have been established, and the various forms required to gather and report cost control information have been identified. They are:

- Daily cashier's and sales reports
- Daily stock and order forms
- Weekly stock and order form
- Daily record of invoices
- Weekly summary of purchases and expenses
- Weekly time cards for hourly employees
- Weekly payroll summary
- Weekly operating report

A total of three daily and five weekly operating forms are required to gather and report all of the information necessary to the cost control system. Each of these, except the accounting department payroll summary report, must be designed to fit the specific operational requirements of each facility.

Daily Cashier's and Sales Report

Figure 9.2 is an example of a daily cashiers report (Cash Reporting Form) used by a contractor-operated facility comparable to our case example. Note that the form is designed to accommodate the service areas of the facility, the number of cash registers used, and other information. This is an actual form used by a location in mid-Manhattan, New York City, in a large office building with a single main tenant, the client.

Figure 9.3 is an example of a similar report used by a smaller, independent B&I operation. The location has a population of only 500 and the foodservice is

DAILY SALES AND CASH REPORT				DATE			WEATHER			
			Prepared By			Approved By				
CASH SALES		REGISTER READINGS	GROSS SALES	OVER SHORT	TAX READINGS	NET SALES	CUSTOMERS	CHECK AVERAGE		
Register 1 *LOBBY*	Closing									
	Opening									
	Net									
Register 1 Breakfast	Closing									
	Opening									
	Net									
Register 1 Lunch	Closing									
	Opening									
	Net									
Register II *LUNCH*	Closing									
	Opening									
	Net									
Register III Lunch	Closing									
	Opening									
	Net									
Register IV Lunch	Closing									
	Opening									
	Net									
Register *A.M.* *COFFEE SERVICE*	Closing									
	Opening									
	Net									
Register V Coffee Service	Closing									
	Opening									
	Net									
Register V Cash Sales	Closing									
	Opening									
	Net									
SUB-TOTAL	Deposit									
Register V Charge Sales	Closing									
	Opening									
	Net									
Outside Sales										
TOTAL SALES	Deposit									
TRANSFER COSTS: 35th and 50th Floor										
Special Functions										
TOTAL TRANSFER COSTS										

SUMMARY	DEBITS	CREDITS	REMARKS:
Cash			*misc. Key I*
Cafeteria Sales			*II*
Accounts Receivable			*III*
Breakfast			*IV*
A.M. Coffee Run + *LOBBY*			
P.M. Coffee Run			
Cash Sales (D.R.)			
Sales Tax (Cash)			
Charge Sales (D.R.)			
Sales Tax (Charge)			
Outside Sales			
Outside Sales Tax			
TOTAL			

FIGURE 9.2 Daily Cashier's Report

Manager's Signature _____ Day & Date _____ Location: _____

BREAKFAST, LUNCH, WAGONS, ETC.		Register	Amount Rung Up	Over	Short	Net Cash Sales	MDSE. REC'D		
							VENDOR	ITEM	AMOUNT
1	CUR PREV								
2	CUR PREV.								
3	CUR PREV								
4	CUR PREV								
5	CUR PREV								
6	CUR PREV								
7									
8									
9									
10									
11									
12									
TOTAL CASH SALES									
CHARGE SALES COLLECTED: DATE OF CHARGE FROM WHOM									

MDSE. OR CONTAINERS RETURNED

MISC. INCOME:

CASH DEPOSITED (DATE   19   )

SUMMARY

CHARGE SALES: (Indicate to Whom Charged)   AMT.

COMMENTS: (PLEASE INDICATE SHUTDOWNS FOR VACATIONS, HOLIDAYS, ETC., OR ANY OTHER CAUSE FOR SALES VARIATIONS.)

TOTAL CHARGE SALES

CASH SALES

TOTAL

DEDUCT—SALES TAX

SALES FOR DAY

FIGURE 9.3   Small B&I Daily Cashier's Report

operated by a chef/manager. To minimize administrative work, the report shows both sales and cash information and a daily record of merchandise received. This eliminates the need for a separate daily record of invoices for this unit.

Figure 9.4 is an example of a standard Daily Cash Register Reading Report used by a national contract management company. It has been developed in a generic manner to suit the needs of all of the company's B&I locations.

Each individual location requires a form compatible with its own sales and cash reporting needs. Figures 9.2 and 9.3 have been designed for specific locations. Figure 9.4 has a generic design for use at multiple locations. Where a generic form is used—often the case with contract management companies—adjustments are usually made at individual locations.

Daily Stock and Order Form

Figure 9.5 is an example of a Daily Stock and Order form used by an independent operator. Note that there are daily inventory and order columns for each item. The separate columns at the right are for recording and evaluating the sums of weekly inventories for reporting purposes.

Weekly Stock and Order Form

Figure 9.6 is an example of a weekly stock and order form (Weekly Inventory Order Sheet) used by the same independent operator. This form is used for items that are ordered weekly or monthly. It covers four weeks on a single sheet, minimizing record keeping while providing sufficient information for a four-week accounting period.

The national contract management companies all use similar daily and weekly order forms.

Daily Record of Invoices

Figure 9.7 is an example of a Daily Record of Invoices form similar to that used by many independent operators. Note that it breaks down food purchases into six categories:

- Meat, fish, and poultry (MFP)
- Produce
- Dairy
- Baked Goods
- Coffee/tea
- Groceries

In addition, it provides a column for some direct expenses:

- Paper goods
- Laundry
- Cleaning supplies
- Other

OPERATION _____ AT _____ DAY _____ DATE _____ 19 _____
CITY   STATE

CUSTOMER COUNT	NO.	REGISTER READING		SALES RUNG-UP	TIPS	VOIDS OVERRINGS	SALES	CHARGE SALES	MEAL TICKETS	OVER (SHORT)	NET CASH
		E									
		B									
		E									
		B									
		E									
		B									
		E									
		B									
		E									
		B									
		E									
		B									
		E									
		B									
		E									
		B									
		E									
		B									
		E									
		B									
		E									
		B									
		E									
		B									
		E									
		B									
		E									
		B									
		E									
		B									
		E									
		B									
TOTAL STAND SALES							S	CS		O/S	CT
GRAND TOTAL	FORWARD TO FORM 1										
				LINE 12			LINE 1	LINE 2	LINE 3	LINE 4	LINE 5

ATTACH TO WEEKLY CASH REPORT - FORM 1

PREPARED BY _____ APPROVED BY _____

S RUNG–UP = E–B   SALES = SALES RUNG-UP–TIPS–VOIDS–OVERRINGS   O/S = SALES—CHARGE SALES—MEAL TICKETS—NET CASH

FIGURE 9.4   Daily Register Reading Report (Courtesy of Canteen Corporation, Spartanburg, SC)

UNIT NO.   W/E

ITEMS	MONDAY		TUESDAY		WEDNESDAY		THURSDAY		FRIDAY		INV.	UNIT PR.	TOTAL
	INV.	ORD.	INV.	ORD.	INV.	ORD.	INV.	ORD.	INV.	ORD.			

LIST HERE ALL ITEMS REQUIRED FOR YOUR UNIT

FIGURE 9.5 Daily Stock and Order Form, Independent

Unit No.			Date			Date			Date			Date		
Items	Unit Pack	Inv./Ord.	Unit Price	Total	Inv./Ord.	Unit Price	Total	Inv./Ord.	Unit Price	Total	Inv./Ord.	Unit Price	Total
LIST HERE ALL ITEMS REQUIRED FOR YOUR UNIT														

FIGURE 9.6 Weekly Stock and Order Form

PREPARED BY: _____   DAY : _____   DATE: _____

INVOICE DATE	INVOICE #	VENDORS NAME	M.F.P.	PRODUCE	DAIRY	BAKED GOODS	COFFEE TEA	GRO-CERIES	PAPER GOODS	CLEAN. SUPPLY	LAUNDRY	EQUIP.	COMMENTS
		TOTAL											

MW-S-202001

FIGURE 9.7   Daily Record of Invoices, Independent

198

Among the items of information required are invoice date, invoice number, vendor's name and the cost of the merchandise. The cost amount is summarized on the weekly operating report.

Some foodservice directors desire a different breakdown of categories. These are defined by what information that FSD needs. The categories shown are fairly standard, but they can be adjusted to suit the manager.

Figure 9.8 is a form used by a national contractor. Note the similarities to the form shown as Figure 9.7. Both forms serve the same purpose.

National contractors design their forms to work with their accounting system. All unit reporting systems must be compatible with a single corporate reporting system.

Weekly Summary of Purchases and Expenses

The summary of purchases and expenses may be an internal location document or an accounting department form. It serves to process the accounts payable information from the receiving point to the accounts payable clerk. For a self-op, accounts payable would likely be on the premises, while at a contracted location, the form might be sent to the corporate accounting department at a separate location. In either case, the same form will suffice.

Figure 9.8 is also an example of such a form used by a major contractor. It may be used either daily or weekly. Note that this report designates accounting codes to be used with a computerized accounting system.

A weekly summary of purchases and expenses (the compilation of daily invoices) initiates both the accounting and the cost control process. The accounting department uses it as part of the monthly (or specific accounting period) income statement. The foodservice director uses it as part of the internal cost control system via the weekly operating report.

Weekly Time Cards for Hourly Employees

The daily/weekly reporting document for hourly employees is usually the time card, which records the employee's number of hours worked. It is also the source document for the payroll department, on premises or at the contractor's headquarters, to prepare a paycheck for each employee.

Time cards track the number of hours worked by all hourly employees. For our case example they would be sorted by department (production, service, sanitation and maintenance) and the results compared to the standards listed in the operating budget. The hours worked can be compared to the labor hours plan, and the dollar amount can be compared to the financial plan.

Time cards vary with the system used; some are direct source data for computerized operations, and others are manual data that timekeepers use to prepare payroll summaries.

Weekly Payroll Summary

Payroll methods vary from company to company. The major contractors utilize their own standard systems, usually from centralized payroll sources. Some of the smaller contractors employ the services of a specialized payroll data processing subcontractor. Self-operators generally use the in-house payroll department.

Regardless of the system used, the payroll department usually produces a payroll summary. That summary details the total number of employees, the

200

DATE PREPARED ___ / ___ / ___   PERIOD ___   OPERATION ___   PAGE ___

LINE	SUPPLIER		P.O. # OR LOCAL REFERENCE NUMBER	INVOICE DATA			MEAT CHEESE 4110714	ROLLS BREAD 4110722	DESSERT ICE CR. PASTRY 4110748	BEVERAGE MILK JUICE 4110763	SUNDRY FOOD 4110771	NON-FOOD ITEMS 4110789	CAN/FROZ. FRUIT/VEG. 4110862	FRESH PRODUCE SALADS 4110854			PAPER 4110755	LAUNDRY CLEANING 6741003	CLEANING SUPPLIES 6741029	
	NAME	CODE		DATE	NUMBER	AMOUNT														
1																				
2																				
3																				
4																				
5																				
6																				
7																				
8																				
9																				
10																				
11																				
12																				
13																				
14																				
15																				
16																				
17																				
18																				
19																				
20																				
21																				
22																				
23																				
	TOTAL																			

FINAL FOR PERIOD ☐   _____
                            MANAGER'S SIGNATURE

FORM NO. 1861 (REV. 8 90) PRINTED IN U.S.A.

FIGURE 9.8 Daily Record of Invoices, Canteen Corporation (Courtesy of Canteen Corporation, Spartanburg, SC)

number of regular and overtime hours worked, and other information designed into the system. Properly planned, the report will provide a summary of payroll costs by department for the foodservice director. This report provides the cost results that are compared to the standard detailed in the financial plan. The comparison alerts management to any problems requiring remedial action.

Figure 9.9 is an example of a Payroll Time Sheet for a contractor-run operation. Other institutional foodservice operations use similar reports.

Weekly Operating Report

The weekly operating report is the primary cost control document for the location foodservice director. It summarizes, on a weekly basis, all the necessary financial results for comparison to financial standards. Each segment of the industry requires a specialized weekly operating report to identify specific informational needs.

The weekly operating report (often called the WOR) uses detailed information from all of the other listed reports:

■ Sales information from the daily cashier's or sales report
■ Inventory values from the daily and weekly order forms
■ Purchase information from the daily record of invoices and the weekly summary of purchases and expenses
■ Payroll information from the daily time cards and the weekly payroll summary

Most foodservice directors in any segment of the industry utilize some form of weekly operating report. The major contractors have distinctively designed reports for the various segments of their activity. Most smaller contractors have similar reports. The self-operators may or may not have a WOR, depending on the nature of the organization. In some cases, their accounting departments provide a different type of reporting. Following are examples of different WORs.

Figure 9.10 is an example of a weekly operating report developed by a small independent contractor for management fee operations. Note that the WOR records data that fulfills seven basic informational needs:

Titles: Headings indicate the unit name, the unit accounting code number, the week ending date, the menu cycle number, and the weekly accounting calendar number. This information is consistent with both unit and accounting department needs.

Sales Breakdown: This section receives data from the daily cashier's or sales reports recording each day's sales by area or category. This daily information is summarized and a weekly total provided. The resulting sales information can be compared to the previously forecast standards of the financial plan. If there is a variance, an analysis of customer counts and check averages will uncover it.

Customer Count and Check Average: This section receives customer count and sales information from the cashier's reports and sales reports, respectively. The result is an evaluation of daily and weekly customer counts and weekly check averages. This allows for a comparison to participation percentages and check averages projected in the financial plan. If sales are reported below the expected standard, it's easy to determine whether the problem is poor participation or low check average.

Cost Breakdown: This section receives purchasing information from the daily record of invoices and the daily and weekly stock and order sheets. A total value of expenditures and a ratio to sales by cost category are figured for the week and period to date. Information regarding food cost is evaluated in total and in selected

WEEKLY PAYROLL TIME SHEET

FOR WEEK ENDING

Unit Name _____   Unit No. _____   Dept. No. _____

EMPLOYEE NAME	JOB CODE	EMPLOYEE NO.	HOURS								DAYS		PAY	TIPS REPORTED FORM R12 NOT TO BE PAID	OTHER EARNINGS-DOLLARS			MISC.		REMARKS SECTION
			REGULAR	OVER-TIME	DOUBLE TIME	VACA-TION	HOLI-DAY	SICK OR PER-SONAL	OTHER	PAID	ACCUM H.O. USE ONLY	2 or WEEKS		GRAT/ COMMIS	SHIFT JOB RATE DIFF OR PREM		AMOUNT	C	VACATION	
			14	18	21	24	28	31	35	39		42	44	49	55		60	67 68		

ENTER TOTALS ON LAST PAGE ONLY

PAYROLL DEPARTMENT USE ONLY

ENTER ALL HOURS IN TENTHS

ENTER IN RED OR CIRCLE AMOUNTS TO BE SUBTRACTED EXCEPT FOR MISC. SEE REVERSE SIDE.

ORIGINAL COPY TO CORPORATE OFFICE, DUPLICATE COPY TO BE RETAINED.
FOR COMPLETE INSTRUCTIONS ON USE OF FORM SEE REVERSE SIDE.

PREPARED BY _____   DATE _____   APPROVED BY _____   DATE _____

FIGURE 9.9 Payroll Summary (Courtesy of Canteen Corporation, Spartanburg, SC)

202

UNIT NAME: _____ NO: _____ WEEK ENDING: _____ WEEK NUMBER: 1 – 2 – 3 – 4 – 5 MENU CYCLE NO: _____

COST BREAKDOWN

DAY	M.F.P.	PROD- UCE	DAIRY	BAKED GOODS	COFFEE TEA	GRO- CERIES	TOTAL	DAILY FOOD COST	Paper Goods	Clean. Supplies	Laun- dry	Equip- ment
SAT.												
SUN.												
MON.												
TUES.												
WED.												
THURS.												
FRI.												
WEEKLY TOTAL												
% TO SALES												

	Period Sales		
WEEK No. 1 – 2 – 3 – 4			
TOTAL			
% TO SALES			

COMMENTS

SALES BREAKDOWN

MEAL PERIOD	SAT.	SUN.	MON.	TUES.	WED.	THURS.	FRI.	TOTAL
								Check Aver.

CUSTOMER COUNT BREAKDOWN

MEAL PERIOD	SAT.	SUN.	MON.	TUES.	WED.	THURS.	FRI.	TOTAL

Summary per client Budget	This Wk.	%	Year to Date	%	WEEK NUMBER BUDGET	%
SALES		100		100		100
FOOD COST						
SALARIES AND WAGES						
PAYROLL BENEFITS %						
PAPER GOODS						
LAUNDRY						
CLEANING SUPPLIES						
REPAIRS						
REPLACEMENT & EXPEND.						
OFFICE SUPPLIES						
LICENSES						
MISC.						
TELEPHONE						
INSURANCE & TAXES						
RENTAL						
Adm. Fee						
TOTAL COST						
NET PROFIT (LOSS)						

WEEKLY PAY ROLL ANALYSIS

Summary	Total	$	Labor / Hrs.
Wk.			
REGULAR			
1	OVERTIME		
2	VACATION		
3	SPECIAL		
4	SICK PAY		
	HOLIDAY		
	MEMORIAL		
	Transfers.		
	Cash		
	TOTAL	$	L / H
	% TO SALES	% Budget	L / H

UNIT MANAGERS SIGNATURE: _____

FIGURE 9.10 WOR from a Self-Operator

203

breakdowns. This allows for a comparison of results to standards and for an evaluation of deviation from standards when they exist.

Weekly Payroll Analysis: This section receives payroll information from the weekly payroll summary and details the number of regular hours, overtime hours, and dollar amount of payroll. In this case, space has been provided for reporting holiday, vacation, sick pay, and memorial pay. These can be used if desired. Information is compared with the standards established in the financial plan. If standards have been exceeded, the area of their excess can be identified. The labor hours worked and overtime hours paid are the usual areas of comparison.

Summary per Client Budget: Remember, this is a weekly operating report for a management fee client. As such, the manager is interested in the financial results—for the week and year to date—compared to the budget provided the client. Space is provided to identify the week's number, and to produce a memo-type income statement for the week and year to date. There is a column for the original financial plan for purposes of comparison to the year to date.

Comments: Every effective cost reporting system allows for the recording of why something happened. The comments section serves this purpose. A manager may wish to detail an item that will be referred to at budget preparation time, an exceptionally low cost, a high check average, or similar items. This information is usually used for further planning and/or corrective action (for a discrepancy to standard). Sample comments might be:

■ High labor cost due to excessive overtime for servicing client's special function
■ Low participation caused by a snow storm
■ High check average accomplished by a promotional special; not expected to repeat

Anything that a manager may wish to recall for later planning is recorded in the comments section.

The weekly operating report provides the foodservice director with all of the information required by step 2 of the control process—comparing results to standard. The four critical areas of sales, cost of sales, labor costs, and direct expenses have all been reported. In addition the manager has the week's results, year to date information, and comparisons to budget.

Any deviations from standard will be evident. The manager can now take necessary action to correct the deviations.

A Contractor's WOR

Figure 9.11 is a weekly operating report, used for the business and industry division of a major contractor. The same information is provided as in Figure 9.10, but the format has been changed to suit this contractor.

Titles: Headings indicate the information needed by the contractor, the unit name, unit number, and week ending date and number. Note the difference in these headings from the ones in Figure 9.10.

Cost Computation: This section lists the dollar amount of purchases (from the daily and weekly summary of purchases) by food group category plus controllable direct expenses. Note that there are small numbers across the top (2016, 2017) to identify the account codes of the contractor for a computerized accounting system. These are listed in a table of accounts and are used to prepare the weekly summary of purchases and expenses and the period P&L statements used by this corporation. Space is also provided for information from the daily and weekly stock and order sheets regarding opening and closing inventories. The resulting evaluation provides the cost of food by category and some direct expenses. These are carried forth to the operating summary section.

WEEKLY OPERATING REPORT
INDUSTRIAL FOOD UNITS

DIVISION OFFICE

WEEK ENDING	UNIT NAME	UNIT NUMBER
1 2 3 4		

COST COMPUTATION	TOTAL	2014 VEND/ OTHER	2016 MEAT & SEAFOOD	2017 GROCERIES	2038 FRUITS & VEGETABLES	2039 DESSERTS & BAKED GOODS	2042 MILK & MILK BEV.	2043 BREAD & ROLLS	3242 PAPER & OTHER	3260 CLEANING SUPPLIES
TOTAL PURCHASES										
PLUS: BEGINNING INVENTORY										
SUB TOTAL										
LESS: ENDING INVENTORY										
COST										

OPERATING STATISTICS

DAY	SHIFT OR SATELLITE UNIT					
	CUSTOMER COUNT	DAILY SALES	AVG. SALE PER CUSTOMER	CUSTOMER COUNT	DAILY SALES	AVG. SALE PER CUSTOMER
Saturday						
Sunday						
Monday						
Tuesday						
Wednesday						
Thursday						
Friday						
TOTAL						

DAY	SHIFT OR SATELLITE UNIT			TOTAL UNIT		
	CUSTOMER COUNT	DAILY SALES	AVG. SALE PER CUSTOMER	CUSTOMER COUNT	DAILY SALES	AVG. SALE PER CUSTOMER
Saturday						
Sunday						
Monday						
Tuesday						
Wednesday						
Thursday						
Friday						
TOTAL						

NUMBER OF EMPLOYEES		AVERAGE SALE PER HOUR WORKED	
HOURS WORKED	REGULAR	PLANT POPULATION	
	OVERTIME	AVERAGE SALE PER PLANT EMPLOYEE	
	TOTAL		

COMMENTS:

*Explain in detail.

MANAGER'S SIGNATURE   DATE

OPERATING SUMMARY

	BUDGET %		CURRENT WEEK	%	PERIOD TO DATE	%
		Register Sales				
		Cart or Wagon Sales				
		Dining Room Sales				
		Vending Sales				
		Net Other Sales				
100.0		TOTAL SALES		100.0		100.0
		Vend / Other				
		Meat & Seafood				
		Groceries				
		Fruits & Vegetables				
		Desserts & Baked Goods				
		Milk & Milk Beverage				
		Bread & Rolls				
		Sales at Cost, Grease, etc.				
		TOTAL FOOD COST				
		Payroll Regular				
		Cash Payroll				
		Vacation and Holiday Accrual				
		Payroll Related Costs				
		Payroll - Transfers Net				
		TOTAL LABOR COST				
		Paper and Other Supplies				
		Cleaning Supplies				
		Laundry				
		Replacements				
		Repairs & Maintenance				
		Insurance				
		Depreciation				
		Other Expense*				
		TOTAL DIRECT EXPENSE				
		TOTAL COST & EXPS.				
		Operating Gain (or Loss)				
		Commission Receipts and Other Income				
		NET INCOME (LOSS) FROM OPERATIONS				
		Due to or (-) from Client				
		AVAILABLE FOR OVERHEAD AND PROFIT				

PRESS HARD — OMIT CENTS

FORM F-17 (7/73)

FIGURE 9.11 WOR from a Contractor

Operating Statistics: This section provides space to report customer counts and sales and check averages by shift or satellite unit. Results are available by day, by week, by area, or whatever breakdown suits the specific need.

Labor Cost: Labor cost is recorded in two areas; first in number of employees and second in the regular, overtime, and total hours worked. This is used to compare results to standard for labor hours. An additional item, average sale per hour worked, provides information on productivity. The contractor uses this to compare one location to another. This is not usually found in the independent's WOR.

Operating Summary: This section provides a weekly profit and loss statement and a period-to-date (two, three, or four weeks) profit and loss statement. It has space for budget percentages also. The completed summary allows the manager to assess the total operation's performance for the week and for an accounting period to date.

This section is used differently by different units to suit their specific needs.

Comments: The comments section fills several of a contractor's needs. It provides space for a manager to record his or her own needs. It is also a communication device between management levels. The WOR for a contractor is sent "up the line" to the district manager and, in some cases, to an accounting department representative. The comments section allows the unit manager to certify that he or she has recognized a deviation from standard and is taking action to correct it.

The example WOR for a B&I location of a contractor has been designed to accommodate the needs of numerous and varied locations and levels of management. Every contractor endeavors to use a single report for multiple needs. This allows for easier training of managers, better communications between management levels, and coordination of the WOR with accounting department data.

Most of the major contractors have WORs designed specifically for each industry segment. Some examples follow.

Vending WOR

Figure 9.12 is an example of a WOR used by a contractor for a vending location. By analyzing the WORs previously covered, a knowledgeable evaluation of this vending WOR is possible.

College and University WOR

Campus dining operations usually have a weekly operating report specifically designed to provide relevant information required by a foodservice director. Sales information would include board plans, faculty clubs, food courts, and other areas present on a campus. Labor cost information would include the separate cost of student labor. Summaries would compare all categories of sales and costs each week and period to date for the financial plan previously prepared for that specific campus dining operation.

Health Care

Health care foodservice operators have several types of WORs. They differ in need and reporting format based on the type of contract; a P&L requires a different WOR than a management fee. Each WOR fulfills the specific informational need.

There are as many WOR forms and designs as there are companies. Most of them have the same basic format and report the same basic information. What's important is that the form used at a specific location reports the information that managers need.

WEEKLY OPERATING REPORT

BUSINESS & INSTITUTION GROUP

VENDING UNITS

Week Ending	Period No.	Unit Name	Unit Number
1 2 3 4			

DETAIL

Payroll	Current Week	Period to Date
Payroll Regular		
Holiday & Vacation		
Payroll Transfers		
TOTAL PAYROLL [1]		
Operating Expenses		
Vehicle Expense		
Repair/Maintenance		
Cash (Over) Short		
Taxes/Licenses		
Uniforms		
Laundry		
Theft Loss		
Replacements		
Paper/Other		
Cleaning Supplies		
Insurance		
Freight		
Equipment Rental		
TOTAL OPRTG. EXPENSE [2]		
Warehouse & Office		
Rent		
Repairs & Maintenance		
Utilities		
Warehouse Supplies		
Property Tax		
TOTAL WHSE. & OFFICE [3]		
General & Administrative		
Telephone & Telegraph		
Office Expense		
Travel		
Bank Charges		
Money Hauling		
TOTAL GEN'L & ADMIN. [4]		

FORM V-19 (9/74)

OPERATING SUMMARY

Budget %		Current Week	%	Period to Date	%
	SALES		100.0		100.0
	Cost of Sales: Merchandise				
	Rebates & Allowances				
	Commissions				
	Sales Tax				
	TOTAL COST OF SALES				
	GROSS PROFIT				
	Other Income				
	TOTAL GROSS PROFIT AND OTHER INCOME				
	Operating Expenses: Payroll [1]				
	Cost Related to Payroll				
	Operating Expenses [2]				
	Selling				
	Equipment Charges and Vehicle Rentals				
	TOTAL OPERATING EXPENSES				
	OPERATING PROFIT				
	Facilities & Administrative Expense: Warehouse & Office [3]				
	Facility Depreciation				
	General & Administrative [4]				
	TOTAL FACILITIES AND ADMINISTRATIVE EXPENSE				
	NET INCOME (LOSS) FROM OPERATION				

COMMENTS:

Unit Manager's Signature   Date

DIVISION OFFICE

FIGURE 9.12 Vending WOR

THE FOOD COST CONTROL CYCLE

Over 85 percent of all cost control problems in the institutional foodservice sector are in three areas: food cost, labor cost, and cash control. A system that methodically reports and ultimately controls these three areas has a spillover effect, controlling all other areas of costs.

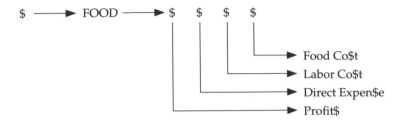

FIGURE 9.13 Warner's Law

Labor cost can easily be controlled by reporting the number of labor hours worked each week and their related dollar cost. Cash can be controlled by adhering to basic accounting and audit practices. The cash is either there, or it is not. When there is a discrepancy, there are some standard procedures to follow.

Food cost control is a different matter. The food used by a location is handled by many people—receiving personnel, cooks, and servers. Theft can be a major problem driving food costs out of hand. A food cost reporting system must cover every occasion of raw material handling, serving, and inventory and ordering.

One principle for an institutional foodservice operation is what I modestly call Warner's Law. That is: $ → FOOD → $$$. Translated, that means "Money to Food to *More* Money." That "more money" must be sufficient to pay for food, labor, direct expenses, and profit. Figure 9.13 represents Warner's Law.

The law covers seven basic steps. Each step requires some administrative effort to contain costs as the food is processed and sold to the customer. These seven basic steps are:

Step 1: Predict food production requirements.
Step 2: Order those requirements systematically.
Step 3: Receive materials properly checked and stored.
Step 4: Produce the menu items to be sold.
Step 5: Sell the results of production.
Step 6: Record the results of the sale.
Step 7: Analyze the recorded results and predict again.

Figure 9.14 is a representation of this cycle.

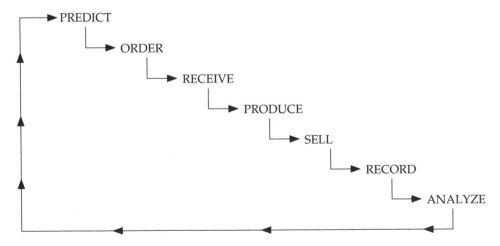

FIGURE 9.14 The Food Cost Control Cycle

Step 1: Predict

Every well-managed institutional foodservice uses some form of production sheet. That form provides details of the forecast sale of each menu item, the number of each item actually produced, the number sold, and comments. Figure 9.15 is an example of such a form used at the urban office building.

Note that the heading on the form provides desirable secondary data:

CYCLE: Which menu cycle is in effect?
DAY: Which day of the week is the service?
DATE: What is the date of planned service?
WEATHER: What is the forecasted weather?
EXPECTED CUSTOMERS: How many customers are expected?
HELP: How many employee meals are to be served?
TOTAL: What is the expected number of meals to be produced?

The answers to these questions are used to predict the day's production needs and to establish an historical database for future planning.

The main body of the form then allows for a listing of the menu, a record of average sales for the last three times an item was served, a prediction of the number (units) expected to be sold this time, the total amount actually produced, the actual sales of each item, and a space for the comments of the production manager.

The prediction of the number of units to be sold requires a fact-gathering system (step 6), which consists of past sales records, menu cycles, past production sheets, cashier's reports, and similar data.

The production sheet provides the manager a detailed forecast of what he or she can expect to sell. A food order is then prepared to fulfill the production needs. By summarizing the production forecast for the coming week, a manager has a detail of the next week's order requirements.

Properly and accurately preparing the production sheet and recording its results is the first point of control. A good production sheet leads to good predictions, which is step 1 of our cycle.

Step 2: Order

Daily and weekly stock and order forms were shown in Figures 9.5 and 9.6. These two forms are the control devices used to order the necessary foodstuffs to fulfill production needs.

Ordering is not purchasing. Purchasing is selecting vendors and negotiating prices. Ordering is merely deciding how much of each item is needed for a specific period. Ordering decisions are based on production requirements (number of items or units) arrived at from predictions.

After units of expected sales have been established, the food orders can be properly evaluated. This is the second point of control. The daily and weekly stock and order forms allow a review of inventory to see if requirements are in stock or need to be ordered. Controlled inventories are a prerequisite to correct ordering and must be a part of the administrative procedures.

A sound control policy is this: Order for production . . . produce for sale. That means placing all orders because you anticipate producing specific menu items. Do not order merely to get those items in inventory.

The dollar amount of any single inventory item should not exceed the predicted one-week use of that item. The dollar amount of total food inventory should not exceed one week's food cost usage.

NAME OF CORPORATION

Cycle	Day	Date	Weather
Expected Customers		Help	Total Expected

PRODUCTION SHEET

ITEM	AVERAGE SALES LAST 3 PERIODS	PREDICTION			TOTAL PROD	SALES			COMMENT TIME OUT

FIGURE 9.15 Production Sheet

By following the "order for production, produce for sale" rule, we maintain control over ordering, step 2 of the cycle.

Step 3: Receive

This step requires administrative and operational procedures to which the managers must strictly adhere. Some of those are:

■ Purchase specifications for all products.
■ Receiving procedures to ensure the proper weight, count, and quality of goods received.
■ Storage procedures to ensure the proper temperature in refrigerators and freezers, conditions in dry storage, and handling of all materials received.
■ The availability of the proper equipment to accurately receive and record. Proper scales, forms, office equipment, and sometimes computer terminals are all requirements for proper receiving.

Receiving is a key step in the control process. It is at this point that you make sure you get what you pay for, in the proper amounts and condition.

Each location requires receiving and storage standards suited to the particular facility. Sometimes the layout of the host organization may create problems. Some self-operated locations such as plants, factories, hospitals, and correctional institutions have one receiving area for the entire facility. Some office building kitchens are on an upper floor, while receiving is on the ground floor.

Regardless of the problems, though, receiving and storage must be controlled. Receiving, step 3 of our cycle, is crucial.

Step 4: Produce

The guide to production is prediction. The same administrative control form used to record the prediction should guide the production. Production must be controlled to conform to the prediction of expected sales. Remember . . . order for production . . . produce for sale. If the sale is not forecast, the item should not be produced.

Overproduction causes leftovers and waste. Underproduction causes shortages and customer complaints. They are equally troublesome.

Production is not complete until yield has been checked at every point of production. For yield to be accurate, a standard recipe is required. When supplies are drawn from inventory to produce a specific amount of an item, those supplies should match the standard recipe or procedure. After production, the yield should be verified to ensure that the expected number of units (portions) were actually obtained from the recipe or procedure.

After production is complete, all menu items are shipped to the point of sale. Various methods are used to maintain temperature from the production point to the selling point. Steam table pans in hot carts, sheet pans in cold carts, bulk items in both hot and cold carts, and more are used to move the completed product to the point of sale. Unless the shipping container is appropriate—properly insulated, heated, or cooled—and correctly handled, waste and loss will result.

Remember, a kitchen is really a production factory. It produces and ships completed products the same as any other manufacturing facility. Production and its attendant controls is step 4 of our cycle.

Step 5: Sell

Items produced in the kitchen and shipped to the cafeteria, dining room, or other point of sale must be merchandised and sold. That sale must be controlled to produce an appropriate yield. Supervision during the selling process is required to ensure that each item achieves the desired amount of sales dollars.

Some items are portion controlled and cause no problems. Other items are portioned by the server, and a control is required. Where a gallon of soup, stew, sauce, or other "loose" item should yield a specific number of portions, management must make sure that it does.

All points of sale require merchandising to ensure that the customer will want to buy the item. Proper cafeteria displays, appropriate dining room menus and service, and similar efforts are all part of the selling process.

Ensuring that the sale achieves the desired check average via good merchandising and that yields are achieved by correct supervision are all part of selling, step 5 of the food cost control cycle.

Step 6: Record

The primary device used to record sales is the cash register. Modern operations have point-of-sale devices connected to computer terminals. While they are still cash registers, they also gather detailed sales and cost information and transmit it to computers for later analysis.

The cash register or point-of-sale equipment is used to break unit sales into as many categories as possible. Where the equipment is a simple cash register, the information will be limited. Other means may be necessary to count the number of menu items that are paid for at the point of sale. Where the equipment is a modern point-of-sale (POS) machine, a complete menu breakdown is available.

The objective is to record the number of items (units) sold. The fact that menu items have been used does not necessarily mean they have been sold. Waste and/or loss may have occurred between the production and selling steps. A complete record of exactly what was sold is required.

A POS system helps control ordering, production, and sales by providing such information as:

■ Sales by units
■ Sales by dollar amounts
■ Sales by meal periods or budget categories
■ Sales by food cost control categories

The management concept of control—establish standards and compare results to standards—begins with a method of recording results, the sixth step to food cost control.

Step 7: Analyze

All predictions made in step 1 of the system are based on an analysis of step 6. The results of selling, properly recorded, can be entered on the original production sheet (Figure 9.15) and on other forms that record sales in dollars.

Completion of the production sheet provides a record of the actual number of each menu item sold, whether or not that item sold out prior to the end of the meal period, if the number sold matches the number produced and shipped to the point of sale, and any other information that the manager wishes to record for later analysis.

Analyzing is the last step in the food cost control process, and probably the most important. Sound and effective analysis allows for sound and effective predictions. These lead to improved production planning and better inputs for the next round of the cycle.

$ → FOOD → $$$$ (money to food to more money). It's more than a rule. It is a process by which the foodservice director ensures that food cost stays within budget.

THE ACCOUNTING FUNCTION

Accounting is the language of business. It is a system used by businesses to record financial information, present it to investors to raise working capital, communicate with the Internal Revenue Service (IRS), and, in general, track performance.

The language of accounting is usually dictated by the Financial Accounting Standards Board (FASB), a nationally recognized organization of Certified Public Accountants (CPAs). This is the guideline under which corporations and other business organizations establish their own accounting standards.

The Self-Operators

Accounting standards in many self-operated facilities are not designed to suit the need of a foodservice organization. They are often governed by standards established for their respective type of business or service activity. For example: A plant or office foodservice must follow the accounting methods in place at the business or industry location being serviced. These will not necessarily be compatible with the foodservice industry.

A hospital foodservice director must follow the standard accounting practices of the hospital. This may be a proprietary, voluntary, or governmental facility. Each will have a different accounting system.

A college or university foodservice director must follow the accounting practices of the university's accounting system. This is usually established by the university's controller. The practices serve the needs of a university and not of a foodservice.

A school foodservice manager must follow the accounting practices of the school district. This may be a county, state, or other municipal entity.

A correctional foodservice director must follow the accounting practices of the governing body. Again this may be a city, county, state, or federal system.

In all self-ops, the needs of the host organization guide the accounting function. The needs of a foodservice organization are seldom considered when the accounting system is established.

The Contractors

Accounting standards in most contractor operations are etched in concrete. Deviation from an accounting procedure is not allowed. Adherence to these procedures is usually reviewed periodically by an internal auditor.

While the accounting methods of a contractor are strict, they are usually designed by individuals familiar with the foodservice industry. All major contractors have an accounting procedures manual to assist the manager in following corporate accounting practices. Where a new situation arises that may cause a question by the manager, a procedure almost always exists to answer his or her query.

Figure 9.16 is a table of contents from a food accounting manual for a national contractor. The table lists the following items:

■ Tables and lists
■ Forms samples
■ Cash procedures
■ Inventory and accounts payable
■ Financial ledger and statements
■ Food account directives
■ Corporate insurance
■ Miscellaneous
■ Index of forms

Every accounting procedure that the location foodservice director might use is detailed. Specific forms used for each procedure are also shown. The manual is updated to reflect new accounting practices, and complete revisions are issued as needed.

Most contractors' cost control systems are compatible with their accounting systems. There are exceptions; in some cases, a unit general manager may require additional or separate information for cost control purposes. In those situations, managers may supplement the cost control system of the company with internal methods of their own.

General managers of a contractor-operated facility are likely to have a previously planned cost control system compatible with the accounting system available to them. Whether contractor- or self-operated, though, the accounting procedures and rules of the organization must be adhered to. These procedures won't always be ideal for an institutional foodservice operation.

BREAK-EVEN ANALYSIS, FUNCTION AND USE

Break-even analysis is a tool used by accountants who specialize in the details of cost control. It can also be valuable for the noncommercial foodservice director in forecasting the results of cost control efforts.

Break-even analysis can be complex; many books use various formulas to detail this concept. The methods and context presented here are simplified for use in a typical foodservice. This is not a complete discourse on break-even analysis as practiced by the cost accountants. It does, however, provide the reader with simple, easy-to-use techniques that can be of value in day-to-day operations.

All managers have two basic functions: they make decisions and they take risks. In every area of daily management, particularly planning and cost control, managers make financial decisions that contain an element of risk. Decision making takes managerial courage. A manager who lacks the courage to make a timely decision is usually an ineffective manager.

Break-even analysis can eliminate some of the risk in making decisions regarding financial management. The basis of the break-even concept is the break-even point (BEP) formula. BEP can answer such questions as:

1. What gross sales amount must be achieved to eliminate the need of an operating subsidy?
2. What must our check average be to reach a given break-even point in sales?

SECTION	FORM NO.	DESCRIPTION	PROCEDURE NO.
		Tables and Lists	
F-1		Code of Accounts	F1-1
F-1		Source Guide	F1-2
F-1		Mailing Schedule	F1-3
F-1		FIT-FICA Tax Tables	F1-4
F-1		Tax Codes	F1-5
F-1		Employee Meals by State	F1-6
F-1		National Stockroom Forms Listing	F1-7
F-1		Document Retention and Filing	F1-8
F-1		Glossary	F1-9
F-2		**Forms Samples**	F2
F-3		**Report Samples**	F3
		Cash Procedures	
F-4		Overview	F4-1
F-4		Cash Collections	F4-1
F-4	12	Imprest Cash Funds and Petty Cash Funds	F4-1
F-4	7, 29	Daily Stand Sales Report	F4-2
F-4	17	Daily Cash Register Reading Report	F4-3
F-4		Endorsement of Checks	F4-3A
F-4	13	Sweda Programmable Cash Register Daily Sales Versus Usage Reconciliation Procedure	F4-3B
F-4	1, 50	Weekly Cash Report and Checks Cashed and Deposited	F4-4
F-4		Tips	F4-6
F-4		Bank Deposits	F4-7
F-4	11	Surprise Cash Register Count	F4-8
F-4		Temporary Imprest Fund Increases	F4-9
F-4	41	Accounts Receivable	F4-10
F-4	714	Function Contract	F4-12
		Payroll	
F-5		Overview	F5-1
F-5		Wage Assignments	F5-1
F-5		FAS Payroll Report	F5-2
F-5	1566	Employee Profile and Change Form	F5-3
F-5	1689	Local Wage Payments	F5-4
F-5	1675	One-Time Employee Payroll Register	F5-5
F-5		State Legal Time Limits to Pay Terminated Employee	F5-6
F-5	1690	Application for Employment	F5-7
F-5	574	Voucher for Payroll Deduction	F5-8
		Inventory and Accounts Payable	
F-6		Overview	F6-1
F-6		Supplier Master File Maintenance	F6-2
F-6	906	Local Purchase Orders	F6-3
F-6	912-C	National Account Supplier Purchase Orders	F6-4
F-6	910-C	National Office Purchase Orders	F6-5
F-6	916	Requisition	F6-6
F-6	1857	Ordering Receiving Inventory Control #1857	F6-8
F-6	1861, 1861-2	Daily Purchase Records	F6-12
F-6	1861-1	DPR Summary	F6-13
F-6	279	M & E Transfer	F6-15
F-6	1859	Closing Inventory and Unpaid Bills	F6-17
F-6	910-C, 911-A	Capital Asset Processing - Overview	F6-18
F-6	910-C, 911-A	Capital Asset Processing - Receiving Operations	F6-19
		Financial Ledger and Statements	
F-7		Overview	F7-1
		Food Account Directive	
F-8		Cash Procedures	F8-1
F-8		Bank Deposits	F8-2
F-8		Purchase of Change	F8-3
F-8		Receiving and Invoice Processing	F8-4
F-8		Charge Sales	F8-5
F-8		Payroll	F8-6
		Corporate Insurance	
F-10	650, FL-314	Certificate of Insurance/Purchase Agreement	F10-1
F-10	661	All-Risk Property Insurance	F10-2
F-10	663, CG-30216-B	Motor Vehicle Insurance	F10-3
F-10	860, CG-30200-D	Comprehensive General Liability	F10-4
F-10	664	Worker's Compensation Insurance	F10-5
		Miscellaneous	
F-11	803	Expense Reports	F11-2
F-11		Change of Management Report	F11-4
F-11	1284, 1285	Open Operation	F11-5
F-11	1284, 1288	Closed Operation	F11-6

FIGURE 9.16 Food Accounting Manual (Courtesy of Canteen Corporation, Spartanburg, SC)

3. What vending sales amount must be achieved to pay a specific commission rate and still achieve a fair ROI? Or attain a desired net operating profit?

Many other similar questions can be answered by the use of simple break-even analysis methods. BEP is a "what if" for financial planning that affects the cost control system.

The Break-Even Point Formula

The basic BEP formula is:

$$\$FC \div (100\% - \%VC) = BEP$$

The formula uses some basic abbreviations:

FC = fixed cost. This is *always* a dollar amount.
VC = variable cost. This is *always* a percentage amount.
BEP = the break-even point.

In addition, the term contribution margin (CM) is used. Contribution margin is the result of the equation:

$$100\% - VC\%$$

Example:

VC is 60%.
CM = 100%—60% = 40%.
CM is therefore 40%.

The BEP formula can now be shortened to read:

$$\$FC \div CM\% = BEP\$$$

Translated, this states that fixed cost (a *dollar* amount) divided by contribution margin (a *percentage* amount) equals break-even point (a *dollar* amount).

An additional term introduced in Chapter 5 and used for financial planning and cost control is return on investment (ROI). Evaluating the necessary sales volume to achieve a satisfactory ROI is one of the uses of break-even analysis.

To review, there are five abbreviations used for financial planning with break-even analysis:

■ FC is fixed costs
■ VC is variable costs
■ CM is contribution margin
■ BEP is break-even point
■ ROI is return on investment

Each of these will be used in our review of the break-even point formula.

Categorizing Costs

To use BEP analysis, all costs in a foodservice must be identified as either fixed or variable. Cost accountants also use other terms, such as semi-fixed or semi-variable, but these are not necessary for our purposes.

- A fixed cost is one that remains at the same *dollar* amount regardless of sales volume.
- A variable cost is one that remains at the same *percentage to sales* amount regardless of sales volume.

Fixed costs, as a dollar amount, remain constant despite any increase or decrease in sales volume. That dollar amount may change to a new figure due to an increase in costs, but it will not fluctuate as a result of an increase or decrease in sales.

Variable costs are those with dollar amounts that increase or decrease in direct proportion to sales. If sales increase, the dollar amount also increases in direct proportion on a percentage basis. The opposite occurs for a sales decrease.

Costs in a Noncommercial Foodservice

There are three basic categories of costs in most noncommercial foodservice operations: food cost, labor cost, and direct or indirect expenses. While different accounting policies may use different category names, these three usually serve to describe any costs incurred by a noncommercial foodservice.

Food cost is always a variable cost. A menu can be costed out to evaluate the ratio (percentage) to sales expected from a specific menu and the resulting sales mix. In Chapter 5, "Financial Planning," a form was used to evaluate the expected food cost of different facilities.

Labor cost in noncommercial foodservice operations is nearly always a fixed cost based on the number of labor hours needed to fulfill the service requirements. Those labor hours in turn become salaries and wages—a fixed cost.

Payroll-related costs have a direct correlation to payroll costs. The four mandated payroll taxes are a direct percentage of payroll. Employee benefits are sometimes related solely to the number of individuals receiving those benefits; however, payroll taxes and benefits are evaluated by most managers as a direct percentage of payroll. As a result, labor cost—salaries and wages, payroll taxes, and employee benefits—can be considered a fixed cost in most cases.

Direct and/or indirect expenses are usually both fixed and variable costs, depending on the specific item. Some have both a fixed and variable nature. For break-even analysis, a table of direct/indirect expenses should be made and each item categorized as either fixed, variable, or a combination of both. Some examples are:

- Paper goods: a variable cost. If paper goods are used to serve food to the customer, their cost will increase or decrease in direct proportion to the number of customers served.
- Cleaning supplies: a fixed cost. The primary use of cleaning supplies is for area cleaning and operation of the dish machine. Since the same area is cleaned every day and the dish machine is usually operated the same number of hours regardless of customer count, the cost of cleaning supplies is fixed.
- Linen and laundry: a fixed cost in most cases. Since the majority of linen and laundry costs go to clean employee uniforms and the head count of employees is fixed, the resulting laundry cost is also fixed.
- Maintenance & repairs: These may have both fixed and variable components. For example, service contracts with an annual fee are a fixed cost. But the annual expected cost of repairs can be budgeted as a percentage to sales, which is a variable cost.
- Depreciation: a fixed cost. In locations where a capital investment has been made, a specific depreciation schedule is usually followed. Annual depreciation will remain the same regardless of the sales volume.
- Fees & commissions: These may be either fixed or variable. If the item is charged

FIGURE 9.17

Fixed/Variable Cost Analysis, Foodservice

Category		Fixed Cost ($)	Variable Cost (%)
SALES	$1,387,500	—	—
Cost of Sales	547,750		39.47
Labor Cost	640,011	640,011	
OPERATING EXPENSES			
Paper Goods	6,937		.5
Cleaning Supplies	6,938	6,938	
Linen & Laundry	27,750	27,750	
Replacements	27,750	27,750	
Insurance	13,875	13,875	
Repairs & Mte.	15,875	2,000	1.0
Pest Control	1,200	1,200	
Admin. Charge	69,375		5.0
Others Costs	33,875	20,000	1.0
Management Fee	69,375		5.0
TOTAL COSTS	$1,460,711	$739,524	51.97%

as a set fee, the category is fixed. If the item is paid or charged as a ratio to sales, the category is variable.

Figure 9.17 is a chart that can be used to evaluate all areas of costs and determine the total dollar amount of fixed costs and the percentage amount of variable costs. The income statement or pro forma budget forecast is used as a model, allowing actual numbers to be used in the evaluation. The numbers shown in Figure 9.18 have been taken from the urban office building example, Figure 5.10.

Each cost is listed under fixed or variable, the resulting dollar or percentage figure is posted under the appropriate column to the right, and a total dollar amount of fixed costs and percentage amount of variable costs is achieved. Total fixed costs are $739,524. Total variable costs are 51.97 percent. These can then be used in the break-even analysis formula.

FIGURE 9.18

Fixed/Variable Cost Analysis, Vending

Category		Fixed Cost ($)	Variable Cost (%)
Projected Sales	$1,750,000	—	—
Est. Product Cost	618,000		35.3
Labor Cost	213,200	213,200	
Other Costs	130,100	7,600	7.0
Depreciation	90,010	90,010	
Branch Charges	35,000		2.0
Commissions	226,550		12.95
Food Ops Subsidy	100,000	100,000	
TOTALS	$1,412,860	$410,810	57.25%

Using the BEP Formula

To answer question 1 on page 216 ("What gross sales amount must be achieved to eliminate the need for an operating subsidy?"), the formula can be used as follows.

Step 1: Evaluate contribution margin (CM):
100% − 51.97% = 48.03%
CM is therefore 48.03%

Step 2: The formula:
FC ÷ CM = BEP
OR: 739,524 ÷ .4803 = $1,539,713

The amount of sales needed to eliminate the subsidy is $1,539,713.

The answer to question 2 ("What must our check average be to reach a given break-even point in sales?") can be found by an analysis of previous budget data. From Figure 5.3, we get the following:

■ 1,790 average customers per day projected for all categories of sales.
■ Sales were forecast as $5,500 per day.
■ There are 250 operating days per year.
■ $1,387,500 annual sales.
■ A resulting overall check average of $3.073 per day ($5,500 ÷ 1,790).

Step 1: Convert projected BEP for annual sales to daily sales:
$1,539,713 ÷ 250 = $6,159

Step 2: Divide BEP daily sales by present average daily customer count:
$6,159 ÷ 1,790 = $3.44

The necessary overall average daily check average must be $3.44, an increase of 37 cents.

Other measurements can be made in a similar manner if a simple cafeteria customer count, a combination of cafeteria and dining room customer count, or any variation is needed. Based on these results, managers can decide to raise menu prices, alter some services, or take other actions, so long as they stay within service guidelines.

The third question, "How much vending sales must be achieved to provide a fair ROI or net operating profit?" requires a different analysis. We'll use the summary pro forma budget (Figure 6.23) from Chapter 6.

Remember the parameters of the example case:

■ 10,000 employees.
■ Two shifts, five days per week.
■ 50 weeks per year of operation.
■ The vending operation must provide $100,000 per year to subsidize the manual foodservice.
■ Capital investment for equipment is projected as $450,000.
■ Desired ROI is 75 percent.
■ Commission structure set at 12.95 percent.

Let's change the example case ROI from 75 percent to a desired 80 percent and evaluate both the sales required to achieve that 80 percent and the weekly per cap to accomplish that objective.

Step 1: Evaluate the CM:
100.0%—57.25% = 42.75% CM

Step 2: Evaluate the 80% ROI as a dollar amount:
$450,050 capital investment
80% X $450,050 = $360,040 desired ROI

Step 3: The desired ROI, as a dollar amount, is now treated as a fixed cost. ADD the desired ROI to the fixed cost and divide by the contribution margin:
$410,810(FC) + $360,040 (ROI) ÷ .4275 (CM) = $1,803,158

The required gross annual sales to achieve an 80 percent ROI is $1,803,158.

To evaluate the necessary weekly per cap required for this result, make the following calculation:

Step 1: Divide the necessary annual sales by the quoted 50 weeks of operation to get average weekly sales:
$1,803,158 ÷ 50 = $36,063 average weekly sales

Step 2: Divide average weekly sales by population to evaluate the necessary average weekly per cap:
$36,063 ÷ 10,000 = $3.606 per cap

The required per cap to achieve an 80 percent ROI is $3.60–$3.61.

In our original pro forma budget, a 75 percent ROI required a $3.50 per cap. If the operator wants to increase the ROI from 75 percent to 80 percent, he or she must find a way to increase the average per cap 10 cents, from $3.50 to $3.60. That might be accomplished by a price increase, a change in the merchandise mix, introduction of new items, or a variety of other options.

In this example, instead of a desired ROI the operator wants a 20 percent net on sales, regardless of the ROI. What per cap must be achieved?

Step 1: The desired 20 percent net is now treated as a variable cost. Evaluate a new CM:
57.25% (VC) + 20% desired net = 77.25%
100.00%—77.25% = 22.75% (CM)

Step 2: Use the formula to evaluate the necessary BEP:
$410,810 (FC) ÷ .2275 (CM) = $1,805,758 (net profit at 20%)

Step 3: Evaluate the required weekly per cap:
$1,805,758 ÷ 50 weeks = $36,115
Divide by the 10,000 population:
$36,115 ÷ 10,000 = $3.61 required per cap.

A per cap of $3.61, with all other statistics the same, should produce a 20 percent net operating profit.

SUMMARY

Cost control management is controlling the operating costs of a business enterprise to carry out the business plan. The plan is rooted in the objective. The cost control system is rooted in the financial plan. Controlling is a method, part of the plan.

Controlling is a basic management process composed of four steps: establishing standards, comparing results to those standards, identifying deviations in operation from standards, and implementing action plans to correct the deviations.

The cost control system must reflect the needs of the individual foodservice operation. A key point is that systems merely report; managers control. A cost control system reports to a manager all of the information to compare results to standards. The action taken by the manager is the control.

Different industry segments have their own control needs and resulting processes. Control systems in an institutional foodservice revolve around four basic areas: sales, cost of sales, labor costs, and direct expenses. There are three questions to be asked in each of these areas to establish a cost control system. What information is needed? How often is it needed? How will it be gathered? Each of the four areas requires an answer to these three questions as part of the cost control system.

Accounting is the language of business. It is also an integral part of the cost control system. Methods will differ from industry segment to industry segment, between self-operated locations, and within contract-managed companies.

Self-operated facilities always follow the accounting procedures of the host organization. These may or may not be compatible with sound cost control practice for their foodservice. In many cases the foodservice director must develop an internal cost control system separate from the accounting procedures in place.

Contract management companies all have accounting practices and procedures manuals. These usually complement sound cost control systems for foodservice operations.

Break-even analysis is a cost accountant's tool valuable to the noncommercial foodservice director in a variety of ways.

10

Sales and Marketing

There is an old salesman's saying, "Nothing happens till somebody sells something." That is certainly true for contract foodservice management.

Selling a new account puts the wheels in motion. It starts the process of:

- Preparing a sales proposal, often in response to a request for proposal (RFP)
- Making the sales presentation and closing the sale
- Preparing a new unit opening plan
- Identifying and training a new management staff
- Recruiting an hourly staff
- Establishing financial and service objectives
- Preparing an operations plan to suit the specific needs of the location, including all of the management tasks described in earlier chapters
- Preparing a marketing plan for the particular location

The sales proposal and RFP start the process. The sales contract brings it to fruition.

Every contract management company expends a great deal of time, money, and effort to selling new accounts. Each year they anticipate losing a certain number of old accounts, selling a greater number of new accounts, and ending the year with an overall increase in total gross sales and bottom-line profits from the new accounts sold.

New accounts alone will not necessarily increase gross sales or improve the profitability of the contractor. The new business sold must be in the right segment and region and must be sufficiently profitable to fulfill the corporation's financial objectives. The type of account (B&I, campus dining, health care, or other) and the method of contracting (profit and loss, management fee, subsidized, or other) all have a bearing on the ultimate profitability of the account. The sales and marketing staff establishes and implements a sales and marketing program.

This chapter provides the reader with an understanding of the new account sales process for a contractor and the marketing work behind it and analyzes the development of a marketing program for a single operation, either contract or self-operated.

The lifeblood of the contractor is the retention of old accounts and the acquisition of new accounts. Success for the location general manager, contracted or self-operated, can result from marketing the existing operation to maximize potential sales and profits.

Upon completion of this chapter, readers should know and understand:

- Sales as part of marketing
- The sales function of the contract organizations
- What an RFP is

- How a bid proposal is prepared, a sales presentation made, an award received, and a contract negotiated
- Client relations, the key to account retention
- Marketing at the location level
- Branding, the latest marketing tool

SALES: A PART OF MARKETING

Marketing is looking at the needs of the buyer rather than the needs of the seller. Marketing is applied management. Marketing is the overall plan to identify the wants and develop products and services that fill the needs of a consumer group. This is all true, and it's all equally applicable in foodservice management.

Marketing, if it's meaningful, involves sales. But in institutional foodservice, it's sometimes unclear who the customer really is.

The buyer of the contractor's services is not usually the consumer, but rather a purchasing agent, committee, or corporate liaison. The consumers are the recipients of the contractor's services: the employees and executives of a B&I facility; the students, faculty, and staff of a campus dining operation; the patients, doctors, and staff of a hospital; and the inmates at a correctional facility. In each case, the buyer purchases a service for use by other individuals, the end users or customers. The seller—the contract management company—must therefore address not only the perceived needs of the buyer but also the actual needs of the end users. These perceived and actual needs are not always identical.

Marketing in a contract foodservice management organization usually has a high priority. A look at each of the organization charts of the four top tier corporations in Chapter 3 shows a marketing vice-president at the corporate level of each. This indicates the importance these organizations attach to marketing.

Each vice-president of marketing helps create the organizational design that best meets market needs. That design reflects the personal philosophy of the marketing executives and changes when the marketing department does.

All of the major contractors place heavy emphasis on marketing. Each contractor has grown to its present position through acquisition rather than internal growth. When a major contractor decides to enter a new segment, it is more likely to acquire a smaller, successful contractor than start a new venture. The histories of the major contractors verifies this.

One example is ARA Services; in its early years, ARA became a full-line service company by acquiring a foodservice contractor (Slater) and adding it to ARA's vending company. That changed its focus from simple vending to full-line foodservice and vending management.

Later, as ARA desired further diversification into the correctional foodservice management market, it acquired Szabo, a company already established in that field. This added a new market segment to ARA's existing foodservice organization.

Each major national contractor grew and diversified in the same way. Today most contractor marketing programs are either marketing or sales driven. Some are a combination. The industry has matured to the point that each company offers about the same services. Only by strong marketing and sales efforts can the individual corporation anticipate further growth and profits.

Target Segments

Recall from Chapter 2 that the following percentages of each noncommercial segments are self-operated:

10–20 percent of business and industry
40–50 percent of campus dining
50–55 percent of all hospitals and other health care operations
90–95 percent of all schools
95–98 percent of all correctional facilities

Each of these markets (B&I less so) is the target of the sales efforts of the major contractors (and most of the minors). While some new business is obtained by winning an account from its present contractor, the greatest potential for growth in all segments is among companies never before contracted.

SELLING THE CONTRACT FOODSERVICE

Increasingly, corporations are downsizing—cutting whole layers of management and moving decision-making authority and responsibility to lower levels of management. In the contract foodservice business, this means individual segment executives and their subordinate regional and district managers are usually responsible for getting new accounts.

Most of the contractors have developed a sales staff specializing in one or more industry segments. While there are similarities in selling new accounts in each segment, there are also major differences in locating the potential buyer, soliciting the RFP, preparing the sales proposals, and making the sale.

Each contractor has its own method of selecting and training sales personnel. They all place a strong emphasis on operational knowledge and/or experience. It is common to develop a sales team whose key members have substantial operating experience to better identify prospects and sell new accounts.

The sales team for a segment, district, or region usually consists of a sales representative, a district or regional executive, and, in some cases, one or more foodservice directors or staff specialists in that district or region.

The sales representative is responsible for finding prospective clients, making the initial contact, getting the RFP, and coordinating the sales effort.

The district or regional executive assembles a survey team to evaluate the potential service needs and financial prospects and provide the details of the pro forma (Remember that a pro forma is a forecast of one or more years' income and expense—the same, in essence, as a budget forecast.)

The foodservice directors or district staff personnel may be part of the survey team. Each contributes his or her specialized knowledge and skills to the evaluation of the site and the potential service needs and financial opportunities.

On occasion, a sales team may encounter an opportunity beyond their ability to respond effectively. Usually the next executive up the corporate ladder will enlist help from the marketing personnel, borrowing staff experts for the occasion. These people may come from another segment of the corporation or from another division within the same segment.

This is often the case when a district or regional manager encounters a sales opportunity in a segment where he or she has insufficient knowledge or experience. A manager may have little experience, for example, with correctional institutions or elementary school systems. Usually a sales team will be established to get that account.

Identifying Prospective Clients

Each area sales representative identifies prospective clients in his or her geographic area(s) or industry segments. Usually there are three basic areas of opportunity:

- As mentioned above, any self-operated facilities in the area
- Any location currently operated by a competitive contract company
- Any new, newly opened, or relocated business in the area

Each sales rep has methods of tracking this activity. Corporate staff services can provide information on major corporations considering a move to the region, new building permits issued in the area, local self-operated facilities, and so on. Whatever the level of assistance, the sales representative is the bird dog, responsible for making the initial contact and opening the way for the sale.

The Request for Proposal

Bids from contractors are most often solicited by the RFP. All government and most major corporate sites will issue an RFP. While many new sales are made by direct contact and negotiation, a large percentage are made by a response to an RFP.

A routine schedule is usually followed by both the agency or company issuing the RFP and the contractors preparing the bid. The following is a typical sequence of events:

1. Preparation and disclosure of the RFP to potential bidders
2. Holding of a pre-bid conference to allow prospective bidders to clarify the (RFP's) contents
3. Site visit by the sales team to compare information received from the RFP and actual conditions at the site
4. Preparation of the pro forma
5. Preparation of the bid proposal
6. The sales presentation
7. Obtaining and negotiating the contract

The RFP is usually prepared by the purchasing department. For new construction, the RFP may be prepared for the architect by a subcontractor specializing in this work.

The responsibility for RFP preparation, the solicitation of bids, bid evaluation, and the selection of a successful bidder are performed differently from segment to segment. Contractors' sales representatives are usually cognizant of the standard practices for their particular areas.

The purpose of an RFP is to persuade interested contractors to bid for desired services; a well-written RFP provides the information necessary to prepare a qualified bid. This includes:

- A description of the services to be performed by the contractor
- Existing constraints on those services
- Physical plant facilities that will be made available
- New facilities, if any, that must be provided by the contractor
- A history (if it is an existing operation) of previous financial results
- Employment populations, their historic fluctuations, and expectations for future population levels
- Type of bid desired—management fee, profit and loss, commission, or subsidized (In some cases the bidders are asked to identify *their* favored contract type.)
- Bidder's qualifications, experience, and plans for servicing the account, including staffing patterns, financial projections, operating plans, marketing plans, corporate staff support to the location general manager, and so on.
- Financial capability and responsibility of the prospective bidder (this is usually

secured with a performance bond requirement, proof of insurance, sample balance sheets, and other relevant documents).

The RFP should detail services desired by the organization and how the contractor should perform those services.

Figure 10.1 is a table of contents from an RFP for a campus dining facility. This is typical for that industry segment. Other RFPs are similar but may be more extensive.

An RFP prepared by a U.S government agency might include the need for compliance with federal requirements and laws including the new Americans with Disabilities Act (ADA), anti-discrimination laws, affirmative action programs, and more.

Each respondent to an RFP makes a commitment to fulfill all bid requirements. Obviously, the contractor must be able to do so.

FIGURE 10.1

Example Table of Contents, Request for Proposal (RFP), Campus Dining

PART I
> Bid Schedule and RFP Timeline
> Proposal Form
> Calls for Proposal (Advertisement)
> Bid Proposals

PART II
> Proposer's Qualifications
> Performance Bond
> Mandatory Pre-Bid Conference
> Basis of Proposal Evaluation
> Award Criteria and Decision
> Applicable Law
> Parties to the Contract
> Contract Assignment
> Contract Length
> Contract Commencement
> Contract Termination
> Conditions:
>> Equipment and Maintenance
>> Quality of Service
>> Operating Conditions
>> Cleaning and Sanitation
>> Trash Removal
>> Contractor's Employees
>> Observation of Rules and Regulations
> Save Harmless Agreement
> Bonds and Insurance
> Records and Audits
> Payments and Reports
> Special Provisions

EXHIBITS:
> A: Description of Foodservice Operations
> B: Past Foodservice Sales
> C: University Calendar
> D: Proposed Price and Portion List, Cash Operations
> E: Proposed Board Plans and Prices
> F: Sample Contract
> G: Bidder's Proposal Form

Pre-Bid Conference

In most cases the client schedules a conference to acquaint bidders with the details of the bid and allow them to question points of the RFP that may be unclear. The client's representative who prepared the RFP usually chairs this meeting.

During the conference the RFP is completely reviewed and prospective bidders ask questions. Upon completion of the meeting, an addendum to the original RFP is usually issued to all interested parties. This addendum summarizes questions and answers from the meeting.

At this point, the attendees make the decision to bid or not to bid. Assigning a sales team, making a site visit, and preparing and presenting a bid all cost time and money. Some potential bidders may decide that this opportunity won't meet financial or strategic objectives. As a result they drop out at this point.

Site Visit

If the contractor organization has made the decision to follow through and bid the job, a site visit by the sales and operating team is scheduled. The team compares the original RFP and follow-up addendum with actual conditions at the site and assembles all other information necessary for the sales proposal. This would include:

- The capital investment needed to improve the physical plant to accomplish operational objectives
- Constraints that will have an effect on the financial plan—items such as an existing trade union contract, equipment and other facility constraints, shift populations, distances from the work sites to the foodservice outlets, and so on.

This data is used for the sales proposal and to:

- Quantify the operational plan to derive a financial forecast for the first year of operation.
- Ascertain whether a management fee, profit and loss, subsidized, or commissioned contract is appropriate, and how best to bid that type of contract.
- Prepare a preliminary location marketing plan to use as part of the proposal if awarded the contract.
- Estimate the opening team requirements, and the related costs, if selected.
- Prepare a plan of operation to include in the proposal (and use later if the bid is accepted).

Preparing the Financial Forecast

An RFP usually provides historical financial information, but a bidder will seldom rely on this data. While those numbers can be used as a basis for evaluation, bidders will usually develop their own financial forecast from the RFP data, the site visit, and other research.

Where a forecast is made for a new facility with no history of operations, bidders usually rely on their own experience operating a like foodservice. Contractors experienced in the segment have a major advantage.

If capital investment is required of the bidder and the contract is multiyear (i.e., a five-year term), the bidder will prepare a five-year pro forma. Although exact conditions cannot be predicted for the extended time period, every effort is made to establish precise first- and second-year performances and closely estimate the remaining contract years.

The pro forma is usually prepared by operating personnel with the assistance of the sales representative. Upon completion, it's reviewed by upper management to ensure accuracy. The smaller the potential bid, the lower the level of management review. The larger the potential bid, particularly if a capital investment is required, the higher the level of management review.

Preparing the Bid Proposal

Upon completion of the site visit and preparation of the pro forma and other required research, a bid proposal is prepared. The written bid proposal is a marketing tool; it addresses the financial considerations of the RFP but also presents the bidder in the best light.

Depending on the size of the new account, the bid proposal may be contained in a simple three-ring binder, or a much larger package with several illustrations may be necessary.

Most contractors will include résumés of one or more general managers they would assign to the location if the bid is successful. Some offer the client a selection of managers from the presented résumés. This is done to indicate their depth of commitment and sensitivity to client needs.

Figure 10.2 shows the table of contents of a bid proposal responding to an RFP like the one shown in Figure 10.1. Note that the bidder has answered all of the client's requests as well as provided additional information to make a favorable impression on the decision makers.

Making the Sales Presentation

After completing the previously described steps, the bidder must make a sales presentation. That's usually the job of the sales representative, assisted by various specialists.

Presentations may be made to one person or a committee. This procedure may cull the list of original bidders down to the final three. Those may be passed on to others for final selection.

The sales presentation is usually a carefully planned show led by the sales rep. The use of specialists from operations, nutrition, finance, and marketing provides expertise and bolsters the presentation, which is designed to convince the potential client that the presenters are best qualified to fulfill its wants and needs. All of the previous work in reviewing the RFP, making the site visit, and preparing the pro forma and bid document is on the line at the sales presentation.

The larger and more profitable the potential account and the more interested the bidder in selling the particular client, the more extensive the sales presentation will be.

Remember—nothing happens till somebody sells something. This is the point where the sale is usually made. While the final decision isn't rendered until all bidders have made their presentations, the sale depends on the ability of the sales team to get its message across at the presentation.

Negotiating the Contract

If the sales presentation is successful and the contractor is awarded the bid, a contract must be negotiated.

Sometimes a sample contract is part of the RFP and becomes the first version of the final contract. If not, the client requests that the contractor prepare an initial contract for review. No matter where the first draft originates, the client must review it to ensure that all financial obligations and service requirements are met.

**Table of Contents
Sample Bid Proposal, Campus Operation**

XYZ CONTRACTOR CORPORATION

I. REQUIRED SUBMITTALS
   Proposal Form
   Alternate Proposal

II. PLAN OF OPERATIONS
   Board Operations Plan
   Cash Operations Plan
   Management Plan
   Staffing Plan
   Sanitation and Maintenance Plan
   Employee Training and Development Plan
   Financial Controls and Accounting

III. MARKETING
   Market Analysis
   Product Analysis
   Competition Analysis
   Branded Concepts Use
   Signature Products Use

IV. FINANCIAL FORECASTS
   First Year's Financial Forecasts
   Five-Year Financial Forecast
   Estimated Return to Campus University

V. PEOPLE
   Executive Profile of XYZ
   Organizational Structure
   Résumés of Executives and Proposed General Managers

VI. EXPERIENCE AND RESOURCES
   Corporate Profile
   Corporate Staff Service, Resources and Client Support
   Background in Campus Dining
   Majoring Catering Experience
   Letters of Commendation

VII. EXHIBITS
   Annual Report . . . Employee Handbook . . . Uniform Literature . . .
   Insurance Certificate . . . Marketing Profile

FIGURE 10.2   Index of a Response to an RFP

For the contractor, a review is required to ensure that it is not bound by any undesirable covenants or other restrictions.

Most contractors have a standard contract for each of the four types of arrangements they enter—management fee, profit and loss, subsidized, and commission. (A sample standard contract for a regional company is shown in Appendix A.) Contractors will try to use one of these model documents, modified to suit the existing location, as the ultimate contract. The smaller the new operation, the simpler the contract; the larger, the more complex. Some government agencies have specific contracts they prefer to use. Other major corporate clients have contracts that their legal departments prefer to use. Whoever provides the first draft, though, there is almost always a need to modify it to satisfy the needs of both client and contractor.

CLIENT RELATIONS

Client relations require ongoing effort on the part of the contractor. From the initial sales contact, through the selling and awarding of the new business, to the ultimate operation of the account, the client must maintain high regard for the management company it's selected.

The primary contact for the contractor within the host company is the client liaison. The basic functions of a liaison—and his/her importance—are covered in Chapter 3.

While the liaison may be the official representative of the client—relating client objectives and policies to the local general manager—he or she is not the primary consumer. The employees, executives, students, and anybody else serviced by the contractor are the primary consumers.

Communications

Contractors should maintain an open line of communication with the client liaison. Location managers and visiting district managers should maintain contact with the liaison; an occasional visit by a high-level manager is helpful, also.

Most of the major contractors have periodic publications they send to their operating personnel. Many of them include every client liaison on the mailing list. This provides each liaison with a continuous reminder of the professional management of the operation.

General Managers

General managers usually meet weekly or biweekly with the liaison to discuss all operating problems, potential solutions, upcoming events, and other items of interest.

General managers also maintain a direct line of communication to all other interested groups: labor union shop stewards, social group chairpersons, sales and marketing executives using the foodservice, and all others considered clients. It is the manager's job to stay ahead of wants and needs. This can be done through food committees of employees, students, staff, and other users. Committees can help plan menus, special events, operating hours, and other related issues. Liaisons should be part of this effort.

The clearer the communication among the general manager, the liaison, and all other consumers, the better the chance of providing satisfactory service.

The District Manager

District managers (DM) make periodic visits to all operating locations in their districts. They, too, must maintain satisfactory communication with both the client and the operation.

During their periodic visits, DMs will make an effort to meet with the client liaison and possibly other interested groups. The objective is to show the contractor's depth of management and a sincere interest in *this* client's wants and needs.

DMs often take clients to lunch, sometimes visiting other area locations of interest to that client. This can be a comparable facility or a commercial operation.

In short, direct contact is maintained between every level of the contractor's organization and every potential customer of the client organization.

Public Relations

Contractors should become involved in community affairs that are important to a client. This may mean providing speakers at professional trade organization meetings, assisting in fund-raising drives and blood banks, participating in Little League, PTA, and more.

This is an area of particular interest for large national organizations; there is a continuing need to reassure local clients that although they are serviced by a national company, it has an interest in local activities.

Some contractors will provide an expert to speak to a local group on relevant topics such as the effects of the Americans with Disabilities Act (ADA) on food-service operations or new recycling regulations.

Every effort is made to establish a public relations program as a part of the overall client relations objective.

Corporate and Client Activities

Every client corporation and facility has its own special personality, management philosophy, and resulting operating style. A contractor must stay in tune with its client and know when something might affect the foodservice contract. For example:

■ The client may encounter a difficult financial year and consider changing corporate strategies.
■ A new manufacturing process may change the service need.
■ A new liaison might be appointed.
■ A change in the client organizational structure might force a change in the operation of the foodservice.
■ An existing subsidized operation may become a profit and loss operation.
■ A university may require a capital investment to improve facilities.
■ A hospital may desire to add a new coffee shop for visitors.

Support Services

A corporation will use a contract management company to operate its foodservice because it feels the contractor offers support services it can't—a fact contractors drive home in the sales proposal and presentation. Every contractor, large and small, tries to sell this idea to potential clients: "We are in the foodservice business and can run your corporate foodservice better than you. We are professionals, and we offer extensive support that you are not in a position to offer yourself."

This is the great appeal of contracting. Support services is the key to that appeal.

The contractor company's departments and personnel are available to the client. Following are some of the services they perform.

Financial Planning

A contractor helps develop financial objectives and operating budgets derived from those objectives.

Financial planning needs differ with the fiscal calendar. Management fee clients, for instance, need their particular accounting calendars matched to those of the client. For other types of contracts, objectives are adjusted to suit both client and contractor. The need for forward planning, cost control systems, and related work differs from location to location.

Capital investment requirements differ depending on the condition of the physical plant. A contractor develops the necessary capital investment budgets and provides the investment for physical plants when a client is not capable of obtaining those funds. Contractual arrangements can be made to protect the client's interests while still allowing the contractor a fair return on investment.

Contractors evaluate client information and to develop forecasts of labor and material costs and other operational requirements. They often employ break-even analysis and other forecasting tools.

Human Resources

A self-operator seldom offers a worthy career path for a foodservice manager; they also seldom have a replacement available if and when they lose a competent manager. And the human resource department (HRD) of the host company won't necessarily know where to find another foodservice manager.

A contractor's HRD can offer assistance. The department maintains a pool of management personnel within its organization. Most HRDs also run training programs for all location personnel and maintain industry appropriate wage and salary information. Contractor HR professionals understand local, state, and federal laws and regulations affecting the foodservice operation. Contractors also have labor relations departments to negotiate with any internal trade unions of the client foodservice.

Specialized Staff

Many clients need specialists who are not part of their own organization. Contractors routinely employ nutritionists, dieticians, cost analysts, marketing specialists, labor lawyers, governmental agency lobbyists, and other professionals clients most often don't have on staff. The services of these specialists are offered as part of the client relations campaign.

When a company hires a foodservice contractor, that contractor's staff services become an extension of the client's organization. Successful client relations depend on the degree to which the contractor provides these services and helps accomplish client objectives.

MARKETING

Marketing is the application of management techniques to identify consumers and to promote and sell products and services to these consumers. Every business requires a specialized marketing effort for its particular products or services.

A successful foodservice director must know how to develop a specific marketing program for his or her location. If not, a marketing expert is needed.

In a contract location, this assistance is usually available from a staff department. At a self-op, assistance may or may not be available from the corporate staff. If not, help must be found from an outside source.

Operations-Level Marketing

Each foodservice, whether B&I, campus dining, health care, or elementary or secondary school, has a specific market. That market is the population eligible to use the foodservice. Unlike the commercial segments of the industry, operators of a noncommercial foodservice *cannot* create their own market. But they *can* create markets within the designated population.

For a location general manager, location marketing consists of using managerial skills to meet the personal foodservice and dining needs of the customers. Location marketing also incorporates facility constraints, menu design and merchandising, pricing policy and structure, financial objectives, host organization foodservice policy, and contractual obligations.

Proper marketing sells the foodservice and the contractor to the client liaison, the customers, and even the contract company's own employees, who want to work for a well-run company.

The Marketing Plan

The marketing plan is a blueprint, a commitment, and a set of marching orders. It unites every element of a foodservice's operation, bringing them together into a force aimed at satisfying a client's wants and needs as thoroughly and effectively as possible.

Each component of the foodservice is assessed in terms of the marketing plan. Some elements are beyond the control of the foodservice director like service hours, service locations, customer base, and capital investment. But others such as menu design, specialized pricing, levels of service, employee skills and training, and sanitation and maintenance standards are subject to manipulation by the director.

A marketing plan has a triangular base. Its points are market analysis, product analysis, and competitor analysis. The data found in these three evaluations are used to develop a location marketing plan.

The market analysis is the identification and selection of customers from the designated population. Who is a candidate to buy the services provided?

The product analysis examines all the services offered and their components. This includes the physical plant, staffing, skills of the staff, decor of the location, locations of the various outlets, and all other items relevant to the product. Product analysis determines what tools are available for customer satisfaction.

The competition analysis is a detailed survey of all other foodservice operations available to the market. Any other commercial facility within reach of the population can be considered competition. In addition, food carried from home—brown bagged—is also competition.

All three, market, product, and competition, must be considered when formulating a marketing plan. These analyses will be applied in the following section to a business and industry location. The same principles can be applied to other industry segments.

Market Analysis

Preparing a market analysis for a B&I operation requires detailed questions about specific characteristics of the target population. The answers should reveal:

- Size of the population, by area, shift, and total. This is usually available from the contract liaison, plant manager, or human resources director.
- Gender, age, and ethnic characteristics of the population. These are usually available from the human resources department. Most locations must complete various state and federal reports to comply with EEOC regulations. This same information can be used as part of the market analysis.
- Worker categories. These include blue collar, white collar, salaried, hourly, executive, and other classifications useful for research purposes. Again, these

can usually be obtained from reports prepared by the human resources department.

Product Analysis

What is being offered to the market defined in the market analysis? A product analysis listing includes:

- The meal periods and the basic menu offered at each. How extensive is the menu? How varied? How many menu cycles are used? What *specifically* is offered in each category of service?
- A study of facilities and equipment and its capacity to produce and serve menu items. Can baked goods be offered? Can "home made" foods be offered? Are the facilities at the points of service adequate to offer the desired menu? What is the seating capacity? Can it handle the service load? Do any constraints exist that inhibit the service need?
- The culinary skills of the staff. Can they make ethnic foods? Dessert specialties? Can buffet catering be offered? How about specialized items such as ice carvings? What type of decorating/garnishing is available? Any special skills on the staff?

Competition Analysis

There was a time when a noncommercial foodservice was thought to have a captive population. While that may still be true for hospital or correctional facilities, it's no longer so for any other noncommercial foodservice. Today the manager at, for example, a college or office building requires a retail mentality to be successful.

A good retailer knows what the competition is doing and develops plans to meet and beat that competition. For a noncommercial foodservice, competition is any restaurant, diner, or other eatery close enough to the target market to draw some of it off during meal periods. Generally, the longer the meal period for the facility, the larger the competitive circle of commercial operations.

Keep in mind the potential competition from the brown baggers. Brown bags may have been replaced by plastic containers, but both the phrase and its effects have survived. Economic conditions can encourage brown bagging. This becomes formidable competition.

Each potentially competitive foodservice must be visited, surveyed, reviewed, and analyzed. A specific form for this should be developed including the following items:

- Name of the facility.
- Exact location of the competitor, including characteristics such as accessibility, parking, and visibility.
- Exterior appearance. Is the restaurant bright and cheery or dull and unattractive? Are the windows clean? Is there an outside patio?
- Interior appearance. What type of decor? Is it well lit or "atmospheric?" Is it clean, well-maintained, and inviting?
- Type of operation. Fast food? A luncheonette/diner? A theme restaurant? Or a bar and grill?
- Menu orientation. Hamburgers, chicken, light fare (salads/sandwiches)? Specialty menu? Ethnic? What, specifically, is offered to the clientele?

- Seating capacity. How many seats are there at counters, tables, bar, or lounge areas?
- Pricing. What meals are served in what price ranges? How does the menu rate for breakfast, lunch, dinner, and snacks? What is the price range and check average for each meal period?
- Hours of operation. What hours are open for each meal period?
- General comments. The survey should have a summary statement of the reviewer's impressions of the facility. Comments include the potential to attract the target market, the products and services offered, accessibility to the handicapped, and any other information not previously detailed.

Based on the findings of the three analyses—market, product, and competition—an in-house marketing plan can be prepared.

Marketing Plan Details

Base the marketing plan on the following model:

Input — Process — Output

Figure 10.3 is a diagram of such an exercise.

The *inputs* are information derived from the market, product, and competition analyses. Toss this information into the *process* hopper. There, it's used to develop *outputs*—the desired products and services.

Following is a closer look at the processes.

Establish Service and Financial Objectives

In Chapter 2, some specific examples were presented for several noncommercial segments of the industry. These are identical to the objectives required to establish a marketing plan and are repeated here.

Service Objectives

1. Provide breakfast service to arriving employees who commute and desire that meal.
2. Provide lunch service to 2,000 employees within 90 minutes; employees released 500 at a time in 20-minute intervals.
3. Provide morning and afternoon coffee break service, via vending machines, at appropriate locations throughout the building.

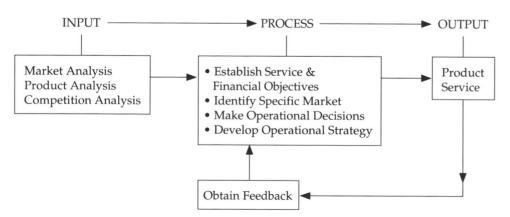

FIGURE 10.3 Input-Process-Output Marketing Model

4. Provide a quality dining room and guest dining room service to the 100 executives of the company plus 30 to 40 executive guests per day. Fulfill special catering requirements for board of directors' luncheons, sales meetings, and similar functions. The cost of corporate catering will be borne by the company.
5. Provide corporate catering services as required by both employee and executive groups, within company policy.

Financial Objectives

1. Offer all employee cafeteria and vending services at selling prices substantially below the outside commercial market. A sufficient price differential will exist to allow employees to perceive the service as a company benefit.
2. Offer executive dining services at a menu price sufficient to cover the cost of food and service labor only.
3. Priced company-catered services (board of directors' meetings, sales meetings, and other functions) at operational cost.
4. Price catered events offered to employees at least 25 percent below comparable commercial operations.
5. Recover, within the foodservice department, the costs of all food, labor, direct expenses, and management fee if contracted. The cost of capital investment, space charges, and related costs will be borne by the company.

Each of those original management objectives are also marketing objectives. While a foodservice director may have some influence in establishing them, in most cases they are dictated by company policy and/or client contract.

Identify Specific Markets

The market analysis previously discussed identified:

■ Size of the population
■ Gender, age, and ethnic mix
■ Social characteristics, (i.e., blue collar, white collar, and other)
■ Related information

Specific percentage participation targets can be established for each group of potential customers, for each foodservice area, and for each meal period. (This would be the same as the population percentage forecast for the budget plan in Chapter 5.)

Make Operational Decisions

Using the service and financial objectives as the driving force and the market identity to channel that force, operating decisions are made.

All the previous chapters—which examined financial planning, menu management, labor hours planning, and so on—dealt with operating decisions. Each will come into play again as part of the facility's operating strategy.

Develop Operational Strategy

Developing an operational strategy to achieve marketing objectives is identical to the planning task of management. In Chapter 2 we defined planning as making the best use of the resources available to a manager. Those resources, again, are:

■ Men and women
■ Money
■ Materials

- Methods
- Machines

Each is now applied to identifying and satisfying the wants and needs of the target market—developing marketing strategy. Operating strategies bring into play each manager's own operating experience.

A manager's knowledge and skill in *every* operating area and all help available from staff should be used to develop an operating strategy for each manager and location.

Such skills as merchandising, promotion, menu planning, labor scheduling, employee training, public relations, client relations, and other talents are all relevant to strategic planning. Marketing strategies are the what. Operating strategies are the how.

Obtaining Feedback

Obtaining marketing feedback is part of management control. As with any other standard, information about actual performance is needed for comparison.

Types of Feedback

There are two types of feedback that help us to evaluate the effects of marketing in a noncommercial operation: direct and indirect.

Examples of direct feedback include customer surveys and guest comment cards, personal observations, comments from foodservice employees, and any other direct evaluations from either customers or employees. A marketing program should be designed to provide as much direct feedback as possible.

Indirect feedback comes from financial and service data used as part of management controls. All of the reports that provide operational data also provide indirect feedback.

One example is the weekly operating report (WOR). This will provide all the information necessary to evaluate a variety of marketing programs.

If a special promotion is designed to increase the participation percentage and/or the check average, the WOR will show whether it worked. If a new menu cycle and merchandising program is started to increase participation, the WOR will provide details on the results of that effort. To evaluate a marketing campaign of advertising and couponing, use the WOR. It provides details of cost percentages to measure success.

The production sheet provides information on menu item popularity and, therefore, on the success of any marketing plan undertaken. A manager can track such information as:

- The sales mix and its effect on gross profit margins.
- Popularity (unit sales) of menu items used as part of a promotion.
- Menu shortages that cause customer discontent.

Other management reports can also be used to assess the results of a marketing program. There is no need to reinvent the wheel; where an information system is already in place and working, it can be used to extract marketing data. *A manager must maintain a retail mentality*. It is the key to identifying customer (market) wants and needs and developing a program to meet them. If foodservice directors assume a captive market and meet only the goals and objectives of the seller, the marketing plan will fail. But if managers "think retail," the marketing plan will succeed.

BRANDING: THE LATEST MARKETING STRATEGY

Nothing in recent years has had greater impact on marketing in noncommercial foodservice than branding. It is still new and controversial, and there is little concrete data available to attest to its success.

Branding can be broadly defined as the use of any well-known, advertised national brand as part of the marketing plan of a foodservice operation. This would include Heinz Ketchup on the table, Oscar Mayer hot dogs on the menu, and Yoplait yogurt on the cafeteria service line.

Branding is also the use of nationally recognized restaurant chains, most often fast food companies, as part of a noncommercial food service.

Such national companies as Subway, Taco Bell, Pizza Hut, and TCBY are common sights on college campuses. Some hospitals even have a McDonald's in place of the coffee shop. Almost every national brand of fast food is now available to the noncommercial operator in one form or another.

A recent survey by Fessel International reported that brands are in approximately four percent of the estimated 14,000 points of distribution (there may be several per account) in noncommercial foodservice. This includes all industry segments. That same survey estimates growth of brand item use at 20–30 percent annually.

Every major—and many smaller—contractors now have branding programs. There are two types: house brands and national brands.

House Brands

A house brand is developed by a contractors or a self-operator to tap the noncommercial market they are in. These usually parallel popular franchise operations serving hamburgers, chicken, pizza, Mexican or Italian food, and cookies. The primary objective of the house brand is to capture a menu or theme category without the franchise fees, license fees, or other costs of doing business as a franchisee.

House Brands of the Big Four

One of the foremost developers of house brands is ARASERVE, a division of ARA. Under the direction of its senior vice-president of marketing, ARA has developed a complete line of products and brands, marketing programs, and support services for its foodservice directors.

ARA offers marketing support for managers in the form of the *ASAP Restaurant Collection*, a complete catalog of private-label brand concepts to suit any foodservice director's needs. Figure 10.4 is a page from that publication listing 14 different house brands and their logos. Some of the specific concepts that compete directly with the major fast food franchisors are:

- Allegros Pasta .... an Italian theme operation
- Itza Pizza .... a franchise type pizza operation
- Leghorn's Chicken.. a fast food chicken operation
- Tortillas... a Mexican fast food operation
- Gretel's Bake Shop .... a cookie facility
- The WOKERY.. a Chinese fast food service
- Deli Corner .... a sandwich service

ARA has established a house brand restaurant concept to compete with operations identified in the competition analysis of the marketing plan. The 50-page

Burgundy: 210001 Gray: 210003 Green: 210005 Teal: 210007

Burgundy: 210071 Gray: 210073 Green: 210075 Teal: 210077

Burgundy: 210011 Gray: 210013 Green: 210015 Teal: 210017

Burgundy: 210081 Gray: 210083 Green: 210085 Teal: 210087

Burgundy: 210021   Gray: 210023   Green: 210025   Teal: 210027

Burgundy: 210091 Gray: 210093 Green: 210095 Teal: 210097

Single Sided: Burgundy: 210031 Gray: 210033 Green: 210035 Teal: 21037
Double Sided: Burgundy: 210032 Gray: 210034 Green: 210036 Teal: 21038

Single Sided: Burgundy: 210101 Gray: 210103 Green: 210105 Teal: 210107
Double Sided: Burgundy: 210102 Gray: 210104 Green: 210106 Teal: 210108

Burgundy: 210041   Gray: 210043   Green: 210045   Teal: 210047

Burgundy: 210111 Gray: 210113 Green: 210115 Teal: 210117

Burgundy: 210051   Gray: 210053   Green: 210055   Teal: 210057

Burgundy: 210131 Gray: 210133 Green: 210135 Teal: 210137

Burgundy: 210061   Gray: 210063   Green: 210065   Teal: 210067

Burgundy: 210141 Gray: 210143 Green: 210145 Teal: 210147

FIGURE 10.4   ARAServe House Brands and Marketing Logos (Courtesy of ARA Services, Philadelphia, PA)

catalog provides managers with everything necessary to set up any of the 14 concepts. The available support material includes guidelines for signs, banners, customized signs, custom shop details, coordinated menu paper, menu boards, apparel, decor, and general merchandise.

This provides each manager with the entrepreneurial ability to assess individual client needs and develop a marketing plan to fill those needs.

ARA has carried over its corporate marketing plan, using the concepts of house brands and individual entrepreneurship, into its recruitment efforts. Figure 10.5 is one of its classified ads for management personnel.

Canteen Corporation has developed a line of house brand specialty items for its B&I operations, which it markets in similar fashion to ARA. Some of its specialty menu items are:

- Bigger Better Biscuits ....An oversized biscuit
- Chic Chick.. specialty chicken breast sandwich
- Classy Cookies...on-premise baked cookie operation
- Pazzelli's Pizza .... franchise-type pizza operation
- Spicey Fries .... A Cajun-spiced oversized french fry
- Light Choice...a menu with a nutrition emphasis

Each of these is part of a total marketing program that includes special menu items and promotions for the other noncommercial segments Canteen operates.

Other major, and some smaller, contractors have marketing programs for their in-house brands and products. The items differ but the concept is the same: Compete with the national franchise brands while foregoing franchise fees, license fees, and other costs of using a national brand.

House Brands of the Self-Operators

Many self-operators have also developed house brands. Self-op colleges, for instance, are the beneficiaries of a complete line of house brands developed by the National Association of College and University Food Service (NACUFS).

Universities are well into the concept of marketing their total foodservice programs. Rather than assume the students, staff, and faculty are a captive market, some schools have developed very sophisticated marketing programs. One example is Cornell University.

Cornell Dining has a number of board dining rooms and cash operations, a student union, faculty and staff dining, and foodservice vending. Cornell developed a marketing program to provide identity and pizazz to each individual facility.

Figure 10.6 is a collage of logos that identify some of the food operations at Cornell. Each location has a specific identity, its own logo, a special menu package, and a complete marketing program. This provides the students, staff, and faculty with choices and competes effectively with the commercial operations off campus. The results have been quite successful.

National Brands

Many well-known fast food franchisors have convinced noncommercial operators to use their name, products, and national identity in their foodservices. Such companies as Pizza Hut, Taco Bell, and Kentucky Fried Chicken, (all PepsiCo subsidiaries), Burger King, Dunkin' Donuts, Sbarro, Subway, TCBY, Mrs. Fields Cookies, Nathan's Famous Hot Dogs, and Popeye's Chicken all sell their products

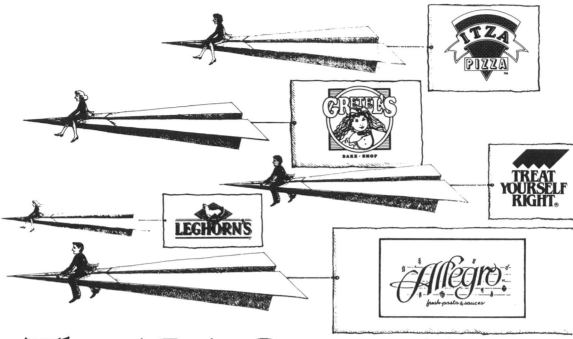

The ARA Creative Force

If you want to see your ideas fly, join up with a team that reaches for the sky.

Find out more about ARA's Creative Force-a team concept that encourages *intrapreneurial* spirit in every job, every location, and every level of our organization.

The results have been forceful. Itza Pizza™...Leghorn'ssm chicken...Allegrosm fresh pastas and sauces...Gretel's Bake Shops™...Treat Yourself Right® nutrition awareness program...Bagel Wagonsm carts...the list goes on and on.

As an ARA Manager, you're a key member of this creative force. You'll be encouraged to use your ingenuity to tailor existing ideas for your customers and clients. You'll be asked to develop your own ideas or test concepts in your unit and help us fine tune them. You could even participate on special teams that develop new concepts.

If you want to make your ideas fly, think about joining the ARA Creative Force. Call *Intrapreneur Match* at 1 (800) 966-1272 ext. WBX-W99 (Lines Open 7 Days/Week). Tell one of our recruitment representatives about yourself. Then we'll try to match your background and interests with our current openings. Equal Opportunity Employer.

© ARA Services, Inc. 1992

FIGURE 10.5 Example of Recruitment Ad as Part of a Marketing Program (Courtesy of ARA Services, Philadelphia, PA)

in noncommercial foodservices. This is accomplished via franchising, licensing, or other means.

Branding in a noncommercial foodservice requires different management than the typical franchisor-operated freestanding building. The menu items are usually the same, but the site is nonstandard. To operate in a foodservice, franchisors have developed three custom programs for the display and delivery of their specialized products:

FIGURE 10.6 House Brand Logos of Cornell Dining Services (Courtesy of Margaret Lacey, Cornell University)

- Towers and counter top units for cafeterias
- Kiosks for add-on fixed operations
- Mobile carts for various and variable uses

These are becoming standards for branded fast-service concepts.

Towers and Counter Top Units

Towers and counter top units are designed to fit into an existing cafeteria counter service. They can often use an existing or slightly modified piece of equipment.

A tower or counter top unit is always self-service, has a limited number of the branded menu items, and has clearly defined price and merchandising points. A so-called core menu is the basic variety offered. This might be an individual pan pizza, a special burger, or other signature item of the franchisor.

A typical investment of $5,000 to $8,000 is required to convert an existing six to eight foot space on a cafeteria line to a branded section of the counter. This includes overhead signage, display equipment, and other brand identity items. Sales potential of a tower/counter unit is between $140 to $150 per foot, per week.

Most production takes place in an existing kitchen with existing equipment and personnel. In some cases products have been partially prepared off premise by the franchise's purveyors.

Kiosks

A kiosk is a small, freestanding unit placed strategically and connected to existing utilities. Requiring 300 to 450 square feet of space, the kiosk can be installed in secondary service areas of a cafeteria, adjacent to vending machines in a manufacturing plant, or other points where additional service is desired.

Food is sold over the counter, similar to any commercial fast food operation. Menus are usually limited, again featuring core items from the product line. The ability to prepare and display the menu items in the kiosk dictates the menu.

A typical investment for a kiosk is $35,000 to $50,000, which provides a completely equipped unit, ready for hookup to existing utilities. Each of the franchisors has its own specifications. Sales potential for a kiosk is between $500 and $600 per day or shift. Much depends on location, population, and desire for the service.

Most kiosks are self-contained, that is, all menu items can be produced and sold from the kiosk. They are usually supported by the backup service, storage, and other facilities of the regular operation.

The kiosk is an add-on, requiring no sacrifice of existing facilities in the way towers or counter top units do.

Mobile Carts

A mobile cart is similar to a kiosk but is reconfigurable, self-contained, and movable. On a cart, operators can produce or hold core menu items and sell them to the customer.

The cost of a mobile cart varies with its built-in cooking and holding capabilities and overall technological sophistication. Prices range from $7,000 to $10,000 per cart. Sales off a cart run between $700 and $750 per day, depending on population and location.

Mobile carts are very versatile. The same cart can be used at multiple locations with different needs. Like kiosks, they offer over-the-counter service of a core menu and require off-cart production and storage areas.

Contractual Arrangements

There are four basic types of contractual arrangements governing the right to sell a franchisor's products: franchising, licensing, operating agreements, and leasing. There are also a variety of hybrid deals between franchise companies and operators. Branding is too new to assess which type of contract—or hybrid—is prevalent. A standard contract will most likely evolve as franchisors and operators find out what works and what doesn't.

Franchising is the arrangement between fast food companies and operators—who usually pay a one-time franchise fee plus a monthly percentage of sales—for the right to sell the company's products and the attendant visibility that a well-know brand offers. Some of the major national noncommercial contractors have franchise agreements that allow them to operate in multiple locations under a single franchise agreement.

Licensing is a limited franchise for a substantially smaller monthly fee. There is no initial one-time fee. The licensee can serve the franchisor's menu items, use its logos, signage, marketing/advertising campaigns, and other items for a negotiated fee. The primary difference between licensing and franchising is the absence of an initial franchise fee.

Under an operating agreement, the brand company provides the service at the location in question—for instance, operating a kiosk at a manufacturing plant. The company makes the investment, pays all operating expenses, and provides the foodservice a rental or commission.

The fourth arrangement, leasing, is in some ways the simplest: the foodservice subleases space to a brand operator, and they enter into a tenant-landlord relationship.

Arrangements vary, but as a rule, major contractors obtain franchise rights for use throughout the company, while self-ops usually license individual locations.

The PepsiCo Story

PepsiCo, the parent company of Pepsi Cola, Taco Bell, Pizza Hut, Kentucky Fried Chicken (KFC), and Frito-Lay, exemplifies the fast food franchisor aggressively hunting noncommercial locations for its branded products. Figure 10.7 is an example of one of its advertisements placed in industry trade journals. Notice that the ad mentions CARTS of Colorado, a PepsiCo subsidiary.

PepsiCo recently acquired a substantial interest in CARTS, a manufacturer of state-of-the-art mobile carts, and has effectively frozen out competition in this market. CARTS also produces technologically sophisticated kiosks and counter top units. By controlling this advanced means of product delivery, PepsiCo has been able to make quick and substantial inroads into all segments of noncommercial branding.

Each of the three PepsiCo companies does its own marketing. Figure 10.8 is an example of a Taco Bell campaign; Figures 10.9 and 10.10 show Pizza Hut and KFC, respectively. All three ads stress the ability to provide either counter top, kiosk, or mobile operations for any noncommercial situation.

Mobile carts have opened new areas of opportunity for Pepsi. The acquisition of CARTS has provided PepsiCo and its operators a major marketing advantage. Figures 10.11, 10.12, and 10.13 are examples of mobile cart operations in Taco Bell, Pizza Hut, and KFC. In some cases they've grouped these three operations in a food court quite successfully. Where this happens, Taco Bell is the primary liaison, providing the operator with a single contact for all three PepsiCo companies.

To increase your profit flow,

TAP YOUR RESOURCES.

PEPSI
The Brand Resource
DRIVING PERFORMANCE WITH PROVEN PARTNERS

When you're looking for increased sales and profits, you need to tap into all the resources you can. Pepsi: The Brand Resource is the way to tap into such profit resources as Taco Bell, Pizza Hut*, KFC*, FRITO-LAY* and other brands that your customers know and trust. Brands that can help open the door to higher sales and profits. You also get access to Carts of Colorado – the foremost mobile cart designer and manufacturer in the country. When you pour Pepsi, you not only get a commitment to build your soft drink sales – you become part of a team that helps grow your total business. To increase your profit flow, remember: *Tap Your Resources.*

PEPSI and PEPSI-COLA are registered trademarks of PepsiCo, Inc. FRITO-LAY is a registered trademark used by Frito-Lay, Inc. © Recot, Inc., 1992. © 1992 Taco Bell Corp. Pizza Hut is a registered trademark of Pizza Hut, Inc. © 1992 Pizza Hut, Inc. KFC and the Image of Colonel Sanders are trademarks of KFC Corp.

FIGURE 10.7 PepsiCo Corporation Trade Journal Advertisement for Noncommercial Branding Concepts (Courtesy of PepsiCo Corporation, Purchase, NY)

9-Ft. Cart
- Space requirement: 75 sq. ft.
- Investment: $35,000
- Equipment sales capability: $200,000–$400,000 annually
- 5–7 core menu items with rotating promotional products available and optional breakfast program

Outdoor Kiosk
- Space requirement: 120 sq. ft.
- Investment: $75,000
- Equipment sales capability: $300,000–$500,000 annually
- 5–7 core menu items with rotating promotional products available and optional breakfast program

Custom Facade
- Space requirement: 200–900 sq. ft.
- Investment: $95,000
- Equipment sales capability: $400,000–$1,000,000 annually
- 12–16 core menu items with rotating promotional products available and optional breakfast program

The Taco Bell complete support program includes:

- versatile state-of-the-art equipment
- menu options
- customized training
- cost effective, easy start-up
- lease programs available

The TACO BELL. Express program brings you systems designed to minimize your time, space and labor and maximize your bottom line profits.

For higher bottom line profits, give us a ring

1 (800) 487-8226

TACO BELL IS A REGISTERED TRADEMARK OF TACO BELL CORP © 1992 TACO BELL CORP

DRIVING PERFORMANCE WITH PROVEN PARTNERS

FIGURE 10.8 Taco Bell Advertisement in Trade Journals for Noncommercial Branding Concept (Courtesy of PepsiCo Corporation, Purchase, NY)

FIGURE 10.9 Pizza Hut Advertisement in Trade Journals for Noncommercial Branding Concept (Courtesy of PepsiCo Corporation, Purchase, NY)

FIGURE 10.10 Kentucky Fried Chicken Advertisement in Trade Journals for Noncommercial Branding Concept (Courtesy of PepsiCo Corporation, Purchase, NY)

FIGURE 10.11 Mobile Cart for Taco Bell Branding Concept (Courtesy of Don Gallery, Executive Vice-President, Carts of Colorado, Denver, CO)

FIGURE 10.12 Mobile Cart for Pizza Hut Branding Concept (Courtesy of Don Gallery, Executive Vice-President, Carts of Colorado, Denver, CO)

FIGURE 10.13 Mobile Cart for KFC Branding Concept (Courtesy of Don Gallery, Executive Vice-President, Carts of Colorado, Denver, CO)

To help market products to the noncommercial segments, PepsiCo subsidiaries have an informal organization called Pepsi Partners consisting of executives from the four concerned subsidiaries of parent Pepsico: Pizza Hut, Taco Bell, KFC, and CARTS.

Other fast food franchisors have either entered or are entering noncommercial foodservice. Burger King, for example, has a unit called Expressway, a scaled-down store offering core menu items.

Products and Equipment

The franchisors who have entered noncommercial foodservice have made changes in both their products and equipment.

For example, Pizza Hut has developed a means of handling pizza dough specifically for the noncommercial market. Frozen dough is delivered exclusively to noncommercial units. It's tempered overnight in the refrigerator, proofed, cooled, and then topped and baked. This is a complete change from the "to order" production method used at freestanding locations.

KFC has developed a freezer-to-fryer product for the noncommercial market as well as a new piece of equipment: the ventless fryer. This allows the operators of a kiosk or portable cart to prepare food at the sales site, thereby retaining the quality associated with the regular stores. KFC says its chicken has a maximum two-hour holding time. So production can take place in the location's kitchen, and name recognition at the point of sale (counter top) will do the rest.

Taco Bell's Kitchen Minus system uses prefried taco shells, precooked meat, preshredded lettuce, dehydrated and seasoned beans, and diced onions. Taco Bell, like KFC, feels that the quality difference is overcome by the brand identity.

Equipment and production methods continually improve. The lure of entirely new markets and more thoroughly penetrable existing markets has motivated fast food franchisors to develop ever more streamlined production techniques. It remains to be seen which brands will make the greatest inroads.

TOTAL QUALITY MANAGEMENT AND MARKETING

Marketing is applied management. Management is the mortar that holds the building blocks of the corporation together, including the marketing department. One of the more recent management theories is total quality management (TQM).

Marriott and its Marriott Management Services subsidiary have adopted TQM as corporate policy. TQM guides their corporate management philosophy and, therefore, their marketing program.

Marriott defines TQM as a way of doing business that emphasizes continuing improvement, with the assumption that meeting or exceeding the needs of its clients and customers will improve its competitive position and profitability.

Figure 10.14 is a copy of the mission statement for all Marriott Management Services operations. Marriott believes that adding these principles will set it apart from its competitors.

Marriott feels that TQM is a major corporate undertaking that not only changes ways of doing business but also changes strategic and operational planning.

SUMMARY

Sales and marketing are two strategic tasks of foodservice contractors. Sales does not stand alone. It is part of the contractor's overall marketing effort.

Selling new accounts and keeping existing accounts is the lifeblood of all contractors. Each year, contractors must achieve a positive balance of new account acquisitions versus lost accounts with a solid gain in overall gross sales and net profits.

Marketing, among other things, is looking at the needs of the buyer rather than the needs of the seller.

Contractor marketers may adopt either the marketing concept or the selling concept.

Each industry segment requires a specific marketing program to identify wants and needs and develop a marketing plan and corresponding sales program.

The primary target markets for new sales are self-op locations. Others are locations operated by other contractors and new facilities resulting from a corporate move or new construction.

Contractor sales teams are the primary tool used to sell new accounts.

Requests for proposals (RFPs) are presented to prospective bidders to acquire new contracts. The sellers (contractors) respond to an RFP with a site visit, preliminary operation plan and pro forma, and, finally, a bid presentation.

Client relations is one of the most important aspects of a contractor's marketing effort.

Marketing, which is applied management, has a triangular base: market analysis, product analysis, and competition analysis.

Branding is the latest marketing tool in noncommercial foodservice. There are two basic types: house and national brands.

There are four basic types of contractual arrangements used to obtain the right to sell a franchisor's products: licensing, franchising, rental, and leasing.

Marriott Management Services
Making The Difference

VISION

We will be recognized as the best international management services team. Guided by our shared values, each one of us is fully empowered to consistently exceed the expectations of the clients we work for and the customers we serve.

CORE VALUES

INTEGRITY

Always act fairly, ethically and honestly in dealing with our people, our clients, and customers, and in all situations.

CUSTOMER DRIVEN

Clients we work for and customers we serve drive all of our actions. We continually listen to them, anticipate and understand their needs, and exceed their expectations.

CONTINUOUS IMPROVEMENT

We encourage creativity and innovation, initiative, and risk-taking to continuously improve our products and services as measured by our clients and customers.

EMPOWERMENT

All associates are fully empowered to serve our clients and customers as individuals and teams. We are responsible for removing barriers to service excellence, always recognizing and dignifying the diversity of our primary resource: *"Our People."*

SUSTAINABLE ECONOMIC GROWTH

We will create sustainable economic growth to provide resources to better serve our clients and customers, enhance the financial security and career opportunity for all associates, and reward our shareholders for their faith in us.

BALANCE

We encourage our associates to balance their personal and professional lives, including health and family, work, and community. We respect the decisions they make to achieve this balance.

FIGURE 10.14   Marriott Mission Statement Embodying the Principles of Total Quality Management

11

Outlook

Lincoln Steffens once wrote, "I have seen the future and it works." While no one knows what lies ahead, the past can help foretell the future.

This chapter will consider the past, apply it to the present, and offer predictions for the future of noncommercial foodservice management, both contracted and self-operated. It will take a separate look at industry segments, technology, and management.

This is not a comprehensive analysis, nor is it intended to be. It is the views of one who has been in this industry for over half a century and has seen many changes.

BUSINESS AND INDUSTRY

Since Robert Owen established the first employee foodservice around 1800, there has been only one good reason to operate an employee or executive foodservice: *it's an employee benefit.*

Recently many companies are questioning that rationale. While most corporate foodservices began either free or subsidized, many now desire to break even on operating expenses. The idea of the foodservice as a benefit has diminished with wide-scale corporate downsizing and cost containment policies.

The difference between commercial and noncommercial foodservices is profit versus productivity. The commercial foodservice's primary objective is to make a profit, a fair return on investment. The primary objective of a noncommercial foodservice is (or should be) to increase worker productivity through worker satisfaction. This results in greater profit from other activities of the company, though not directly from the foodservice. Many employers have forgotten this basic premise.

The current corporate trend is for all parts of the operation to cover their operating costs. While this may contain costs, it is impractical to expect the foodservice, operating within the confines of the company, to cover all operating expenses.

A company must determine if the foodservice is part of the employee benefit package or a cost center expected to make a profit (or at least not lose money).

There has been some movement towards the latter because of lean economic times, but things will probably shift again. Those companies that value an employee and/or executive foodservice will again consider part of the cost an operating expense. Those companies who don't see employee foodservice as a benefit will eliminate it.

While a return to the days of heavy subsidies or free meals is unlikely, any service that provides a greater benefit than its operating cost will probably be maintained. Most employee foodservices fall into that category.

The current trend to contract rather than self-operate will continue and grow. Some historically self-operated facilities will contract as present management gives way to the next generation.

The importance of executive dining rooms will diminish as the baby boomers take over; clients still need to be entertained, but increasingly managers are eating in the cafeterias with the rest of the employees. This trend is especially visible in high-tech industries and will expand to the more traditional manufacturing businesses as well.

Management fee contracts, presently less popular than profit and loss contracts, will have a revival. Although clients will demand a professional foodservice with a contained cost, they will desire to control all corporate policies, including those involving the foodservice (hours, types of service, prices, and other). That's possible only with a management fee contract.

Business (offices, essentially) and industry (factories) will both shrink, with implications for foodservice. Ever-improving technologies will allow corporations to reduce staff even more. As a result, large employee foodservices will become increasingly rare.

Manufacturing, another beneficiary of technology, will also produce more with less staff, and huge in-plant cafeterias will shrink along with the work force.

Although the various foodservices may be smaller they will continue to be viewed as employee benefits. The meaning of "benefit" may shift; lower selling price will be supplanted by availability, convenience, and quality.

CAMPUS DINING

The colleges and universities of America have grown greatly in the past 20 years. The days when only middle- and upper-class families could send their children to college are past. Now every American has the opportunity to obtain a college education.

As a result of social and economic changes, many administrators are questioning the suitability of the board plan versus a declining-balance debit card. But the board plan is alive and well on most older campuses and will probably remain that way. This is particularly true among self-operators.

Contractors will continue their growth in this industry segment. In the next ten years, they will obtain another 10 to 20 percent of the market. New contracts will replace the traditional board plan with the declining-balance debit card. The traditional all-you-can-eat for a fixed board rate will lose popularity.

Self-operators currently meeting the financial and service needs of the college or university will continue. But they, too, will at least consider the declining-balance debit card concept.

Recent experiments with branding have been very successful in campus dining. While it may have limited potential in other noncommercial segments, branding will prosper on campuses.

HEALTH CARE

It is difficult to forecast the future of health care in America and the effects on health care foodservice. As this is being written, the administration and the country are debating health care reform, further muddying the waters.

Despite the uncertainty, the health care industry (particularly hospitals) is already putting its financial house in order in preparation for future legislation. Many institutions have established cost containment measures and, as a result, have reassessed the nutritional services department.

Like colleges, if hospitals are efficiently and effectively self-operated, this will continue. If the administration feels that contracting will reduce costs, they'll contract. Cost alone will be the deciding factor. If a contracted service is unsatisfactory, the institution will merely re-bid and change contractors. But they will not return to self-operation. The primary type of contract will be profit and loss, whereby the contractor provides a stable price for proposed services. The key element will be identifying the contracted services: patient foodservice, employee cafeterias, and in-house catering.

The fringe benefits of free or subsidized doctors' dining rooms and other non-patient services will become rare or obsolete.

The visitors foodservice operation will receive strong review as a potential profit center. While many are now operated by volunteer groups, this will change. If the visitor service can make a profit, the hospital will try to capture that profit.

Other areas of health care—nursing homes, assisted living centers, and all institutions covered by health insurance—will become cost driven. As the means of payment (reimbursement by either private or national health insurance) becomes fixed, the need to contain costs will become stronger. This will be another reason to use a contractor.

ELEMENTARY AND SECONDARY SCHOOLS

The National School Lunch Program is politically driven. Some are trying to change the present subsidized breakfast and lunch to a universal free meal program. Others want to reduce government involvement in subsidized school foodservices. It's unknown which side will prevail.

Contractors have become increasingly skilled at operating school foodservices on a profit and loss basis. They have sharpened operating techniques, marketing programs, and management to obtain a greater share of this market.

A much larger percentage of this market will probably go to contractors within the next ten years. Many segments of government services, at all levels, are privatizing operations. These run the gamut from airports to trash collection agencies. School systems will follow, moving strongly towards contractor operations.

Operators of school systems will offer auxiliary services. School kitchens might serve programs such as Meals on Wheels, day care centers, elder care centers, and other community services.

CORRECTIONAL FOODSERVICE

As noted earlier, this segment is the latest to receive recognition as a bona fide profession. The lack of cell space has caused crowding in our country's prisons, making their professional operation—including foodservice—an issue of national concern.

Capital requirements for new correctional facilities are a major problem for state or local government. Like schools, privatization is making inroads.

The construction and operation of correctional facilities will probably become privately financed and operated to a great degree. Government entities will contract with investors and management companies to construct and operate prisons.

Correctional foodservice will begin to mimic other sorts of feeding. Professional managers supported by staff nutritionists, training directors, purchasing specialists, and others will become standard. Thus, the contractors' role will grow because they have the organization in place to provide these services.

It's likely that correctional foodservices will become involved in inmate rehabilitation. The kitchen as a training facility for rehabilitation programs will be more common. This is another plus for contractors.

FOODSERVICE VENDING

Vending provides service where it's either economically or physically impractical to offer a broader foodservice. This will continue.

The service will change as equipment gets more and more sophisticated. The debit card has been introduced to vending with modest success. Its use will expand dramatically, especially where the handling of cash is a problem, like college campuses. Declining-balance concepts are installed and other campus services are available to the student via the debit card.

Debit cards will reduce the need for expensive bill and coin changers and working capital. This will in turn effect the investment requirements of contractors and potential commissions. Debit cards will penetrate other segments, not just campus dining.

Vending machines will continue to offer the standard hot drink, cold drink, and food machine product lines. Food quality and merchandising will certainly improve.

TECHNOLOGY

Technological improvements over the past 25 years have had a dramatic impact on manufacturing and service industries. The impact on the foodservice industry has been slighter, particularly in the noncommercial segments.

Kitchen production must still take place to match service requirements. That production has changed more from management techniques than from technological improvements. Changes lowering required labor hours for meal production have not been due to technology but to changes in management policies such as the use of convenience foods.

Technology will probably not dramatically improve productivity in the kitchen. A roast that requires three hours in the oven, or a cake that takes 45 minutes to bake, will still require that same time. Unless kitchen production methods are changed, technology will not enable the production of more goods or services per labor hour. The primary means of reducing labor costs will be purchases of pre-prepared foods, more instances of self-service, and changes in the basic service offered.

MANAGEMENT

Historically, the foodservice industry has been slow to accept even basic management practices. Some old hands were prone to say, "That's great, but not for the food business." Well, they were wrong. Sound management principles will work in *any* business, particularly in the noncommercial foodservice business.

Professional foodservice directors understand the fundamentals of professional standards and conduct. They have a personal performance standard and a code of ethics: they belong to one or more professional associations, read food-service trade publications and journals, and continue their professional and managerial education.

Appendix A lists professional associations representing the various segments of the industry. All those making a career in noncommercial foodservice are encouraged to join and become active in one or more of these organizations.

Future foodservice directors who do not develop and use management skills will probably fail. Technological advances will make the manager's job easier, but they will not replace the practice of sound management.

Appendix A

Professional Associations and Trade Publications

There are associations of professional managers, such as the American Management Association, whose members represent a broad spectrum of American business and industry. Other associations address the management interests of specific industries.

Listed here are several noncommercial foodservice professional organizations as well as publications devoted to the industry and its segments.

PROFESSIONAL ASSOCIATIONS

BUSINESS AND INDUSTRY

Society for Foodservice Management (SFM)

> 304 W. Liberty Street
> Louisville, KY 40202
> Phone: 502–583–3783
> Executive Director: Greg Jewell

SFM is an organization whose members are primarily in the business and industry segment. Over 1400 members represent all major national and regional foodservice contractors, independent operators, corporate liaison personnel, and companies providing products and services to the industry.

CAMPUS DINING

National Association Of College and University Food Service (NACUFS)

> 1405 S. Harrison Road
> Suite 303
> Manly Miles Building, MSU
> East Lansing, MI 48824
> Phone: 517–332–2494
> Executive Director: Joseph H. Spina

NACUFS is a professional association for campus foodservice directors and support staff at over 500 colleges and universities throughout the United States, Canada, and abroad.

FOODSERVICE VENDING

National Automatic Merchandising Association (NAMA)

> 20 N. Wacker Drive
> Chicago, IL 60606
> Phone: 312–346–0730
> President: James A. Rost
> Director of Communications: Sheldon Silver

NAMA is an organization whose interests are commercial and foodservice vending. Their members operate vending machines in all segments of the industry. Some members are manufacturers of vending machines and related equipment and others are suppliers to the vending industry.

ELEMENTARY AND SECONDARY SCHOOLS

American School Food Service Association (AFSFA)

> 1600 Duke Street, 7th Floor
> Alexandria, VA 22314
> Phone: 800–877–8822

The American School Food Service Association (ASFSA) represents professionals active in elementary and secondary school foodservice operations. ASFSA is an organization whose membership is composed of both hourly and salaried personnel. It provides educational and training programs offering certification status from the lowest hourly position to the highest management positions. In effect, they have established performance standards for their industry segment.

HOSPITAL AND HEALTHCARE

American Society for Hospital Food Service Administrators (ASHFSA)

> 840 N. Lake Shore Drive
> Chicago, IL 60611
> Phone: 312–280–6416
> Executive Director: Kathleen Pontius

The American Society of Hospital Food Service Administrators (ASHFSA) is a subsidiary of parent American Hospital Association (AHA). Its members are all professional foodservice directors of health care institutions.

CORRECTIONAL FOODSERVICE

American Correctional Food Service Association (ACFSA)

> 2040 Chestnut Street
> Harrisburg, PA 17104
> Phone: 717–233–2301
> Executive Director: M. Colleen McCann

The American Correctional Food Service Association is an organization dedicated to the professional management of foodservice operations in the nation's correctional institutions. Its members, both self-operators and contractors, represent over 1,200 adult institutions in an industry segment comprising $1 billion in food purchases annually.

NUTRITION AND DIETETICS

American Dietetic Association (ADA)

> 216 W. Jackson Blvd., Suite 800
> Chicago, IL 60606
> Phone: 800–877–1600
> Executive Director: Bonnie Pear

The ADA is an association of professionally and technically trained dieticians. They are active in all segments of the foodservice industry with a strong emphasis on the noncommercial and institutional segments, particularly health care.

Trade Publications

Restaurants & Institutions

> Cahners Publishing Co.
> Cahners Plaza
> 1350 E. Touhy Ave., P.O. Box 5080
> Des Plaines, IL 60017
> Phone: 708–635–8800

Food Management
270 Madison Ave.
New York City, NY 10016
Phone: 212–951–6700

Food Service Director
630 Third Ave.
New York City, NY 10017
Phone: 212–986–4800

Nation's Restaurant News
425 Park Ave.
New York, NY 10022
Phone: 800–447–7133

Restaurant Busines
Bill Publications
633 Third Ave.
New York, NY 10017
Phone: 212–986–4800

Automatic Merchandise
Johnson Hill Press
1233 Janesville Ave.
Fort Atkinson, WI 53538-0803
Phone: 800–547–7377

Vending Times
Vending Times, Inc.
545 Eighth Ave.
New York, NY 10018
Phone: 212–714–0101

Correctional Foodservice Magazine
665 La Villa Drive
Miami Springs, FL 33156
Phone: 305–887–1700

Appendix B

Dining Service Agreement*

DINING SERVICE AGREEMENT

Between

CLIENT
Address

and

_____

_____

_____ , 1992

BD P&L Model
1/15/92

*Courtesy of Robert C. Wood, Wood Foodservice Management Company

DINING SERVICE AGREEMENT

Agreement is hereby made this month of _____, 1992 by and between CLIENT (hereinafter called CLIENT), and CONTRACTOR, a Pennsylvania corporation, (hereinafter referred to as CONTRACTOR), for the provision of dining service management.

In consideration of the premises and mutual promises and agreements herein, and intending to be legally bound hereby, the parties agree as follows:

1. EXCLUSIVE RIGHT

CLIENT hereby grants to CONTRACTOR the exclusive right and privilege to provide and manage the dining services at or upon the total CLIENT premises at _____.

2. GENERAL RELATIONSHIP

It is agreed that in all matters relating to this Agreement, CONTRACTOR shall render services as an independent contractor. No relationship of employer-employee is intended nor created by this Agreement, and employees of CONTRACTOR are not employees of CLIENT under the meaning or application of any federal or state unemployment insurance laws, or other social security law or any worker's compensation law, industrial law, or otherwise.

3. ASSIGNMENT

This Agreement may be assigned in whole or in part by CONTRACTOR upon notice in writing to CLIENT.

4. CONTRACTOR SERVICES AND OBLIGATIONS TO CLIENT

CONTRACTOR will furnish nutritious and tastefully prepared food, and adequate and sufficiently trained personnel, to provide the services hereunder. CONTRACTOR will also provide necessary administrative, executive, management, dietetic, and personnel supervision, and other related services to support CLIENT's dining service. In performing its obligations hereunder, CONTRACTOR will:

A. At all times maintain an adequate staff of employees on duty at CLIENT for efficient operation of the dining service. Such staffing level shall be mutually agreed upon between CLIENT and CONTRACTOR.

B. Employ and pay all labor and management necessary for the efficient operation of all dining services.

C. Provide dining services hereunder according to a mutually agreed upon schedule, which may be adjusted from time to time upon reasonable advance notice from CLIENT.

D. Provide a menu, including portion sizes and prices. CONTRACTOR will notify CLIENT of any price increases in advance of implementation.

E. Provide bartending services and/or pour wine if said alcoholic beverages or wine are purchased directly by CLIENT or other authorized customer, however, CONTRACTOR will not purchase any alcoholic beverages except those used in cooking.

CLIENT shall indemnify and hold harmless CONTRACTOR and its employees from and against all claims, damages, losses and expenses; including reasonable attorney's fees, arising out of or resulting from the service of alcoholic beverages by CONTRACTOR.

DINING SERVICE AGREEMENT ■ 263

F. Assume responsibility for the cleanliness of the food preparation and service areas (including floors in such areas) and food service equipment used by CONTRACTOR in the performance of its obligations under this Agreement, pursuant to requirements of federal, state, or local health authorities having jurisdiction over the premises.

G. Allow authorized representatives of CLIENT access to dining service areas, and allow such authorized representatives the right to inspect the dining service premises.

H. Require that employees under WOOD's direct supervision use due care in handling CLIENT's equipment. CONTRACTOR will return to CLIENT at the expiration of this agreement such equipment and utensils in the condition in which received, except for ordinary wear and tear.

I. If required, separate trash according to state or local municipality regulations and/or CLIENT policies regarding recycling.

5. **CLIENT OBLIGATIONS TO CONTRACTOR**
   CLIENT will:

A. At no cost to CONTRACTOR, provide adequate facilities (including office space) for the efficient operation of the dining service, and furnish the necessary utilities (including but not limited to heat, water, electricity and telephone service) required for CONTRACTOR to perform its obligations under this Agreement.

B. At no cost to CONTRACTOR, provide, and permit CONTRACTOR to utilize, CLIENT's dining service equipment (including but not limited to equipment required for the preparation and service of food; dishes, flatware, glassware, utensils, smallwares; office furniture and standard office equipment, personal computer, time clock, and safe) necessary for CONTRACTOR to perform its obligations hereunder.

C. CLIENT will provide the initial inventory of china, flatware, glassware, etc., and will be responsible for all replacements of same.

CLIENT and CONTRACTOR will jointly inventory the china, flatware and glassware, etc., and both parties will be provided with a copy of the inventory. CLIENT and CONTRACTOR will mutually agree that the inventory is at an adequate level for normal operational requirements. If CONTRACTOR is to provide dining services for additional CLIENT customers, it will be the financial responsibility of CLIENT to provide adequate operational levels of the above mentioned items as required to provide the additional service.

D. Maintain, repair and replace such aforementioned equipment and facilities at CLIENT's own expense, and keep equipment and facilities maintained in a safe operating condition. CLIENT shall provide any necessary repairs and replacements within sufficient time so that CONTRACTOR will not be unduly interrupted in its performance of its obligations under this Agreement.

E. Assume responsibility for cleanliness of dining room/cafeteria table tops, chairs, walls, etc., and provide janitorial services for all floors from service counters forward (i. e., customer areas). CLIENT will also be responsible for cleaning hoods and ducts.

F. Assume the expense of, and liability for, the removal of trash and garbage (including removal of grease) from CLIENT's premises.

G. Assume the expense of, and liability for, pest control.

H. Reserve the right to use all dining service areas, from time to time, for non-dining service functions, provided, however, that CONTRACTOR is given prior notice regarding non-dining service functions and that CONTRACTOR will not be unduly interrupted in performing its obligations hereunder. CLIENT will be responsible for any costs involved in setting up and cleaning up of dining service areas used by CLIENT for non-dining service functions.

6. PREMISES

a. Occupational Safety and Health Act

At the commencement of this Agreement and for the entire term thereof, CLIENT agrees to provide premises and equipment free of conditions which violate the Occupational Safety and Health Act (OSHA) of 1970 or the applicable standards promulgated under the Act. CLIENT agrees to pay the cost of all repairs, modifications, new equipment, and labor necessary to correct all conditions in premises and equipment which violate the Act. Determination that a specific condition violates the cited Act shall be made by a competent safety engineer, safety consultant or other appropriately recognized specialist engaged by CLIENT. CONTRACTOR will be responsible to use the equipment and facilities under its care, custody and control in a manner which would not cause violation of the OSHA Act of 1970, including reports and record-keeping required under the law.

b. Environmental Compliance

CLIENT shall keep or cause the premises to be in compliance with all applicable federal, state and local environmental laws, ordinances, rules and regulations, and shall obtain and comply with any and all approvals, registrations or permits required thereunder. CLIENT agrees to defend, indemnify and hold harmless CONTRACTOR from and against any claims, demands, suits, adjudications, administrative proceedings, penalties, fines, liabilities, settlements, damages, costs, or expenses of whatever kind or nature, including without limitation, attorney and consultant fees and expenses, investigation and laboratory fees, court costs, litigation, and costs of abatement and clean-up, except to the extent that CONTRACTOR is directly responsible for any such violations hereunder.

7. PERSONNEL

A. CONTRACTOR agrees that it will use its best efforts to employ qualified, trained, and competent employees in accordance with the standards in the food-service industry, and will endeavor to assure the proper conduct of said employees.

B. CONTRACTOR is an Equal Opportunity Employer. It is CONTRACTOR policy that no person shall be discriminated against in employment because of race, age, color, religion, sex, national origin, physical handicap or veteran status. This policy applies to all personnel including executive management, technical, professional, and supervisory personnel, and to all personnel actions including recruitment, employment, promotions, transfers, lay-offs, and any action related to the determination of compensation and benefits; and to the administration of Corporate sponsored training, education, tuition assistance and social programs.

C. During the term of this agreement and until one year has elapsed after termination of this agreement, neither CONTRACTOR nor CLIENT shall hire or enter into any contractual arrangements of any kind whatsoever with any management and/or supervisory persons (EMPLOYEES) who are employed by the other party. Exceptions may only be made by written agreement between CONTRACTOR corporate president and CLIENT's authorized representative.

CONTRACTOR and CLIENT acknowledge that the restrictions contained in this Agreement, in view of the nature of the business in which CONTRACTOR is engaged, the training CONTRACTOR will provide EMPLOYEES in connection with the duties of EMPLOYEES required hereunder, CONTRACTOR providing

EMPLOYEE with knowledge of WOOD'S trade secrets and recipes, and CONTRACTOR providing EMPLOYEES with knowledge of WOOD'S past, present, and prospective clients of CONTRACTOR, are reasonable and necessary in order to protect the legitimate interest of CONTRACTOR and CLIENT, and that any violation thereof will result in irreparable injuries to CONTRACTOR and CLIENT, and therefore, CONTRACTOR and CLIENT each acknowledge that, in the event of violation of any of these restrictions, CONTRACTOR and CLIENT, as the case may be, shall be entitled to obtain from any court of competent jurisdiction, preliminary and permanent injunctive relief as well as damages, including reasonable attorney's fees, expenses, and costs incurred in connection with the enforcement of these restrictions by CONTRACTOR or CLIENT, and that if anything in this Agreement is deemed by such a court to be unduly restrictive, such court shall nevertheless have the right to enforce this Agreement to the fullest extent the court deems equitable.

8. INSURANCE

A. CONTRACTOR shall procure and maintain insurance of the types and minimum limits enumerated hereunder, as such respects the functions of CONTRACTOR under this Agreement. CONTRACTOR shall furnish CLIENT with certificates of insurance evidencing such coverage, and will include CLIENT as an additional insured under the CONTRACTOR Comprehensive General Liability Policy. The certificate will provide for thirty (30) days written notice to be given to CLIENT in the event of cancellation.

1) *Worker's Compensation*
   In accordance with the Laws of the State of _____ or such laws as may be applicable for work done under this agreement.

General Liability	$ 1,000,000
Bodily Injury & Property Damage	Each Occurrence
Auto Liability	$ 1,000,000
Bodily Injury & Property Damage	Combined Single Limit
Product Liability	$ 1,000,000
Bodily Injury & Property Damage	Each Occurrence

2) *Umbrella* $10,000,000

B. CONTRACTOR shall indemnify and hold harmless CLIENT, its agents and employees from and against all claims, damages, losses, and expenses, including reasonable attorney's fees, arising out of or attributable to the willful acts or omissions or negligence of CONTRACTOR, its agents and employees, except to the extent that same is attributable to the willful actions or negligence of CLIENT, its agents and employees.

C. CONTRACTOR agrees to carry Fire Insurance, including Extended Coverage and Special Extended Coverages to protect the property of CONTRACTOR while situated on the premises of CLIENT.

D. Each of the parties hereto expressly waives all rights and claims they may have against the other, their parents, subsidiaries and affiliates for loss or damage caused by fire or other perils normally defined in Fire, Extended Coverage, and Special Extended Coverage policies. Each insurance policy procured by CLIENT and CONTRACTOR shall, if possible, affirmatively state that it will not be invalidated because the insured waived its rights of recovery against any party prior to the occurrence of a loss. The failure of either party to request such a waiver or the failure of any insurance carrier to execute such a waiver shall not nullify this waiver.

E. CLIENT shall notify CONTRACTOR immediately upon discovery of any claim or possible claim relating to aforementioned insurance by contacting _____ .

9. FORCE MAJEURE

If, because of riots, war, public emergency or calamity, fire, earthquake, act of God, government restriction, labor disturbance or strike, business operations at CLIENT shall be interrupted or stopped, performance of this Agreement, with the exception of monies already earned or due and owing, shall be suspended and excused to the extent commensurate with such interfering occurrence. At the request of CLIENT, CONTRACTOR will make every reasonable effort to continue providing dining services during such occurrences, according to specific financial terms and conditions to be mutually agreed upon between the parties.

10. LAWS AND ORDINANCES

CONTRACTOR shall comply with all laws, ordinances, rules and regulations of federal, state, county or municipal authorities or departments relating to or affecting the provision of dining services by CONTRACTOR.

CONTRACTOR will procure all necessary licenses and permits required for CONTRACTOR to perform its obligations under this Agreement.

11. GOVERNING LAW

This Agreement shall be construed and interpreted, whether in matter relating to contract or tort, in accordance with the governed by the laws of the Commonwealth of Pennsylvania.

12. FINANCIAL ARRANGEMENTS

A. CONTRACTOR will provide the services described herein on a profit and loss basis. CONTRACTOR will operate on its own credit and, except as otherwise provided herein, CONTRACTOR will be responsible for all costs of managing the dining service. In consideration of such services, CLIENT will pay CONTRACTOR a fixed subsidy in the amount of _____ Dollars ($000.00) per week.

On or about the first day of each accounting period, CONTRACTOR will invoice CLIENT for the aforementioned subsidy. CLIENT will pay CONTRACTOR such subsidy within fifteen (15) days from the date of the invoice.

B. Prices to be charged for special services, such as catered lunches or dinners, will be determined by mutual agreement between CLIENT and CONTRACTOR. CONTRACTOR will invoice CLIENT for such special services.

C. CLIENT agrees to pay a late charge of one and one-half (1-½%) percent per month on any invoice or portion thereof which is not paid within fifteen (15) days from the date of the invoice.

D. The financial arrangements set forth in this Agreement are based on existing CLIENT conditions (including by way of example, population, personnel practices, etc.) and labor costs, commodity costs, Federal, State, local sales and excise taxes, and license fees now in effect. In the event of a material change in any of the aforementioned items, upon mutual agreement, the financial arrangements herein may be renegotiated to reflect such change.

13. INITIAL PAYMENT

Prior to the commencement date of this Agreement, CONTRACTOR will invoice CLIENT for an Initial Payment in the amount of _____ (00,000.00). This Initial Payment will be used by CONTRACTOR to fund the working capital requirements under this Agreement. CLIENT will pay such Initial Payment to CONTRACTOR within fifteen (15) days from the date of the invoice. CONTRACTOR will retain the Initial Payment for the term of this Agreement and any subsequent renewals or extensions thereof. The Initial Payment will be reviewed and may be adjusted annually.

Should either party terminate this Agreement, CONTRACTOR will return the Initial Payment to CLIENT, or, at WOOD's option, apply the Initial Payment to any outstanding invoice balances due CONTRACTOR by CLIENT.

14. ACCOUNTING

A. Fiscal Calendar

CONTRACTOR will operate under a fiscal calendar consisting of eight 4-week accounting periods and four 5-week accounting periods (52-week year). However, approximately once every five years, the calendar will be adjusted to consist of seven 4-week accounting periods and five 5-week accounting periods (53-week year).

B. Inventory

CONTRACTOR will maintain ownership of the entire inventory of food and supplies purchased by CONTRACTOR for use at CLIENT.

15. CONFIDENTIALITY

All financial, statistical, operating, proposal, contract, and personnel data relative to or utilized by CONTRACTOR, shall be and remain the property of CONTRACTOR and shall be kept confidential. CLIENT agrees to keep such information confidential and so instruct its agents, servants, employees and independent contractors. The use of such data by CLIENT in any manner, shall not destroy WOOD's ownership or its confidentiality.

16. NON-WAIVER

No delay or failure by either party to exercise any right under this Agreement, and no partial or single exercise of that right, shall constitute a waiver of that or any other right, unless expressly provided herein.

17. HEADINGS

Headings in this Agreement are for convenience only and shall not be used to interpret or construe its provisions.

18. BINDING EFFECT

The provisions of this Agreement shall be binding upon and inure to each of the parties and their respective successors and assigns.

19. NOTICE

Any notice to be given hereunder by either party to the other shall be in writing and may be effected by certified mail, return receipt requested. Notice shall be sufficient if made or addressed as follows:

TO CONTRACTOR: **TO CLIENT:**

Either party may change the address for notice by giving notice of such change in accordance with provisions of this paragraph.

20. COSTS OF SUIT AND COLLECTION

If any action at law or in equity is brought by either party to enforce or interpret the provisions of this Agreement, the prevailing party shall be entitled to recover costs of suit and collection, including reasonable attorney's fees, from the losing party, which fees shall be in addition to any other relief which may be awarded.

21. UNENFORCEABLE PROVISIONS

In case any one or more of the provisions contained in this Agreement shall for any reason be held to be invalid, illegal or otherwise unenforceable in any respect, such invalidity, illegality or unenforceability shall not affect any other provision thereof, and this Agreement shall be construed as if such invalid, illegal or unenforceable provision had never been contained herein.

22. AUTHORITY

CLIENT represents that any provisions of this Agreement requiring approval by CLIENT's Board of Directors have been so approved and authorized.

23. TERMINATION

In the event that CLIENT shall fail to pay any invoice or portion thereof, including any late charges incurred, within the fifteen (15) day period specified herein, CONTRACTOR may, at its option, terminate this Agreement and withhold further performance of its obligations hereunder, unless CLIENT cures the default within ten (10) days after written notice from CONTRACTOR specifying the nature of CLIENT's default.

In the event CLIENT should be adjudicated a voluntary or involuntary bankrupt, institute or suffer to be instituted any proceeding for reorganization or rearrangement of its affairs, become insolvent or have a receiver of its assets or property appointed, CONTRACTOR shall have the right to cancel this Agreement forthwith and without notice.

24. COMMENCEMENT & CANCELLATION

This agreement shall commence on _____ , 1992, and shall extend thereafter until terminated by either party, without cause, by serving notice in writing to the other party at least forty-five (45) days prior to the effective date of termination.

25. ENTIRE AGREEMENT

This contract constitutes the entire agreement between the parties and supersedes all prior proposals, agreements, arrangements and/or understandings between said parties regarding the subject matter hereof. This Agreement may not be modified or changed in any manner whatsoever except in writing and by mutual agreement of both parties.

26. SIGNATURES

IN WITNESS WHEREOF the parties hereto have caused this Agreement to be executed by their duly authorized officers the day and year so noted below.

ATTEST: CLIENT

_____   BY: _____

Date: _____   Title: _____

ATTEST: CONTRACTOR:

_____   _____

Date: _____   Title: _____

Appendix C

Budget Work Kit

BUSINESS & INDUSTRY FOODSERVICE FACILITY

For use in preparing an annual operating budget for an institutional or contract foodservice operation.

FORM A: Sales Forecast Planning Form
FORM B: Sales Mix/Cost Mix Analysis Form
FORM C: Labor Cost Planning Form
FORM D: Payroll-Related Costs Planning Form
FORM E: Operating (Direct) Expenses Planning Form
FORM F: Summary Projected Annual Budget Planning Form

FORM A

Sales Forecast Planning Form

A. Location: _____

B. Population Employees: _____

Executives: _____

(1)	(2)	(3)	(4)	(5)	(6)
Meal Period or Shift	Participation Percentage	Average Daily Customers	Estimated Check Average ($)	Estimated Average Daily Sales ($)	% Sales Mix
BREAKFAST					
LUNCH					
AM Break					
PM Break					
TOTAL BREAKS					
Service Dining Room					
Executive Dining Room					
Special Functions					
Others (list):					
_____					
_____					
_____					
_____					
(C) Total Estimated Daily/Annual Sales				$_____	100.0%
(D) X _____ Days = Estimated Annual Sales				(E) $_____	

FORM B

Sales Mix/Cost Mix Analysis Form

(1)	(2)	(3)	(4)	(5)
Meal Period or Shift (From Form A)	Projected Sales Dollars ($)	Projected Food Cost (%)	Projected Food Cost ($)	Manager's Comments
TOTALS	(A) $_____	(C) B ÷ A = __%	(B) $_____	

FORM C

Labor Cost Planning Form

(1)	(2)	(3)	(4)	(5)
Position	No. of Workers	Total Weekly Labor Hours	Present Wage/Salary Rate ($)	Present Weekly Cost ($)
I. MGE./ADMIN.				
———————				
———————				
———————				
Subtotal				
II. PRODUCTION				
———————				
———————				
———————				
Subtotal				
III. SERVICE				
———————				
———————				
———————				
Subtotal				
IV. SAN.& MTE.				
———————				
———————				
———————				
Subtotal				

TOTAL: Present weekly wage and salary cost   (A) $_____

Present weekly wage and salary cost (weekly cost X 52)   (B) $_____

PLUS: _____% Reserve for wage and salary increases   (C) $_____

TOTAL: Projected annual labor cost   (D) $_____

FORM D

Payroll-Related Costs Planning Form

I. PROJECTED ANNUAL PAYROLL COST (From FORM C)

        A. Management and Administration (Salaried) $_____

        B. Hourly Wages $_____

        TOTAL SALARIES AND WAGES (payroll) $_____

II. PROJECTED NUMBER OF EMPLOYEES (From FORM C)

        C. Salaried   ____

        D. Hourly   ____

        TOTAL EMPLOYEES   ____

(1)	(2)	(3)	(4)
Cost Category	% of Total Payroll Cost	Fixed Cost per Employee ($)	Total Cost ($)
Social Security			
Medicare			
TOTAL F.I.C.A.			
State Unemployment			
Federal Unemployment			
TOTAL UNEMPLOYMENT			
Workers Compensation			
State Disability			
Health Insurance			
Life Insurance			
Pension Plan			
Union Welfare Plan			
Others (list):			
TOTAL VARIABLE COST %	(A) _____%	$ _____	$ _____
TOTAL DOLLAR COSTS $	(B) $_____	+ (C) $_____	= (D) $_____

FORM E

Operating (Direct) Expenses Planning Form

Projected Annual Sales: $_____
(From FORM A)

(1)	(2)	(3)	(4)
Item of Cost	Variable Cost %	Fixed Cost ($)	Total Cost ($)
Paper Goods			
Laundry			
Cleaning Supplies			
Trash Removal			
Exterminator			
Maintenance/Repair			
Uniforms			
Insurance			
Advertising			
Others (list):			
TOTAL COST %	(A) _____%	$ _____	$ _____
TOTAL COST $	(B) $_____ +	(C) $_____ =	(D) $_____

FORM F

Summary Projected Annual Budget Planning Form

I. SALES (Income)	$_____	100.0%
II. COST OF SALES	$_____	___._
III. GROSS PROFIT	$_____	___._

IV. LABOR COST

Salaried	$_____		
Hourly	$_____		
TOTAL PAYROLL		$_____	___._
PAYROLL-RELATED COSTS		$_____	___._
TOTAL LABOR COST		$_____	___._

V. OTHER OPERATING COSTS

Variable Costs	$_____		
Fixed Costs	$_____		
TOTAL OPERATING EXPENSES		$_____	___._

VI. OPERATING PROFIT	$_____	___._

VII. OTHER COSTS

Depreciation	$_____		
Administrative Charge	$_____		
Rent	$_____		
Others (list):			
_____	$_____		
_____	$_____		
_____	$_____		
_____	$_____		
TOTAL OTHER COSTS		$_____	___._

VIII. OTHER INCOME

Vending Commissions	$_____		
Management Fee	$_____		
Other	$_____		
TOTAL OTHER INCOME		$_____	___._

NET UNIT AVAILABLE	$_____	___._

Appendix D

Vending Pro Forma Work Kit

FORM A

Sales and Cost Analysis

(A) Population: _____

(1)	(2)	(3)	(4)	(5)	(6)
Machine Type	Vend. Price	Weekly per Cap Sales ($)	Annual Gross Sales ($)	Merchandise Cost (%)	Annual Merchandise Cost ($)
(B) TOTALS	—	$ _____	$ _____	_____ %	$ _____

FORM B

Labor Cost Analysis

(1) Position	(2) Number	(3) Rate ($)	(4) Hours per Day	(5) Projected Weekly Cost ($)	(6) Projected Annual Cost ($)
Manager					
Supervisor					
Mechanic					
Routeperson					
Host/Hostess					
Others (list)					
(A) TOTALS				$ _____	

(B) _____ % Payroll-Related Costs $ _____

(C) Forecasted TOTAL Annual Labor Cost $ _____

FORM C

Direct and Indirect Expenses Analysis

A. Projected Annual Gross Sales from FORM A: $ _____

(1) Item of Cost	(2) Variable Cost (%)	(3) Variable Cost ($)	(4) Fixed Cost ($)	(5) Total Cost ($)
Vehicle Expense				
Installation				
Retail Sales Tax				
Licenses/Permits				
Sales Commission				
Mte. & Repairs				
Utilities				
Other (list):				
(B) TOTALS	_____ %	$ _____ +	$ _____ =	$ _____

FORM D

Depreciation Schedule

(1) Machine Type	(2) Number of Machines	(3) Unit Cost ($)	(4) Total Machine Cost ($)	(5) Freight Cost ($)	(6) Sales Tax ($)	(7) Total Investment ($)
Hot Drink						
Cold Drink						
Merchandiser						
Pastry						
Candy						
Hot Food						
Cold Food						
Milk						
Microwave						
Coin Chge.						
Other (list):						
TOTALS			$ _____ + $ _____ + $ _____ = $ _____			

(A) Equipment Depreciation ÷ _____ years = $ _____

(B) _____ Vehicles @ $_____ = $ _____ ÷ _____ years = $ _____

(C) Office Equipment $ _____ ÷ _____ years = $ _____

(D) TOTAL ANNUAL DEPRECIATION $ _____

Enter TOTAL ANNUAL DEPRECIATION on Form F

FORM E

Proposed Commission Schedule

(1)	(2)	(3)	(4)
Product Type	Annual Sales	Commission Rate	Annual Commissions
Hot Drinks	$ _____	_____ %	$ _____
Cold Drinks	$ _____	_____ %	$ _____
Merchandiser	$ _____	_____ %	$ _____
Pastry	$ _____	_____ %	$ _____
Candy	$ _____	_____ %	$ _____
Hot Food	$ _____	_____ %	$ _____
Cold Food	$ _____	_____ %	$ _____
Milk	$ _____	_____ %	$ _____
Cigarettes	$ _____	_____ %	$ _____
Others (list)	$ _____	_____ %	$ _____
TOTALS	(A) $ _____	(B) _____ %	(C) $ _____

FORM F

Summary Pro Forma (Budget)

Projected Annual Gross Sales		$_____	100.0%
Estimated Product Cost		$_____	___.__
Gross Profit		$_____	___.__
OPERATING EXPENSES			
Labor and Related Costs		$_____	___.__
Other Costs: Fixed	$ _____		
Variable	$ _____		
TOTAL Other Costs		$_____	___.__
Depreciation		$_____	___.__
_____ % Branch Charges		$_____	___.__
TOTAL OPERATING EXPENSES		$_____	___.__
OPERATING PROFIT		$_____	___.__
(Commissions)		$_____	___.__
NET AVAILABLE		$_____	___.__
TOTAL INVESTMENT		$_____	
RETURN ON INVESTMENT		_____ %	

Index